PRAISE FOR *HEI*

"With wisdom and common sense, Lori Day provides a much-needed point of view for our society. I wish that she had written *Her Next Chapter* ten years ago, so I would have had her insight when my daughter was four! Mother-daughter book clubs are such a great step in the right direction. I know what I'm giving my young mother friends and relatives this year for birthdays and holidays!"
—BRENDA CHAPMAN, **writer and director of** *Brave*

"This book is an indispensable guide for anyone who cares about raising girls to be leaders. Lori Day identifies and articulates so many of the challenges that can hold girls back or trip them up. Her gentle, intuitive suggestions make it easier to start a meaningful conversation on these tricky topics. This book also offers a treasure trove of inspiring heroines. Whether it's a daring heroine in a novel, a professor giving a great talk, CEOs and scientists profiled in documentaries, or simply the other moms in the mother-daughter book club, role models for girls abound in this delightful book." —JUNE COHEN, **executive producer, TED Media**

"*Her Next Chapter* is a smart and incisive guide for mothers raising daughters in today's toxic media culture, where hypersexualization and gender stereotypes are the norm. Lori Day shares with mothers important insights about media literacy, brilliant recommendations about healthy media, and discussion guides for book clubs—which offer mothers and daughters the opportunity to strengthen their relationship. A must read for moms!"
—ELENA ROSSINI, **writer, producer, and director of** *The Illusionists*

"Looking for a wonderful way to bond with your daughter? Look no further than *Her Next Chapter*. Using mother-daughter book clubs as the backdrop, *Her Next Chapter* provides tools and strategies for discussing the issues today's girls face, while promoting media literacy and empowerment. What more could you ask for from a book?"
—JENNIFER L. HARTSTEIN, **PsyD, author of** *Princess Recovery:*
A How-to Guide to Raising Strong, Empowered Girls Who Can
Create Their Own Happily Ever Afters

Her Next Chapter

How Mother-Daughter Book Clubs Can Help Girls
Navigate Malicious Media, Risky Relationships,
Girl Gossip, and So Much More

Lori Day, M.Ed., with Charlotte Kugler

CHICAGO
REVIEW
PRESS

For Geof, who loves Charlotte as if she were his own.

Published by Chicago Review Press, Incorporated
814 North Franklin Street
Chicago, Illinois 60610

ISBN 978-1-61374-856-5
Cover design: Rebecca Lown
Interior design: Sarah Olson
Cover illustration: David Trumble

Library of Congress Cataloging-in-Publication Data

Day, Lori.
  Her next chapter / Lori Day, Charlotte Kugler.
    pages cm
  Includes index.
  Summary: "A guide to using book clubs to open up dialogue about and explore issues facing
young girls today Mother-daughter book clubs are a great way to encourage your child's
reading and for girls and moms to bond with each other while also socializing with friends,
but they can do much more than that, suggests educational psychologist and parenting coach
Lori Day. They can create a safe and empowering haven where girls can openly discuss,
question, and navigate some of the challenges of girlhood today. In Her Next Chapter, Day
draws from experiences in her own club and her more than 25 years in education to offer
a unique, timely, and inspiring take on mother-daughter book clubs. She provides clear,
succinct overviews of eight of the biggest challenges facing girls and young women today,
giving mothers the information they need to moderate thoughtful conversations, while
weaving in all the carefully chosen book, movie, and media recommendations; plentiful
discussion questions and prompts; and suggested related activities that guide and extend
discussions and make clubs fun. It outlines precisely how mothers can work together, using
the magic of books, to build girls' confidence and lessen the negative impact of media on
self-image. Also included are relevant quotes and experiences from a wide range of mothers,
a list of further resources, and chapter-closing reflections from Day's now-adult daughter,
Charlotte, who shares memories about what the club did for her as a child and observations
on today's girl culture"—Provided by publisher.
  ISBN 978-1-61374-856-5 (pbk.)
  1. Mothers and daughters. 2. Girls. 3. Self-esteem. 4. Parenting. 5. Book clubs (Discussion
groups) I. Kugler, Charlotte. II. Title.

HQ755.85.D394 2014
306.874'3—dc23

                    2013045732

Printed in the United States of America
5 4 3 2 1

Contents

▶ PART ONE ◀

Setting Up Your Club *and* Keeping It Strong

▶ PART TWO ◀

Let's Get the Dialogue Going

Acknowledgments

|||||||||||||||||||||||||||||||||||||||||||||||||||||||||||||||||||||||||||||||||||||||||||||

Writing is never truly a solitary endeavor. I had so many muses, here and elsewhere, living and dead.

Right here, every day, my husband Geoffrey ate, drank, and slept this book with me. He provided everything from the most patient tech support to the deepest emotional support, and believed in me even when I did not believe in myself. He also began almost every evening meal with the admittedly tiresome but somehow eternally endearing quip, "How was your day, Mrs. Day?" followed by caring inquiry into whatever book-related triumphs and travails had characterized the last several hours. Geof, Mrs. Day's day was always better when you were around.

One hundred miles away, at Mount Holyoke College in western Massachusetts, my coauthor and dear daughter, Charlotte Kugler, was juggling all of the writing necessary as a double-major in English and anthropology, plus her part-time writing job for the communications department of the college, plus working on her own novel, plus her contributions to this book. I don't know how she managed such a load. I could not be more grateful for the opportunity to write with my daughter, whose incisive editorial input and beautifully written reflections helped this book blossom. Charlotte, when you were in the second grade, you announced to me that I would be buying your books one day. I know that is true—although I hope you'll give me free, autographed copies! What I never imagined was that your first book would also be mine, and I am so honored.

From the United States and various countries around the world, my globetrotting brother Deron Triff opened countless doors for me with some of the most influential female leaders across the country, and I can't thank him enough.

At Chicago Review Press, my editor, Lisa Reardon, discovered me on a soda fountain stool at the Huffington Post and offered me an opportunity to fulfill my life's dream. I am now a published book author thanks to her vision, faith, and guidance.

To David William Trumble across the pond, tremendous admiration and appreciation for lending your artistic talent to the cover of this book. There is no one who is more fun to work with.

I give heartfelt thanks to Lisa Francine, librarian at the Fenn School in Concord, Massachusetts, and Jordana Shaw, librarian at the Nashoba Brooks School in Concord—two friends without whom I literally could not have pulled this off. Your expertise in children's literature and generosity with your time was integral to this book—and to my sanity! Thanks also go out to Margot Magowan, founder of Reel Girl, who helped me choose the inspiring movies recommended in this book. Margot, the tagline for your website, "imagining gender equality in the fantasy world," perfectly describes my hope for the moms and daughters who will be watching many of the movies you suggested.

Much gratitude to all of the amazing women and men who granted me interviews and lent their wisdom to this book: Pam Allyn, Lyn Mikel Brown, June Cohen, Pam Garramone, Carrie Goldman, Jean Kilbourne, Peggy Orenstein, Jeff Perera, Stuart Schmill, Jennifer Shewmaker, Robyn Silverman, Rachel Simmons, Michele Sinisgalli-Yulo, Melissa Atkins Wardy, Marci Warhaft-Nadler, and Regina Yau.

Much appreciation to everyone who read part or all of my manuscript and/or book proposal and gave me the perfect "feedback sandwiches," especially my fellow writing group members Rebecca Hains and Christa Terry, as well as Bethany Bateman, Soraya Chemaly, Geoffrey Day, Lisa Kaplin, Gabrielle Tenn New, Melanie Parker, Jennifer Shewmaker, Michele Sinisgalli-Yulo, Debbie Triff, and Ainslie Wallace.

I thank my parents, Bob and Edrea Triff, for giving me a world-class education, the kind I wish every girl (and boy) around the globe could have. I offer special gratitude to my favorite high school English teachers at the Lovett School in Atlanta, Georgia. Mr. Hall, you saw something in me as a writer and helped me to see it in myself. Mrs. Schaum, you introduced me to Walt Whitman's "There Was a Child Went Forth," my favorite poem and an inspiration for this book. And Mr. Schaum, you taught with a Maine accent that I could not wrap my head around at the time but would later grow to love, living in New England. You told my mom at a parent-teacher conference that I was the best *Beowulf* student you'd ever had, and that meant a lot to me, because *Beowulf* was wicked hard!

I am grateful for all of my favorite childhood authors—for Laura Ingalls Wilder, E. B. White, Judy Blume, and so many others. I carry you with me always.

Thank you to the Concord Bookshop for providing the spark that led to my own mother-daughter book club and, eventually, this book. Thank you to the members of our own special book club. You know who you are!

Finally, thank you to everyone throughout my life who has ever said, "You really should write a book." It was the road not taken for me, until now. I did finally listen.

Introduction

|||||||||||||||||||||||||||||||||||||||||||||||||||||||||||||||||||||||||||||||||||||||

Like many mothers, I tend to be hard on myself. Because I make a living advising other parents on all kinds of issues related to their children, you'd think I have it all figured out. You'd be wrong. I have always second-guessed myself and often looked for creative ways to garner support from other moms in this extreme sport called parenting. I have also been aware that if the typical challenges of motherhood sometimes rest heavily on my own shoulders, then how must it feel for other mothers? We all have our moments of throwing darts in the dark. Perhaps that's best done as a team. And in the finest of circumstances, someone will know where the light switch is.

One of the happiest and most memorable undertakings of my early parenting years was the formation of a mother-daughter book club, a collaboration with my daughter and coauthor, Charlotte Kugler, and four other mother-daughter pairs, that would last for six years. My decision to establish a mother-daughter book club evolved from several different parenting goals, in addition to a desire to spend more special time with Charlotte.

When Charlotte was a young child, the monumental shift in pop culture toward the sexualization of girls was of growing concern to me. Unfortunately, this tendency is something we see even more of now than we did in the late '90s. I attribute the beginnings of my advocacy work for girls to a specific date: September 7, 1999. I had one of those eureka flashes when this sense of purpose became clear to me. I was reading the *New York Times* and, in a watershed moment, I became acutely aware of my vulnerability as the mother of a daughter in what seemed to me like a society gone haywire.

After reading an article about the ways in which young girls were being turned into consumers of what had previously been strictly adult fashions, I became so angry I went straight upstairs to my clunky old Dell desktop computer that ran a Windows 95 operating system, opened up WordPerfect, composed my first-ever letter to the editor, and sent it over my dial-up connection via my free Juno e-mail account. I barely knew what the Internet was back then.

I recently looked at the letter, excavated from the early Internet archives of the *Times* by my tech-savvy husband, Geof, Charlotte's stepdad. I remembered that it had to be shortened by the editorial team from its original multiparagraph rant, but it remained essentially authentic to my feelings, conveying my dismay about the new girl fashions, the shifting landscape of raising daughters, and my disconnect from other mothers who did not share my concerns or values.

From this point on, I noticed *everything.* As a mother, once your eyes are opened to the sexualization of girlhood, you cannot unsee it. Looking back now on the *NYT* article that so disillusioned me, it is rather tame compared to what I read these days about girl fashions and what I see in schools and out in public. The clothes girls were starting to wear the year of that article were inspired by Britney Spears, whose hit song and music video ". . . Baby One More Time," released in 1999, forever changed the image in my mind of girls' private school uniforms. Britney was the gateway drug.

My sudden inability that year to find a basic T-shirt for my seven-year-old daughter that was not chopped off just below her nonexistent breasts was enough to send me into a silent rage as I walked in—and directly out—of all of the children's clothing stores at the mall. Would I need to hire a seamstress to make appropriate apparel for Charlotte to wear so that she would not have to run, jump, and climb in a ridiculous half-shirt that was no longer just being marketed to teens, but had trickled down into the little girls' department?

And it was not just sexualized clothes. In parallel to that trend was another one—the escalating gender divide in toys. The year after T-shirt-gate, in 2000, the Walt Disney Company launched a marketing blitz that led to the creation of the $4 billion princess franchise and, ultimately, the onslaught of more than forty thousand Disney princess items that are currently being sold on the children's market. It is no secret that Disney's highly profitable, widely accepted, corporate-created definition of what it is to be a girl has become today's norm. This new normal has obliterated any collective memory of what childhood was like for girls before all of the gender-neutral toys were bulldozed into the aisle marked Boys, making room on the girls' aisle for other corporations to join Disney with their own merchandise contributions in creating what is now known colloquially as "the pink ghetto." Not since the sacking of Troy has there been such a plundering! This trend was just beginning when Charlotte was in elementary school, and was nowhere near the monster that it is today, but it was growing, and, it seemed to me, the imaginations and aspirations of girls were simultaneously shrinking.

I also remember noticing how few of my daughter's books had female protagonists—certainly fewer than half of them—and of the ones that did, few of those portrayed women and girls in strong roles in which they demonstrated authentic agency in their own lives. Female characters were often tokens, sidekicks, or love interests. It's not that there were no books about girls—of course there were. But I noticed that girls did not seem to mind reading books about boys, while boys had no interest in—and in fact outright avoided—reading books about girls. You may have noticed the same dynamic at play in the adult world.

Here's a good example. The book *Holes* by Louis Sachar won the Newbery Medal, and Charlotte loved it, as did most kids her age. It is a darkly humorous mystery about a bunch of boys sent to a camp for boys that is really a juvenile detention center . . . where they have to dig holes all day. If that book had been about girls at a girls' facility digging holes all day, I maintain that boys would not have been interested. But as it was, boys and girls loved it. The story revolves around boys because, by default, their stories are everyone's stories. There is no male equivalent of "chick lit." I started talking to other mothers, teachers, librarians, and colleagues about this, and found that they all observed the same gender dance, and all of them felt frustrated too.

The same thing was happening with movies. In the mid-'90s, several wonderful films came out based on critically acclaimed children's books: *Matilda* by Roald Dahl, *Harriet the Spy* by Louise Fitzhugh, and *A Little Princess* by Frances Hodgson Burnett, among others. Great books, great movies. But the movies performed poorly at the box office, and production companies went on record saying they would not produce more movies starring girls because they were money losers. Girls went to see these movies but most boys stayed home, and thus the potential ticket sales were cut in half. This was the same dynamic that happened with books about girls. I recall a lot of mothers talking about this and feeling sad and indignant. Everyone wondered whether the *Harry Potter* series (which was brand-new at the time our book club formed) would have received the same voracious following if it were about a Harriet rather than a Harry. We also lamented the fact that Joanne Rowling went with "J. K. Rowling," obscuring her own gender in order to sell more books.

Charlotte has always been a strong reader. She attended the Alcott School in our hometown of Concord, Massachusetts—the Concord of both Revolutionary War and literary fame. The home of Louisa May Alcott, where she penned *Little Women*, was just around the corner from Charlotte's school, which was named after Louisa's father, Bronson Alcott, the superintendent of the Concord Public Schools from 1859 to 1865. At the time of this writing, Concord is ranked the second-best school system in Massachusetts. Despite the excellence of the schools, Charlotte did not feel challenged when it came to reading. I did not want to be one of "those" mothers who complained to teachers about how they were not adequately enriching my child, whining about how bright she was and how teachers were not meeting her needs. I was inclined to augment her reading on my own rather than make waves.

Around this same time, a woman named Shireen Dodson wrote a book entitled *The Mother-Daughter Book Club*, and a companion book called *100 Books for Girls to Grow On*. My local bookstore, the Concord Bookshop, devoted its storefront window to a display of Dodson's books, as well as some of the books Dodson recommends girls read, all of which focus on substantive female protagonists. As my daughter and I walked past the bookshop, the display in the window beckoned to us and we went inside. Within minutes Charlotte said, "Mommy, I want to do that!"

Thus the spark for our club was ignited. Yet when I thought about all of the roads that led to this decision, it seemed that we'd had an appointment with fate all along.

We began our club when Charlotte and the rest of the girls were in third grade. In the beginning, the mothers set most of the ground rules and selected the reading lists. As the girls got older, the mothers handed over the reins to the girls, who chose the books we would read together. Eventually we did not focus exclusively on female protagonists, but simply on good literature that was not being covered in school.

I can say without the slightest hesitation that our mother-daughter book club was the most extraordinary formative experience in my relationship with my daughter. I cannot recommend it highly enough to other mothers looking for ways to expose their growing daughters to female-centric literature and to enrich their emotional bonds with their daughters.

Trust me when I tell you that your daughter will be affected by the club more than she can articulate at the time. Here, in part, is what Charlotte wrote when she was in the eighth grade for her monthly newspaper column in the *Concord Journal*:

> When I was in third grade, my mother and I helped found a mother-daughter book club, which has endured to this day. . . . Since I was an only child with no extended family nearby, my mom wanted to find another way to implement the African proverb "It takes a village to raise a child." She felt she and the other chosen mothers could raise us together in a special and meaningful way, with the good values and confidence necessary for us to become strong young women. Part of the reason she wanted to start this club was because it would always be a place where my friends and I, as teenagers, would feel comfortable sharing our thoughts and lives in the presence of other caring, experienced women. . . .
>
> The discussions we engage in during the meetings often begin as conversations about problems in the text that the protagonist encounters and overcomes, and inevitably shift seamlessly to conversations about similar problems we have experienced and dealt with while growing up. I have always loved this aspect of our meetings, as it allows for everyone to empathize with each other and create a common thread of understanding related to the books and our experiences and daughters and mothers. . . .
>
> We are now in our sixth year together, and our meetings have always been, and will remain, a highlight of my month. Regardless of how hectic our lives are or how many times we have to reschedule the meeting date, we try never to miss a month. In the fall of 2000 we began as five mother-daughter pairs, but busy lives and divergent interests did not allow the original group to continue. However, the remaining three pairs are now carrying on with a renewed sense of connection and devotion to our club, which I believe will take us far in the years to come. . . .

This club has served as an outlet for my passion for literature, and has provided me with both emotional support and the company of good friends for six years. I hope it will continue to do so for many more. I have realized lately that my feelings of dedication and gratitude towards the club come not only from reading enjoyable books, but as much from the members themselves, and it pleases me to know that in return, I am helping to contribute to the experiences of everyone else.

One of my friends in the book club has two cats, just as I do. For Christmas one year I gave her a T-shirt that said "Books . . . Cats . . . Life Is Good," and got one for myself as well. I do not know what life has in store for me, but hopefully there will be plenty of books and cats and good friends, and if I ever have a daughter of my own, a mother-daughter book club for the next generation.

When I look back on our mother-daughter book club, which ended in 2006, I feel proud of what we accomplished. By the time our club dissolved—something neither Charlotte nor I anticipated at the time Charlotte wrote the above newspaper column—we were down to three pairs from our original five, and those three girls were entering high school. Although there are things in retrospect I wish we'd done differently that I believe would have allowed the club to endure until the girls left for college—and which I'll explain in chapter 3—I am grateful for the six years we had together. We all learned and grew tremendously from the experience, and I think the girls are more confident, happier, and healthier young women today due to the supportive environment created by our club.

If I were starting another mother-daughter book club today, there are many things I would do differently in response to how much more challenging our culture has become for girls. A modern club would function even more as a support group. I'd use a very similar structure, and still focus on girls age eight to fourteen-plus, but I would want to be able to tackle head-on some of the known obstacles to healthy emotional development for girls and young women. It would be important to me to have this sharper focus, and to build a club with other mothers who shared these same concerns and values, and whose parenting style, like mine, was to talk openly and directly about the sensitive and difficult passages our girls were navigating. I would take all of the benefits of reading empowering girl-centric literature, of mother-daughter bonding, and the collaborative development of media literacy skills, and I would help our group harness all of that energy to push back against a media culture that tells girls their greatest value lies in how they look, and that the world they are inheriting places gendered limits on who they can be and what they can do. And all of this is exactly what I've tried to do!

This book is about much more than how to form a mother-daughter reading club. It is about the imperative and value of a more contemporary version of these clubs, one that addresses directly the negative aspects of today's culture for girls and women, and how to overcome these influences through discussions and activities that are engaging, empowering, and fun. It outlines precisely how mothers can join arms with each other and with their daughters to proactively shape their daughters' sense of self in positive ways despite the obstacles embedded in society. Mothers will learn to identify the cultural impediments that women face, to understand more fully why and how they occur, and to recognize in themselves how they as adults are affected. Moms will also learn to use suggested books, movies, and other media to create a place outside the modern girlhood box that their daughters can inhabit and in which they can thrive.

Written in concert with my daughter, this book is a way to share our joint vision with other mothers and give them the tools to become a powerful village. In a culture that can make the job of raising girls intimidating and isolating, it is crucial to have ways of coping and persevering that bring mothers and daughters together in uplifting and pleasurable ways. We hope this book will serve you well.

Author's Note

|||||||||||||||||||||||||||||||||||||||||||||||||||||||||||||||||||||||||||||||||||||||||||||

Before digging into the specifics on forming and running clubs, as well as the particular girl-empowering topics that are a focus of this book, I'd like to first speak to some of the terms that are used, the way the book is structured, and for whom the book is written. While this book has not been written to address the needs of fathers and sons, men and boys—which is a worthy effort, just not the one undertaken here—the terms "mother" and "daughter" are expanded to include several variations on this relationship, such as:

- stepmother/stepdaughter
- foster mother/foster daughter
- aunt/niece
- guardian/girl
- grandmother/granddaughter
- daughter with two moms

It is important to move beyond the traditional and biologically defined mother-daughter relationship and include all of the other caring, mentoring roles that women can play in a girl's life, and that more fully reflect our society as it is today. *Throughout this book, words like "mother," "mom," "daughter," and "girl" should be taken to represent all of these other possible variations, and others.* The common thread is that this is a book about adult females collectively nurturing female children.

Along those lines, *Her Next Chapter* is also intended to be a resource to a variety of other adults who work with girls: teachers, school administrators, psychologists, social workers, librarians, and other mentors. The challenges faced by girls and women today are considerable, so the more adults in positions of advocacy and mentorship who read about the issues the better. For example, a teacher reading this book might recognize the ways he or she inadvertently reinforces gender stereotypes, or gender-segregates the toys and play areas in the classroom. There are many uses for this book in addition to a mother-daughter book club, and it is my hope that it will fall into the hands of as many adults as possible who share the mission of helping all girls reach their full potential.

Her Next Chapter is divided into two parts. The first three chapters in part one are best read in sequence, because these are the chapters that help mothers start their clubs and that include all of the information needed to make good decisions that position the club for long-term success.

Part two comprises eight "issue chapters," chapters 4 through 11, that each articulate a specific challenge faced by girls and/or women. Woven into these chapters are numerous book, movie, Internet media and activity recommendations, along with discussion questions and prompts that can open up positive discussion about—and provide guidance on—these issues. Two leading experts are interviewed for each of these chapters who lend their expertise to the exploration of each issue. Topically related quotes by mothers—gathered in response to questions I posed to my friends, to fans on my author Facebook page, and via other interactions on the Internet— bring further context to how these issues affect women and girls in their daily lives. All of these chapters end with a reflection from Charlotte.

Part two is not intended to be strictly linear or prescriptive. The chapters are arranged in a loosely chronological way that felt right to me when I wrote them. They may be read and used in that order if you like, but by no means must they be read in that manner. Mothers may have their own reasons for creating a different sequence, for skipping certain chapters entirely, for exploring some chapters with younger children and others with older children, for repeating favorite chapters with additional books or movies, and so forth. Moms may have other ideas to add.

This book is certainly not intended to be an eight-month-only project! These eight topics can be revisited over and over again, with others added along the way, for as long as your mother-daughter book club stays together. You may eventually choose not to concentrate entirely, or even at all, on female-centric themes, books, and movies. *What matters most is being a club that remains focused on providing a nurturing small community for your daughters as they grow up.*

This book is a starting point for you, and a resource to keep returning to, but a successful club will eventually move beyond this book. That is how it is designed. When you no longer need to rely on this book, you will have developed your own skills for choosing topics, books, movies, and running discussions. That is my goal: to guide, support, and launch lots of self-sufficient mother-daughter book clubs that, in turn, will provide mentoring for other start-up clubs. Raising the next generation of empowered young women who are able to think critically about pop culture and are willing to be engaged about important issues, especially those related to women's rights and female leadership, is the objective of this book.

PART ONE

SETTING UP

YOUR CLUB

and

KEEPING IT STRONG

Why Form a Mother-Daughter Book Club?

One day Charlotte and I were talking politics. I told her that I thought the world would be a better place if half of the political power in every country were in the hands of women, who comprise half of the human population. I don't know if this will ever come to pass, or if the effect would be as I imagine—especially given that we have female politicians with a variety of political leanings—but perhaps we'd have less war, better education for our children, better health care for everyone, a cleaner environment, and in America, for sure, less time spent discussing abortion and birth control instead of jobs and the economy. I told Charlotte that my greatest hope is that in my lifetime I will see more women ascend into leadership roles in government, business, media, and other male-dominated realms where their presence could be a game changer.

"That is why I want us to write this book, because—"

"Because we have to start with the children," finished Charlotte.

That we do.

After this exchange, I remembered a favorite quote from the movie *Babe*. As the narrator said, "little ideas that tickled and nagged and refused to go away should never be ignored, for in them lie the seeds of destiny." This conversation with Charlotte tickled and nagged, and helped us refine our ideas on what the book should be, why mothers should read it, and why we feel mothers and daughters will benefit from starting their own club. So why form a book club?

We Need Small Villages

Mother-daughter book clubs are not only a vehicle for sharing the enjoyment of reading, but they also act as small villages where women can collectively support girls and model healthy femininity for them. As a broader culture, we are failing at this. The best interests of children seem to often come last, behind the best interests of adults and corporations that can make money by selling products and services that reinforce gender stereotypes. As grownups, when we prioritize profit over children, we are robbing our youngest citizens of a healthy childhood in order to line our pockets. It is an act of economic and emotional vandalism. But it doesn't have to go down like this.

Mother-daughter book clubs provide girl-friendly smaller villages, and in some ways they are emotionally safer than school and sometimes even home. For only children like mine, they are a place where they can feel something akin to having sisters. For children with siblings, they are a place where they can feel special and enjoy time spent with their mothers. Most important, clubs can really be the small, intimate groups in which girls experience a measured amount of communal upbringing, something that is sorely absent in today's world.

Clubs Can Meet a Wide Range of Goals

If you talk to people who have been in mother-daughter book clubs or if you read about them, you will quickly see that there are many reasons for forming them, as well as for staying in them over time. Some examples of differing missions include:

- providing more challenging books for strong readers;
- providing additional practice for weaker readers;
- building strong emotional bonds with daughters;
- social opportunities for mothers;
- social opportunities for girls;
- addressing important aspects of family life, such as imparting religious values, reinforcing racial identity, or fostering an appreciation for art or music; and/or
- helping girls become more confident by providing a safe place for them to express their opinions and use their intelligence, apart from the environment of school where some girls dumb themselves down.

This book will help you form and run a specific kind of mother-daughter book club that teaches mothers how to help daughters prepare for—and proactively address—the challenges facing them today. The goal is to raise girls to become confident young women in a culture that makes many girls and women feel insecure and powerless about their looks and abilities and future roles. With the tools you gain from this book, you will be able to instill in your daughters a greater sense of agency about their own lives, and this will lead to girls who are more resilient and more driven to reach their fullest potential.

But even with that specific mission, your club will be poised to accomplish other goals as well, as you come to define them. Once the meeting structure is in place, you can use it to enrich or empower the daughters of the club in whatever ways your own group determines are important. Clubs can and do evolve over time, and that is one of the beautiful things about them.

Clubs Help Moms and Girls Navigate the "Terrible Teens" and Other Clichés

When I was reading and researching in preparation for starting our own mother-daughter book club, and again as I worked on this book, I sometimes felt conflicted about the ways in which mother-daughter communication was discussed. Sure, it is very important and must be cultivated! But sometimes I felt that as the reader, I was presented with various euphemisms for girls and their behavior that were at best incomplete and at worst harmful clichés.

We have the moody, cantankerous "terrible teen," who drags her mother on terrifying roller coaster rides along with herself and all of her hormones. We have the "sullen tween," who stem-winds her mother by saying "nothing" when asked what she did at school that day, heading off to her bedroom with her smartphone and her itchy thumbs.

Of course there are girls like this, and mothers have battled or negotiated some version of these adolescent behaviors since time began. But there are many other kinds of preteens and teenagers, despite the fact that we often paint them all with the same brush. In fact, mother-daughter book clubs, if they are done well and started early, help prevent this kind of overhyped, door-slamming pod person from entering your house in the first place. Of course, there are no guarantees, and this book comes with no money-back offer. Mother-daughter book clubs are just a way of hedging your bet. I don't see these clubs as providing a flyover of some inevitable maelstrom so much as I see them as a way to create the kind of bonds that allow mothers and daughters to persevere through whatever developmental and relationship challenges await *all* of us as we grow older.

We spend a lot of time in our culture talking about strategies for dealing with the "turbulent teenage years," another favorite cliché. But the reality is that, these days, girls are ducking arrows on the frontlines of girl culture *way* before adolescence, and ten is the new fourteen in some respects. Even more interesting, and perhaps ultimately more significant, is that mothers have never been more vulnerable to their own media assault, which tells them they need to be hot from cradle to grave and must stay young and thin and beautiful (*like* their daughters, along *with* their daughters). Some mothers thus position themselves to be their daughters' peers, either due to their own conflicted feelings about aging or to the many books and movies that suggest that mothers and daughters should foremost be friends—even BFFs!

This is a big deal. Girls generally have multiple friends, but only one mother (or maybe two). Even for girls who do not have many or any friends, their mothers should not stand in as direct substitutes. The erosion of the line between girlhood and womanhood goes in both directions. While girls are racing to grow up as fast as possible, mothers, if they fall victim to the type of thinking the marketers count on, are racing in the other direction, toward their daughters and away from middle age. There is strategy behind the name of the popular clothing store Forever 21, which is patronized by both girls and women. I pull no punches when I say that mothers need to be mothers, first and foremost.

Communication between mothers and daughters has never been more complex or more crucial. Mothers in your club may not always agree—with each other or with the points made in this book—and that is OK, and great grist for conversation when it happens. Regardless of individual opinions on individual issues, the book and movie discussion skills taught here will benefit both daughters and mothers, and will help us stay close as females who are all dealing with some of the same unwholesome aspects of our current brand of femininity.

Both mothers and daughters can learn how to push back against some of these pressures. The most exciting and perhaps most transformative part of this process is that mothers and daughters *do* things within mother-daughter clubs that help them *be* things together as females, while still maintaining their separate roles. This happened to Charlotte and me, and it was joyous! She would be the first to tell you that we still butt heads a lot, but she has also told me that we have a depth to our adult relationship that seems unique, and I agree.

Clubs Help Mothers and Daughters See Each Other as Individuals

When Charlotte and I first started our club, we both knew the other four mothers and daughters fairly well. (This won't be the case for all clubs, but it was for ours.) Even so, I recall being pleasantly surprised by the way I got to know the other mothers and daughters so differently, and so much more intimately, within the context of our club over the years.

When we started the club, the girls were in third grade at the same elementary school. They played together. We mothers talked amongst ourselves while the girls played. We even socialized as couples and families. Yet through the lens of the club, I saw a different side of the other girls and moms. I even saw a different side of my own child, and she'd probably say the same about me.

I would characterize the mothers in our club as, on the whole, a mature, competent, and confident group of women. We all seemed to share the most important values that we hoped to pass down to our daughters. We all took our roles as mothers seriously, and viewed our roles as friends to our daughters secondarily. I think we each admitted to certain anxieties about raising girls—I know I did, often!—but together we seemed to know how to row in the same direction.

That said, we were still quite different people in a number of ways. I had one child, and the other mothers had two, two, four, and five children respectively. Over the years of our club, some of us worked outside the home while others didn't, and job circumstances changed from year to year for some of us. We had varying degrees of "craziness" in our lives in terms of how busy and stretched thin we were. We came from different religious and political backgrounds, although we were all Caucasian and middle- or upper-middle class. We had different personalities. While we didn't always agree, we usually tended to come to agreement, which was the important part. Creating and running a club brought out some of our differences because we had to make group decisions about the direction of the club—quite a different dynamic than chatting about the girls' latest math test while waiting to pick them up from school.

The girls always seemed more different than alike to me. Their friendships with each other were in flux at times. They all essentially got along, or we would not have come together for the club, but there were occasional social issues that developed (these will be discussed in greater detail in chapter 3).

In general, during the years of our club, regardless of our membership numbers, the girls each got so much time to speak—about the books, about school, and about their lives—that all of the mothers came to see each of them as wonderfully evolving individuals, not merely as the little girls they were during the early playdate years. Of course, part of this was that they were growing up! But much of it was that they were able to show us—and each other—who they really were as human beings within the comfortable haven of our club. Watching these girls find their voices as young women was extremely rewarding.

Clubs Are a Support Group for Moms

Although much of the focus of this book—and others on the same topic—is on what mother-daughter book clubs can do for girls, I can't stress enough how much these clubs can do for mothers as well. Some mothers will find the endeavor easy, while others may find it less so, at least initially. But everyone will gain the support from each other that they need. Raising kids today is hard, and raising girls comes with its own unique set of challenges for mothers. There were times I felt confident about how I was parenting Charlotte, and other times I looked to the moms in the club for assistance—either through a direct conversation, or simply by watching what they modeled with their own daughters.

Learning from other trusted and respected mothers is perhaps one of the least discussed but most important benefits to a mother-daughter book club, and here's why. In the twenty-five years I have worked with kids and parents, I have noticed a decline in the internal confidence mothers have about parenting. In my educational consulting practice, I am routinely involved with attentive parents who love their children deeply, but seem to seek my advice on everything—from the smallest decisions, such as what music classes to sign them up for, to the largest, such as how to help them stand up to bullies or how to get help for their teen's depression. That's fine, and that's my job. But what concerns me is how dependent upon "expert advice" too many mothers have become in recent years, as if they are birds that have suddenly lost their inner compass while migrating.

I have huge concerns about the parenting culture we now have, especially for mothers. Mothers are under constant media bombardment. You cannot open a magazine or browse articles online or tune in to Facebook without reading some version of how mothers are doing it wrong. Or can't have it all. Or should have it all. Or are not following the "right" method for potty training or breastfeeding or violin instruction or fill in the blank. And none of them, it seems, can regain their figures quickly enough after giving birth, like celebrities do. The cycle is endless.

Back when mothers raised children in literal villages, without the Internet but with grandmothers and aunts and sisters and village elders to guide and support them, were they better able to develop confidence in themselves as parents who could eventually rely on their own methods? And is methods just another word for instincts and communal knowledge?

Contemporary society involves a huge peanut gallery of experts who make a living hawking self-help books (am I one of them?), bloggers blogging bloggerifically throughout the blogosphere on their parenting blogs (am I one of *them*?), marketers instilling insecurity in mothers in order to sell them expensive products and services which promise to solve the insecurities the companies themselves created (nope, I'm not one of them), and so forth. Many mothers are so busy debating which author or talk show psychologist gives the best parenting advice that they can't hear their own inner voices. There is just too much noise in the system. And there is too much money to be made by those fanning the flames of the Mommy Wars. Mothers need to seek less validation for their parenting decisions, judge each other less, and find more ways to form genuine connections with other women who sincerely want to be their allies, not their "mompetitors."

It's no wonder so many moms are adrift today, reaching out plaintively for help navigating a culture that is not always supportive of their parenting. There is always a place for parenting experts. If there weren't, I'd have a different career—and I really love the one I have. However, there is a balance to be struck between seeking expert advice and following your gut instincts as a mom. This book includes many interviews with experts— lots of my favorites!—and recommendations for parenting books. All of this information is valuable. The endgame, though, is for moms to rely on each other as well as popular experts and lesser-known people like me. So this book can be seen ironically as both a parent guide/self-help book *and* a book about developing greater personal and social resources so that parenting books won't be needed as much.

Mother-daughter book clubs are a way to sidestep some of these distractions and instead listen closely to a small group of chosen mothers who you trust. Mother-daughter book clubs are not only a way for girls to find their inner voices, but for mothers to do the same.

Clubs Can Make Difficult Conversations Fun

That is not an oxymoronic heading, nor is it the whiteboard scribbling of an organizational consultant brought in to train employees on how to work out their differences. There really is a way to talk to girls about uncomfortable topics in a reasonably painless way. At the very least, you can spread the pain around a bit in a group setting!

The obstacles facing healthy female development are considerable, and will be thoroughly discussed in upcoming chapters. Some mothers may wonder, *"Is* there any solution?" Hang in there! The breaking news is that the research studies that have explored the ways in which girls are harmed by the current girl culture have universally found that mothers (and fathers and other mentors) have a lot more power to provide an effective counterbalance to all of those destructive messages girls consume every day than they believe they do. And yes, approaching difficult topics can be fun and done with humor. In fact, that is often the best way. As anyone with experience can attest, lectures certainly are not.

Many experts on media literacy caution that we should not place too much responsibility at the feet of parents. I agree that many problems are created by society and can only be solved by wide-scale social pushback. However, I recognize that when parents are overworked or in other ways unable to focus time and energy on fighting media messages coming into their own home or out in the world, their kids will be more vulnerable, and that this is unfair. Cultural change takes time. What are parents to do who feel they can't afford to wait for the culture to become more affirming to girls? My view is that those parents who do feel able to shoulder some of this burden need the tools to do so. That is what this book is: one tool, for those who want it.

Learning how to use books, movies, and other audiovisual media as tongs with which to pick up and examine difficult topics is central to this book. And there is strength in numbers. There were certain topics I found difficult to address with Charlotte one-on-one, but they were not always the same ones with which the other mothers in the group struggled. By approaching them collectively, different mothers can take the lead when they are in their comfort zone, and be followers when they are not.

Our club was a more traditional one, with a goal of empowering girls through reading female-centric literature that portrayed girls and women as strong, adventurous, and independent. *But this book is about forming mother-daughter clubs with the specific purpose of better preparing girls for the difficulties they will face as they grow into women—in school, at work, in their relationships, and out in the world at large.* This means that a club organized around this larger mission will, by definition, potentially grapple directly with more uncomfortable material than we did.

So where does the fun part come in? It comes in through all of the usual ways—the pizza for dinner, the special alone time with mom, the weekend getaways, the unique sense of social belonging that comes from being in a club, the exciting club activities and field trips, and the simple joy of reading and discussing books or movies. But it also comes from the shared and mutually understood task of talking about, you know, girl stuff!

Then there are the adventures! Perhaps one of the most exciting and fun things that happened in our club resulted from our decision to go to our local bookstore to attend a reading and signing by Jane Langton, whose new book *The Mysterious Circus* had just come out. We had read *The Fledgling* as a club, and some of the girls had read other Langton books as well, so it was a real treat. At the end, I got up the nerve to approach Langton and tell her that we were a mother-daughter book club and that we loved her books, but she headed me off at the pass with, "Oh, you must be a mother-daughter book club! I would be absolutely delighted to come to one of your meetings some time!"

You can't imagine the excitement of the girls (and moms!). But it was nothing compared to our excitement when the day came and we had Jane Langton all to ourselves to discuss her book *The Time Bike*. The more you invest in your club and the more you look for outside opportunities to enrich your meetings, the more likely it is that your club will stumble into situations like this one. Serendipity is a beautiful thing.

By way of a different kind of example of what is fun about mother-daughter book clubs, I remember a conversation I had with Charlotte when we were on a special mother-daughter trip to the beach to celebrate her thirteenth birthday—she had become, *gasp*, a teenager! This story doesn't start out super fun, but stay with me . . .

We took our trip during school vacation in December, and the book we were reading for our upcoming book club meeting was *The Secret Life of Bees* by Sue Monk Kidd. We had two bookmarks in the book, and would pass it back and forth on the beach, occasionally commenting on being ahead or behind the other one, and teasing each other about what was coming up that the other had not yet read. That lightheartedness belies the darkness of the story. It was a tough book in many respects, especially for me. I was born and raised in Georgia during the civil rights movement. There were many parts of *The Secret Life of Bees* that caused me pain.

One day Charlotte noticed me crying while reading the book. I don't even remember why, specifically. But it started a conversation about bigotry and hatred and abuse, and how we can respond to that kind of emotional material, that kind of history, and the fact that racism is still very much a part of the American experience today. We shared stories with each other of times we witnessed racism and how we felt and what we said or did . . . or didn't say or do and wished we had.

I obviously had more to share at my age than Charlotte did at hers, but the point is that we were sharing. We talked about different scenarios—some real and remembered, others imagined—and how we could respond in a way that stopped someone from being bullied or helped raise awareness or in some other way confronted racism. Before too long, we were not talking about Lily or any of the other characters in *The Secret Life of Bees* anymore, nor about anything else in life that felt heavy. We were walking across the sand to a snack bar to get some lunch, and Charlotte said to me, "Mom, it's so fun reading the same book at the same time with you and discussing it and getting to talk about *real* things. Things that are *important*. It makes me feel grown up."

I felt the same way. Charlotte was growing up, but so was I. I was learning how to build that bridge that would allow me to reach her and enjoy being with her as she got older. Bridges can take many forms. They can be built with art or music or sports or books or many other things. For Charlotte and me, it was a bridge of books, words, language, and ideas. It still is. Talking about what we read and feel and see in society is a bond that keeps growing. And it's fun. It is really, really fun to have this special connection with my daughter!

2

Getting Started

"When we share the experience of reading with our children, books create a garden, a special sunlit corner where our relationship can grow alongside, but apart from, the crowded landscape of everyday life."
—*from* The Mother-Daughter Book Club
by Shireen Dodson

In a way, starting a mother-daughter book club actually begins long before your daughter is at an age when she is reading chapter books, browsing library shelves, or mulling over which friends to invite to the club. It begins with raising a reader who will one day be excited by (or at least amenable to) the idea of forming such a club at all.

When Charlotte was very little—perhaps three or four years old—I did something on a sheer whim that turned out to be strikingly influential to her development as a reader. I have no idea how I got the idea, but one day I said to her, "You cannot have everything you want. Most things have limits. Toys have limits; you can't have all the toys you want. Candy has limits; you only get it once in a while for a special treat. But do you know one thing that will never have limits for you? Books! You can have *as many as you want.*"

I gave some version of this speech to Charlotte many times, and somewhere along the line she understood it, and she clung to this promise from me and reminded me of it often. It was an easy promise to keep, with the caveat that I did insist that "as many as you want" did not apply to retail bookstores. It applied to the library, the annual library book sale, thrift shops, yard sales, and used bookstores. In any of these places, I handed Charlotte a tote bag and said, "The sky's the limit!" After all, a tote bag full of fifty-cent books would cost me about the same as one new book from a retail shop. By the time Charlotte entered high school, she had more than one thousand well-read and cherished books. This was not a financial problem; it was a storage problem! That is not the worst problem to have.

In whatever creative ways you can muster, help your girls *love* reading, and read to them and in front of them often. By the time you start your club—or even well after—they will learn to feel the magic, and books will remain an important connection between the two of you for a lifetime.

Now that you and your book-loving daughter have decided to start a club, you'll need to think about next steps so that you can give your group the strongest foundation possible, ironing out as many details up front as you can before your much-anticipated first meeting.

Get Ready

When Charlotte and I strolled past the Concord Bookshop in the fall of 2000 and saw the display window dedicated to mother-daughter book clubs, we went inside and I bought a copy of Shireen Dodson's *The Mother-Daughter Book Club*. I read it, took notes, and spent weeks thinking about the concept before formulating a plan for starting a club of our own. It is easier to discuss the issues—from the simplest logistical decisions to the most deeply philosophical ones—when all mothers have the same information as their foundation, so all of the mothers read Dodson's book as well. Likewise, I recommend that all of the mothers who will be joining a club today read *Her Next Chapter*. From there, all of the many discussions that need to take place among the adults can proceed more smoothly. Different mothers will have different preferences, but I've outlined mine, and some questions to think about, below.

Who Will Lead?

I wanted a partner. I felt that reaching out first to one other mom would allow me to test the waters, see if she agreed the club was a good idea, and remove any appearance of me being the sole creator and manager of any club we might start. This worked beautifully. We had coffee and discussed everything from philosophy to practical matters, agreeing on almost everything, including the optimal size for the club and who else to invite. As we moved forward, we did so together, until we achieved a cohesive group of five mother-daughter pairs who were then charting a mutual course by consensus.

There are plenty of other ways to start—on one mother's initiative, or on more than two's. But whatever you do, be mindful of the fact that however you start, you will be proposing an activity that will ideally last for years. Laying the foundation for your club in as democratic and thorough a fashion as possible will serve all of you best in the long run.

What Is an Ideal Club Size?

It's important to place this question in proper context. Enjoyable book clubs can be as small as three pairs, or much larger, but since mother-daughter book clubs will be exploring challenging issues, a smaller, more intimate environment is best, so a club of three to five pairs is probably perfect. Six to ten members should be enough to stimulate discussion, but not so many as to intimidate quieter members or compromise privacy or emotional safety.

There is also the practical challenge of hosting big clubs because most families do not have big enough living rooms for large groups to sit comfortably. Big rooms in communal spaces such as libraries or community buildings do not usually feel cozy, and are often not even remotely private, which can have a chilling effect on discussion. However, I have observed public spaces that do work. Each club needs to choose a meeting space that best fits its needs.

Whom to Invite?

This consideration is important for any mother-daughter book club, but especially for one with our particular mission. For starters, it is crucial to choose mothers who are socially compatible and who share common values. Relationships between young girls can change at any moment, so the relationships between the moms must be the glue that holds the club together over time. If the mothers are on the same page about the purpose of the club and how to pursue it, the club will thrive. If the mothers agree from the beginning to discuss difficult topics directly, there is less likelihood of conflict down the road. After deciding on an ideal number of reading pairs, brainstorm a list of moms who at first glance seem to agree on a few key points:

- Girls and women face unique obstacles.
- A healthy way of guiding daughters is to form a mother-daughter book club.
- It is important for everyone to approach issues sensitively, but without denial.
- It is important to be able to agree on selected books and movies (generally meaning that members will share similar opinions on what is "age appropriate" in terms of book and movie content).

While it is idealistic and appealing to think about creating a club with mothers who have very divergent views, this has specific advantages and disadvantages for a mother-daughter book club, and they bear consideration. For example, if some mothers don't want their daughters exposed to any violence in books or movies, then your club will be unable to read a book such as *Gorillas in the Mist*, the story of Dian Fossey. Likewise you will not be able to watch the movie. If you disagree with this stipulation for your own daughter, you might become frustrated. Longevity is predicated upon the club not falling apart, and when mothers cannot agree on the things that give the club cohesion, it cannot survive. In a classroom, many different voices are educational. In a book club like this one, there is room for differences of opinion about all kinds of things in life, but there are fundamental mission-based values that, if not in sync, will pull the club apart before it ever gets off the ground. Diversity of race, religion, socioeconomic status, and so forth are desirable for any group. What is key is that despite those differences, all of the mothers are united in their vision for the club.

After coming up with a list of potentially well-matched moms, then consider the daughters. In some clubs the mothers and daughters all previously know each other. However, there can be any combination of mothers and/or daughters who are already acquainted, are good friends, or have never even met. Anything can work as long as you begin with very frank discussions about what the moms want to get out of the club for their daughters and themselves, and how they fundamentally view the world. Secondarily, it helps if the girls like each other—or are neutral or have never met. Avoid creating a club with girls who are known not to care for each other or who have had direct conflicts. Girls can go to the same or different schools, but they should be close in age.

What Is the Right Age for the Girls in the Club?

Although I have heard of clubs that started when girls were still reading picture books, I think the optimal time to start is when the girls are reading short chapter books, typically around age eight (the third grade). You can certainly start them later. If you start them earlier, the girls will eventually be able to read the kinds of books that really lend themselves to discussion. For the purpose of this particularly themed mother-daughter book club, I recommend beginning at age eight or older because this is also the age at which girls are able to understand and contribute to conversations about the challenges they face as females.

What About the Reading Levels of the Girls?

When starting our own club, this is a question about which we probably did not make the right judgment call. We wanted the club to be inclusive of different kinds of readers, because that seemed good and right. When the girls we invited were in third grade, there were differences in their reading abilities, but who knew if these would persist or change over time? We started out dealing with the disparity by compromising and choosing books "in the middle." Ultimately that frustrated the one weaker reader *and* the four stronger readers. I have often wondered if things would have been better if the split were three to two in one direction or the other. Socially, I believe it would have been, but in terms of the book selections, the problem would have been the same. And as the girls got older, it became even more difficult, because the stronger readers clamored for more advanced books, and the weaker reader had to face a monthly slog.

Sadly, five years in, that mother-daughter pair dropped out, after having tried really hard to stick with it. It was simply no longer fun for the daughter for whom the reading each month was such a burden on top of homework. I don't wish that this particular mother-daughter pair had never been invited, because they were a wonderful addition in all other ways, but I do regret that perhaps, instead of helping that daughter enjoy reading, the club may have inadvertently made her feel worse because self-comparisons to the stronger readers were inevitable. I have concluded that, to the degree possible, it is best if the girls of the club read on roughly the same level, regardless of what that level is. The bottom line is that all of the girls should feel relaxed, happy, and good about themselves when they are in a mother-daughter book club.

Get Set

You've determined the size and scope of your club and selected the founding members. Now you'll have to think about the logistics of your meetings.

How Often Should Clubs Meet?
When, Where, and for How Long?

The frequency of your meetings is of course each club's choice, but what worked for us were monthly meetings during the school year, with summers off. That allowed the right amount of time to read each book and plan for meetings. More frequent meetings would have been too much work and would have conflicted with the many other commitments each family had to juggle; less frequent meetings would have diminished the cohesion of the group.

I strongly recommend meeting in members' homes rather than public places. However, there are many ways to be creative. As long as members feel physically comfortable, closely connected, and protected from eavesdropping strangers, it should all work out. I know of one club that met in a very small, comfy room in a church basement. Those members felt they had privacy, and enjoyed not having to take turns hosting in their small houses and apartments.

We chose to meet the first Friday of the month for a casual dinner, rotating houses. We came together at 6:00 PM and usually ended by 8:30 PM. This allowed about half an hour for the moms to catch up, share a glass of wine (something we actually discussed: whether or not to drink in front of the kids!), discuss in advance our own reactions to the book, and help the hosting mom pull dinner together while the girls played and chatted. We would usually eat a very simple dinner of pizza, pasta, or some other super easy, kid-friendly food from around 6:30 PM to 7:15 PM—with lots of raucous table conversation—and then clear the table. We'd move to the living room to start the discussion by 7:30 PM. Sometimes we had dessert before the meeting; other times we took a break midway to have dessert.

There are *infinite* variations on my club's routine. I know of clubs that meet for dessert only, after their own family dinners, and ones that meet on Sunday afternoons and serve only a snack. Whatever you choose to do, try to pick a schedule and routine that everyone feels they can commit to. Take my word for it: you will want to avoid rescheduling missed book club meetings. When several families are involved, getting disparate schedules to align can prove tricky. You can always try something out; if you find it is not working, try something else. For our club, the shared meal around the table was an integral part of our experience. We stuck with it even when we felt tired at the end of the week. I'm sure there were times when each of us might have preferred not to host at all. We had a rule that no mom should feel guilty about deciding to order pizza when it was her turn to host. The no-shame pizza rule was a proactive way of alleviating pressure on the host and making sure the meetings happened!

Have a Moms' Organizational Meeting

One of the reasons our club started out so well is that the mothers made the time to thoroughly discuss all of the issues we could anticipate before including the girls and having our first official meeting as a mother-daughter book club. Of course there were ongoing conversations throughout the years about issues that came up as the girls got older, but we built a foundation from the beginning that greatly benefitted us in the long term.

In addition to making sure we were as ideologically aligned as possible, one of the other helpful things we did was to collect our thoughts about what guidelines we wanted for our club *before* bringing the girls in on that discussion. And you do need to eventually bring the girls in on that discussion if you want them to buy in. Some of the guidelines that our club adopted included the following:

- Strive to make the club feel like a fun extracurricular activity, not school.
- Always read the book. (I know, a cliché as guidelines for book clubs go!)

- Reserve meetings as special mother-daughter time. Fathers, other relatives, or sitters took care of any other siblings one Friday evening per month.

- Request that mothers and daughters attend meetings together as much as possible. However, when one was sick or otherwise unable to make a meeting, it was fine for the other to come solo so that the meeting did not have to be rescheduled.

- Do not allow other adults (such as, fathers or babysitters) to accompany girls to meetings.

- Discuss with the girls the importance of not bragging about the club at school or appearing cliquey.

- Agree in advance on a process for deciding whether or how to replace any members who drop out.

- Commit to starting and ending meetings on time.

- Schedule meeting dates and the rotation of hosting duties at the beginning of the school year and for the whole year, so everyone could plan ahead.

All clubs are unique and will have their own details to sort out. Our choices were our own. Another club might be just fine with siblings being around during meetings or putting meetings on the calendar on a month-by-month basis. A club beginning today might want to address the issue of cell phone use during meetings, something that was not a problem in the prehistoric days of our own club ten years ago! As long as the moms can reach agreement on the logistics as well as the goals for the club, that is what counts.

A few words about movies . . .

Our own book club did not watch movies—we were all about books. In order to broaden the ways in which mother-daughter clubs can be enjoyed, I decided to add recommended movies because some clubs may occasionally like to discuss a movie instead of a book, or may want to watch a movie after reading the book, or vice versa. I remember that there were certain months of the year, such as December, when our families were so busy that watching a two-hour movie at home instead of spending many hours reading a book would have been a welcome reprieve. Therefore, mothers are free to decide what balance they prefer between reading and movie watching. I love books, but I was amazed by some of the movies I have discovered, and many of them affected me very deeply. You will have plenty of choices for what you read and watch, both as a club and at home in your spare time.

Choosing Your Monthly Books and Movies

We've all heard the saying "so many books, so little time." Nothing could be more apropos for describing how hard it was to select books (and movies and media) to recommend for this guide. Some of these titles are ones our own book club enjoyed, some are ones Charlotte and/or I enjoyed, and still others were recommended by librarian and movie-expert friends that I thought would make great additions.

My recommendations may well suffice, but mothers should feel free to explore all of the resources out there when selecting books or movies for their own club. There are entire books written about how to select good girl-centric literature. There are also some excellent websites devoted to both books and movies that are recommended for girls. Some of those helpful resources are listed at the end of this book.

That said, how might mothers decide what will work best for their own clubs each month? Here are a few things to consider:

- The lists I present at the end of chapters 4 to 11 are prescreened to work well for each chapter's specific topic.

- I've developed discussion guides for some of the recommendations. So if you want to have a ready-made list of questions to use, perhaps until you are comfortable creating your own, you have the option of choosing some of the books and movies that come with guides.

- Each list of recommended books and movies includes selections that are appropriate for different ages, so you may revisit these lists as your girls get older, making choices that are age-appropriate each year.

- I tried to include a variety of genres of books and movies, so that your clubs may choose among them as you see fit. I remember that the girls in our own club really loved getting into different genres at different times. We might have gone for a while exploring biographies, and then the mood shifted to historical fiction. One day the girls approached the mothers and requested we read some short stories. Get input, and have fun trying out new types of books!

- When our club first began, the mothers chose all of the books. Thought was given to selecting books that were a good match for the expressed interests of the daughter whose family would be hosting in a particular month. For example, in seventh grade, Charlotte really wanted the "short stories" month to be at our house, so it was scheduled that way.

- In the busier months we scheduled shorter books or easier reads, and in less busy months we scheduled longer, more challenging ones.

- As time went on, we sought more feedback from the girls on books they wanted on the list. After a few years, developing the reading list each year was truly a joint mother-daughter endeavor, led by the girls. Mothers always retained veto power, though!

- We tried not to choose books that were out of print and hard to find, or ones that were new and only available for purchase in hardcover.

- We gave the girls veto power over any books the moms suggested that they had already read or knew were going to be read in school.

- We allowed any girl who had already read a book on her own to remove it from our list if she did not want to read it again.

These are just some of the decisions we made on selecting books, and I think the same analysis could be applied to choosing movies. Again, your own club may create other guidelines.

How to Assess the Age-Appropriateness of Books and Movies

If it is possible to be both a liberal and conservative parent at the same time, I was and still am both to Charlotte. When it came to keeping her physically safe and emotionally happy, I was vigilant, cautious, and methodical.

But when it came to giving her as many windows and lenses as possible for viewing our complex world, I bent over backwards, often spontaneously, and learned I could somehow wing it. I was the mother who only let her eight-year-old daughter watch wholesome television, for short periods of time each day, but who talked to her about the horrors of war and why they were fought while letting her watch *PBS NewsHour* right beside me. I did not want her to see programs and commercials that purveyed the most gender stereotypical and sexualizing aspects of pop culture, but I did want her to know, for example, that there were girls around the world who were abused and deprived of education.

I suppose there was a method to my madness. I believed that acknowledging that there were bad things and bad people in the world—while telling Charlotte that her father and I would always do everything possible to protect her—taught her resilience and gratitude. I did not want her to see commercials that made her feel she was not pretty enough, but I did want her to understand her privilege. To this end, I made dozens of split-second decisions each week about what I considered "appropriate" for her to see or hear at her age. Sometimes my parenting was in line with others' and sometimes it was not. I didn't worry a lot about that.

When it came to our book club, I was almost always on the same page as the other mothers when the girls were young. Once they were in middle school, I noticed that I was OK with book content that occasionally made other mothers less comfortable. I pass no judgment on this. There is no one-size-fits-all when it comes to child rearing.

In my own view, there is such a thing as gratuitous sex and violence, and then there is sex and violence that is not excessive and is integral to the story. I recall that some of the books we mothers analyzed in terms of mature content included *Lord of the Flies, Life of Pi,* and *A High Wind in Jamaica.* Bringing up these books and others like them as hypotheticals is a good exercise. It allows moms to determine where their comfort zones lie and how closely aligned their views are or are not—something that is important to ascertain early on.

Within the book and movie recommendations at the end of chapters 4 to 11, you will find a great variety of content suitable for girls of different ages. With the movies it was easy—I simply gave the movie's MPAA rating and stated if I disagreed with it. I leave it to mothers to preview the films, talk to friends, or read parent reviews on the Internet to determine at what age children should be allowed to see each movie. Ratings are sometimes questionable in either direction. And no institutional rating can replace a mother's own good judgment about what is or is not appropriate for her daughter.

I really wrung my hands over how to assign age recommendations for each book. I came up with age recommendations based on what I could read on online book review sites and in book compilations, along with my own opinion after reading the book and consulting my librarian friends and Charlotte on their thoughts. There is nothing scientific about it. The age recommendations are meant as guidelines, and they necessarily take into account both reading level *and* maturity of content. Often, these do not sync up. It is up to moms to research or preview books to determine if the reading level and content are appropriate for their own girls. We moms all have different opinions about content, and our girls might be strong, weak, or average readers.

When assessing the age appropriateness of books and movies, I suggest you do not act overly protective and shield girls from *all* sex and violence, especially after they've graduated from elementary school. They need to be able to process certain realities of our world, and will face them eventually—with or without us present. I think it's best that girls experience some thoughtfully chosen mature content with their mothers first. This way they will have support and guidance, and will be able to filter what they read or view through their mothers' values. If they are confused or worried, their mothers will be there to answer questions and provide reassurance.

It is natural for mothers to assume their girls are more innocent and naïve than they really are. While working in schools, it was never fun to be the one to tell parents that their children were less innocent than they thought. Knowing this, I promised myself that I would try to strike a balance between protecting Charlotte from growing up too fast and leaving her to receive information from her peers before me.

It's impossible to manage this informational balancing art perfectly in our digital world, but girls do thrive when they feel their mothers trust them, respect them, and are honest with them about difficult subjects. This helps keep the lines of communication open. Keeping this advice in mind when choosing books and movies makes the process easier. There is no one-size-fits-all set of book or movie recommendations, so it is important that the mothers of your club agree about how to make selections and, eventually, when and how to give over some of this power to the daughters.

How Should the Questions and Prompts Be Used?

Just as it helps new teachers to create and follow detailed lesson plans, it helps the mothers of a new mother-daughter book club to have plenty of sample questions and discussion pointers at their fingertips. If your club feels this guidance is helpful, there are enough discussion questions offered in this book to allow a club to meet monthly for up to twenty-four months without having to plan any of your own discussions.

It was quite a lot of fun for me making up the questions! I kept a notepad beside me at all times while reading books and watching movies, jotting down ideas. My intention is that all of these questions and prompts will give confidence to mothers as they lead their first discussions. There are more questions per book or movie recommendation than you will likely get through in a given meeting, so you can pick and choose your favorites, or do some at one meeting and the rest at the next, or simply go with what seems most interesting to the girls.

Don't worry if you only get to three or one or none of the questions supplied in the guides from this book. Sometimes discussions take an unexpected turn, and it's best to let it happen if it feels productive. Some of the most magical moments in our own book club happened when a question on the list led to conversation that took on a life of its own. If the conversation is interesting and the daughters are enjoying it and you can feel your bonds being strengthened, just go with it! You can always loop back to questions on the list later, or even individually between mother-daughter pairs on the car ride home or at some other time. If you are anxious about getting through all of the questions on the list, the daughters will sense this anxiety and will experience the club meetings as having some tension and perhaps too much structure, the way it feels in school when a teacher is rushing through material. So relax and take the pressure off yourselves—everyone will have more fun, including you.

Remember that there are no right or wrong answers, just as there really are no right or wrong questions.

Can Moms and Daughters Create Their Own Discussion Questions?

Some mothers and daughters may never feel comfortable creating their own discussion questions. Some may grow to feel comfortable after a few meetings. And still some others may feel comfortable from the start. There are no rules about it. However, if you hope to stay together for a long time and choose other books from the recommendation lists in this book or from elsewhere, you will have to think about ways of planning a discussion. Google is your friend.

As daughters get older and take on increasing responsibilities leading discussions, they might find some online resources helpful as well. There are also plenty of books (see the resources section) that give sample discussion questions. And of course, you can always just wing it. It gets easier with practice. A good way to get started with using your own questions is to use some of mine, add some of your own, and see how the mix-and-match goes!

It's also OK to go completely off script. If mothers thoroughly read and understand the issues articulated in the upcoming chapters, they will be much better equipped to guide club discussions on their own terms or to even veer off into discussions about society in general or the real lives of the girls, related or unrelated to any of the recommended books. This is what teaching media literacy is about: understanding each challenge faced by girls and women, and teaching girls to deconstruct the disempowering messages that are harmful to their self-esteem. The book and movie and media recommendations—and the discussion questions that go with some of the books and movies—are *tools*. Use them as you see fit. If you ground yourself in a solid understanding of the issues so that you are prepared to answer daughters' questions, the rest will follow.

Meeting and *being* are more important than following any particular plan or structure. If you have good chemistry and are comfortable engaging in personal dialogue, you are de facto fulfilling one of the goals of a mother-daughter book club: creating a supportive little community for raising girls to become emotionally healthy, connected to their mothers, and allies to one another.

How Should Mothers and Daughters Use the Media Suggestions?

I love the power of Internet media when it is used for good and not evil! Sometimes the message packed into a two- or three-minute video is unequaled by anything you'd spend two hours watching or ten hours reading. Obviously, we're all interested in powerful *positive* media for girls.

Included in the upcoming recommendations are videos that further educate mothers and daughters. Mothers should preview all media recommendations first to determine which ones they feel are appropriate for their daughters, and at what ages.

These videos can be viewed together as a whole club, at home by mother-daughter pairs, or by mothers only. They are sure to provoke very interesting conversations! Be sure to read the comment threads when you can. Although this always involves some degree of peril from dreaded Internet trolls, I usually find the various points of view on the issues to be fascinating; they very often add substance to any discussion about the video content. Even when commenters hold views that are misogynistic, it is helpful to be aware of these views and to discuss with girls that there are people in the world who have these opinions, why this is the case, and what to do when stumbling upon antiwoman rhetoric. Unfortunately, bigotry is a part of life, and as mothers we owe our daughters a realistic conversation about it in all of its forms, including misogyny. Knowledge is power.

Go!

Now you're ready: your very first mother-daughter book club meeting! Our club had a marvelous first meeting. I still remember it vividly. The mothers had decided that the first meeting with the girls should not involve a book discussion yet, but should be devoted to getting to know each other better and talking about how the club would work. The girls were so excited they could barely sit still!

First-Meeting Icebreakers

We started our first gathering with dinner, as would become our custom, and then played some icebreaking games. You can find many different ones to choose from online or in books, but here's what we did:

1. We had each mother interview her own daughter, and vice versa. The interview questions were pretty straightforward, but there was still a lot of giggling. ("Hey mom, I'm *interviewing* you!") The questions we used were: *What is your favorite book? Who is your favorite author? What is your favorite genre of book to read? What are you looking forward to about being in this reading group? What else would you like everyone to know about you?* To this day I have saved the girls' adorable handwritten answers to the interviews of their mothers, as well as the mothers' written

answers given by their daughters. Once all of the interviewing was done, each member "introduced" her mother/daughter to the group by reading the answers to the questions. Very non-threatening and simple!

2. Next we played a game called "Two Truths and a Lie," where each member wrote down two things that had really happened to her and one that hadn't, striving to recall two amazing truths and inventing one believable falsehood. This was another way to share information about ourselves using the vehicle of a fun and quirky game. I recently came upon my pages and Charlotte's. Charlotte's statements were: *1. I once swung over the bar of my swing set. 2. My favorite meal is mussels marinara. 3. When I went to London, I saw the Queen.* Number one was the lie. Mine were: *1. I used to work in a planetarium. At night I showed visitors the moon and stars through the big telescope in the observatory, and during the day I showed them sunspots. 2. I once jumped out of a plane with a parachute. 3. I met a former president of the United States when I was a little girl and he sat down with me to talk about my favorite books.* Any guesses? Number two was the lie, and number three is an awesome story!

Get Down to Business

After everyone was warmed up, we covered the following items of business:

- The selection process for books.
- The meeting schedule.
- The importance of commitment (reading the books, being prepared for discussions, trying not to miss meetings, etc.).
- Our commitment to making the club fun and not like school . . . not to insinuate school is not fun! (They got it.)
- Reminding the girls not to brag about the club at school, since that might hurt other girls' feelings.
- Soliciting their input on how we can have book discussions that everyone enjoys, where everyone gets a fair turn to speak, where no one talks too much, etc. They had great ideas!

As we wrapped up, the moms announced the first book that we'd all be reading during the next month, as well as the home where the first official book club discussion would take place.

Subsequent Meetings: Tips for Having Fun, Productive Discussions

I have a theory about teaching people how to lead book discussions, and it's the same as my theory about coaching people to speak in public: if you overwhelm someone with too many things she must remember and hold at the front of her brain while executing the task, she will be more anxious and less effective. There is a lot that has been written about leading book discussions, but if you read too much of the logistical minutia, you might be apt to feel increasingly more worried and less confident about pulling it off. You'll wonder, *How in the world can I remember all of this?* Therefore, I believe the most productive way of empowering mothers to lead discussions is to suggest just a few of the most general, most helpful pointers, rather than diving into the weeds on the lesson. So here they are:

- *Remember that your role is to facilitate.* Try to ask questions that get others talking, and then step back and listen.

- *Discourage literary debates between the moms.* There is no better way to alienate the daughters, and they may balk at coming to meetings if the moms appear to be lecturing them on the books, or too wrapped up in their own adult conversation.

- *When possible and relevant, ask questions that help the girls pivot from discussing the characters in the book or movie to talking about their own experiences.* See the discussion guides in this book for examples of how to do just that. This is when conversations really become dynamic and inspiring, because the transitions from academic discussions to personal ones are what ultimately change lives over time.

- *Encourage the girls to take turns.* If one is using up too much time, do not hesitate to step in and politely thank her for her opinions and create an opening for others to speak by simply asking, "What do others think?" or something similar.

- *If a girl is not speaking, ask her if she would like a turn, but do not press her if she chooses not to speak.* You want to ascertain if she is having difficulty getting a word in edgewise, or if she is simply more comfortable listening.

- *Model comfort with silence.* If there is a pause in the conversation, members may be reflecting on what has been said and considering what to say next. Give it a minute. Shier members will often contribute in moments when the pace of discussion slows down. However, if the discussion has truly fizzled, ask the group if anyone has anything else to add and then move on to the next discussion question.

A goal of many mother-daughter book clubs is to eventually encourage the girls to lead discussions themselves. In our club, the girls did an amazing job, even the ones who were more introverted. It seems to me that they modeled themselves on the examples set by the moms!

Running Smoothly

—⟫ ⟪—

"As the girls grew and started middle school, then high school, the books we read and the issues we tackled challenged us in unexpected ways. We ended up talking about many topics we'd never envisioned discussing when our girls were in elementary school, including underage drinking, date rape, deciding whether to have sex with a boyfriend, teen pregnancy and parenthood, and many other types of risky behavior. We also read books that were laugh-out-loud funny, told tales of fantastical worlds, and relayed true stories about people and events. When I look back over the long tenure of both my clubs, I realize we have accomplished even more than we hoped to when we started out."
—*from* Book by Book: The Complete Guide to Creating Mother-Daughter Book Clubs *by Cindy Hudson*

Over time, as the girls in the club get older and family lives change, there are sometimes steps that mothers need to take to keep the club enjoyable and a priority in their lives, as well as their daughters'. By anticipating and communicating about some common growing pains, clubs can stay strong and last for years.

When Family Lives Change

We are all familiar with the notion that tasks and responsibilities tend to get added to our plates but never removed. Life just has a way of feeling busier every year. The decision to form or join a mother-daughter book club should not be made lightly. Committing to the reading and setting aside one evening per month to meet—or whatever other arrangement you make—is a significant investment. It has increasingly fabulous returns, but the commitment becomes harder to maintain when moms and daughters find themselves pulled in more and more directions. Just a few of the issues you might face include:

- increasing homework demands
- girls taking on more extracurricular activities
- girls pursuing separate and busier social lives outside the club
- mothers needing to spend increasing time supporting the interests and activities of other children in the family
- mothers going back to work or working more hours
- mothers and/or girls wanting to reprioritize their commitments

I remember thinking a lot about this when our own club formed. Because I'd worked in schools and been around families for so many years, I knew what lay ahead for me (and the rest of us): life would inevitably speed up. And when it started to happen, I would fantasize about an invisible force field that could materialize around our club and keep the rest of the world out for that one evening a month. Personal and family obligations chipped away at our time together, and it took a joint effort to protect what we had built. Here are two things we did that helped:

- At the end of every school year, we went out to dinner together to discuss how we felt the year had gone for our book club and to look ahead to the next year. It was a chance for us to talk about the highlights and lowlights of the past nine months, to propose any changes we might want in the future, and to officially let each other know if we could commit to another year come September. This conversation generally happened over egg rolls and wonton soup.

▰ Informally during the year, we mothers would discuss any concerns of our own or our daughters. This sometimes happened between just two mothers, and sometimes as a whole group. Nipping things in the bud is always preferable to letting issues simmer. We were fortunate that we all considered ourselves friends and could usually talk about anything that was bothering us or our girls. That's not to say it always worked out this way or was always easy, but we did our best—and this goes back to my earlier point about it being so key that the mothers be the glue for the club. It is healthy to set aside, in one way or another, mothers-only time with each other.

There are bigger challenges than busy lives, of course. There can be serious illness, death, loss of a job, or divorce (as happened to me during the book club years). Even happy milestones, such as the birth of a new baby, can shake things up. How each club collectively weathers these life events will differ. However, the way these clubs can function as support groups for the moms can feel like a port in the storm when one is most needed. And when mothers help each other out, they model that virtue for their daughters.

What to Do When Girls Have Social Conflicts

When we started our own club, the then-five girls went to the same school. They were not all best friends, but they did know each other and had no conflicts. It seemed about as good as one could hope for with five girls. But in the back of my mind, I could not help wondering, *Will it still be this way when puberty hits?* Even in third grade, it is possible to get a glimpse of which girls might be more popular when they are older, and which ones might be more likely to march to the beat of their own drummers. You can see as they approach adolescence which girls are becoming concerned with their physical appearance, which ones are experiencing emerging popularity, and which ones are most likely to embrace their inner nerd. There are no crystal balls, but one thing can be counted on: the girls will grow and change in a few predictable—and many unpredictable—ways.

I wondered how the girls of our group would get along come middle school, when social pressures might push some together and pull others apart. I hoped that when this happened—because to some degree it was inevitable—our club would remain a comfortable respite from the developmentally normal social strivings, competitions, and occasional bullying episodes that arise when middle schoolers try to figure out and claim their places in the social hierarchies of their peer groups. I never thought for a moment we would somehow escape these fun times! I just did not know exactly how the middle school years would play out in our club, and whether, as moms, we would be able to support our daughters through any conflicts that arose between them. Very privately, I wondered if we as moms would be able to handle sticky situations among the girls without becoming defensive about our own kids.

I was right to wonder, because it did come to pass that the girls grew to be more different over time. Each one orbited in her own social sphere at school, so that which still tied them together increasingly became only their shared history and continued participation in our reading club. By middle school we were down to four pairs, and those four girls went different ways beginning in sixth grade. There were two middle schools in town. Randomly, one girl went to one, and the other three went to the other. Among the three, two remained in the same social circle and the other joined a new set of friends.

But on the first Friday of every month, there we all were together, catching up and trading stories and sharing our excitement about reading, just as we'd always done. That bond was still strong. It was not strong enough, however, to prevent a very typical social conflict from arising between two of the girls during their seventh-grade year.

It took a long time for me to figure out what was happening. At first I had the vague sense that there was tension between the girls, but I couldn't tell where it was coming from. Eventually, during one of our mother-daughter weekend trips, the situation became obvious because we were together for two days instead of a few hours. To come right to the point, one girl teased another about her weight. And is there anything surprising about that? No. Body shaming is one of the most common forms of bullying, especially between girls, and I blame myself to this day for not anticipating it and doing something to help us all prepare for the eventuality that someday something like this would happen in our club—because after all, our club existed within, not outside, the real world of girlhood.

If I could turn back the clock, I would have discussed the possibility of girl-on-girl bullying with the mothers first, making sure everyone was on board with the understanding that *any one* of the daughters could be a bully or be bullied. None of our girls were somehow immune to either of these roles, despite what excellent moms we all knew we were! I'd have made sure we were all more explicit in setting expectations for kindness, and that we formed a common strategy about how we would handle any bullying if it occurred. Because our own mother-daughter book club did not have this book's stated mission of proactively addressing challenges faced by girls and women, we did not anticipate the developmentally typical but damaging behavior of girls bullying each other over physical appearance. This will be addressed directly in chapters 6 and 7 of this book, but it was not really on our radar back in 2004.

How did we handle it? Not very well. The classic mom-jitsu move of ignoring troubling behavior until it hopefully goes away is not recommended. It took a long time for the issue to become clear to us, because kids can be rather secretive when they are bullying, being bullied, or being bystanders. It is also rather hard to put your ego aside as a mother and accept that your daughter might be the perpetrator of bullying. It was difficult for us to discuss as mothers because we had not created a blueprint for the necessary discussion earlier, before there was a need for it, and before feelings were hurt. It was a big elephant in the room. I share the lesson with future clubs: *expect* social conflict between the girls. If it doesn't happen, that's terrific. If it does, you'll be better prepared to see the truth and deal with it right away.

Moms Don't Always Agree Either: How to Get Unstuck

A mother-daughter book club can be a very intimate experience. Members' closeness may extend well beyond group reading and into the private details and relationships between mothers and daughters, daughters as friends, mothers as friends, and beyond. There are no substantive human relationships that are completely devoid of conflict, and I submit that conflict can be healthy.

When book club mothers disagree, a few of the most common sources of conflict include:

- Frustration resulting from members not following the agreed-upon guidelines for participation in the club, such as when one pair misses too many meetings, or when one member consistently does not do or finish the reading.

- Difficulty agreeing on books and movies, often related to maturity level of content.

- Differences that arise between moms during discussions that veer onto subjects such as religion or politics.

- Events outside of the club that spill into the club, such as quarrels between girls at school, which cause mothers to feel upset with each other's daughters and often each other.

- Life stressors that affect a mom or daughter and excessively intrude into club meeting time.

My own club dealt with almost all of these, in some measure, from time to time. However, I don't recall a high level of conflict, partly because we were all very close and also somewhat conflict-averse, and partly because we had the good fortune of not running into very much conflict. We did not always agree on book selections, especially when the girls were in middle school. When this happened, we tried to compromise and usually did, but there were times (probably more than we all verbalized) when one mother or another wished we either had or had not read a certain book.

Choosing members at the outset who share similar values cuts down on how often this happens, but when it does, moms need to articulate to one another why they believe a book or movie is a good or a poor choice, and members need to really listen to opposing views and try to either come to consensus, or agree to disagree and propose alternate outcomes so that no mother feels or experiences that her wishes are never considered.

What to Do If Members Quit

I know of very few clubs that have not faced this challenge. No matter how committed everyone is at the beginning, over the years lives and circumstances change. Even the most solid club is likely to lose one or more mother-daughter pairs along the way. The most common reasons members quit include the following:

- moving
- being too busy
- reshuffling priorities
- being unhappy in the club

Our club started with five mother-daughter pairs and we lost two of them during our six years together. It is important to acknowledge that members may quit, but also to agree upon a plan for whether or how to replace pairs if they do leave. Our club did discuss this, but I don't recall that we took it quite as seriously as we should have. We were very confident we'd go the distance together. What we had decided in the first year was that if a pair left we would:

1. Decide *if* we all wanted to replace them, or whether we preferred to move forward as a smaller group.

2. Agree on who would replace the departing pair if we chose to do so. Anyone could have veto power over a choice if she did not feel comfortable with it; *everyone* would have to agree on whom to invite. If we could not agree unanimously, then by default we would not invite anyone new and would move forward as a smaller club.

This all sounds logical, right? Well, hindsight is twenty-twenty, and I no longer think so. Here's why: it was simply too easy not to replace pairs when they left. It was *much* easier to say:

- "We're fine as a smaller group!"
- "It would be hard to agree on the same mother-daughter pair, so let's not bother."
- "We've known each other so long, it would be awkward for another pair to enter now—for them *and* for us."
- "Since the rest of us are fully committed and no one else will leave, this won't happen again."

See the problem? Right—magical thinking. By the time our second pair quit, we were down to three pairs who'd been together for five years, and at that point the idea of inviting someone new just felt impossible. We were not happy to be reduced to three pairs but agreed to make the best of it, and again recommitted to staying together through high school—another five years! The assumption was, again, that no one else would quit, and we'd be fine.

One year later, another pair quit, citing busy lives as the reason. The girls were about to begin high school. The two pairs remaining—including Charlotte and me—were now very upset. Can two pairs constitute a club? We decided not, and that we'd cut our losses there and try to stay in touch in other ways. I recall a particularly sad dinner at which the four of us—the two moms and two fourteen-year-old girls—met at a restaurant to discuss everything. The girls were even more disappointed than the moms. Both of them adored the club and desperately wanted it to continue until it came to a natural ending, when the girls went off to different colleges. They felt shocked that it had ended the way it did. Now, looking back on it, we should not have been surprised. We should have had a different mind-set from the beginning.

Had we replaced the first pair who quit early on in the club, we could have set a precedent for how to handle further departures down the road. It would not have been that hard to do in our second year together, and we'd have adjusted our expectations regarding variable club membership in a healthy way. I so wish I could get a redo on that one, but sometimes there are no mulligans. My advice is probably obvious: if at all possible, *do* try to replace any pairs who leave using an agreed-upon method that is determined from the outset. This will set your club up to last as long as possible.

The transition of the girls to high school is a common time for long-running clubs to end, and something I often hear from other mothers. I think it's a wonderful goal to stay together through the high school years, but it does not mean that our club—or yours—is a failure if that doesn't happen. Our club had six great years together that changed our girls' lives for the better. I know that it also changed mine for the better. Invest time and energy in your club, do what you can to keep it together, and when the time comes for it to end, whenever it may be, think about what you gained. You'll be surprised by how much!

How to Incorporate New Ideas and Activities That Will Reenergize Your Club

There are many things you can do to ensure your club remains fun and exciting over time. None of this guarantees that pairs won't quit, or that your club will never come to a premature end, but clubs tend to last longer when members find ways to spend more time together, enjoy special experiences outside of the meetings, and add creative elements to the meetings themselves. All of this needs to be balanced in terms of how much time mothers and daughters have to devote to the club. If clubs are *too* time intensive, some members may be driven away. It makes sense for clubs to consider the different ways in which they can enhance their time together and then to pick and choose a small number of options that appeal to everyone. Here are just a few ideas:

- *Keep a scrapbook to chronicle the books your club reads.* There are many creative ways to do this. Our club kept scrapbooks for each of the first several years we were together. At each meeting, the scrapbook was passed to the daughter who would be hosting the next meeting. She would take it home and make a page to add to the scrapbook during the month in which she had it. There were no rules about how the girls created the pages. Those who liked to write might do a book review of that month's reading selection, or write a poem about it. Those girls who were artistic could draw or create a collage or any other relatively flat type of artwork that could fit inside a scrapbook. Some girls did a combination of writing and drawing. At the end of the year, we all had a marvelous time flipping through the scrapbook and reminiscing about all of the books we had read. Over the years, this became even more fun because we could look back fondly at all the cute pages the girls put into the scrapbooks when they were very young! Today, digital scrapbooking is another option some girls might enjoy; an added benefit is that everyone can keep a copy.

- *Try some of the suggested activities that accompany each book and movie guide.* Following each discussion guide in this book is a recommended field trip, game, or other activity related to the theme of each book or movie. Or make up your own!

- *Attend children's author events and book signings.* If your club is anything like mine was, the girls will have books or authors about which they are very passionate. Subscribe to your local bookstore or public library's newsletter and find out in advance when those beloved authors are coming to town.

- *Go to the movies or a play together.* Pay attention to girl-centric movies and theater productions (professional, community, or school) coming to your area and make it a club event to attend and discuss it afterward, perhaps over ice cream.

- *This takes some doing and requires family collaboration and planning, but if your club can go away together for one weekend a year, you will be amazed by how much that strengthens friendship bonds between girls and moms.* Our club went away every October to a cozy B&B about an hour away. We were sensitive to the demands this placed on busy families and the financial constraints that differed for each mother, so we would leave on a Saturday morning, stay over only one night, and head back on Sunday afternoon. During our special mother-daughter weekends, we went on short hikes and picnics, visited flea markets, went apple picking, hung out together reading, and made plans for the coming year. It is possible to do all of this fairly inexpensively. Some clubs go camping together, which is a thrifty way to do it. Or perhaps someone in your club has access to a free place to stay. If you make it an annual event, everyone really looks forward to it, and you will create many fond memories. Remember to take lots of pictures!

There are so many ways of keeping your club interesting and fun, and not letting it get stale. Seek feedback periodically from both moms and daughters about what is working and what is not, as well as any ideas they may have for spicing things up. Simply having this conversation will help you make necessary changes that will further improve your experience together.

PART TWO

LET'S GET
the
DIALOGUE
GOING

4

"What a Pretty Dress!"

HELPING GIRLS TRANSCEND
GENDER STEREOTYPES AND SEXISM

"How shall I describe the person I once was? At the age of thirteen I was very much a girl, having not yet begun to take the shape, much less the heart, of a woman. Still, my family dressed me as a young woman, bonnet covering my beautiful hair, full skirts, high button shoes, you may be sure, white gloves. I certainly wanted to be a lady. It was not just my ambition; it was my destiny. I embraced it wholly, gladly, with not an untoward thought of anything else."
—from The True Confessions of Charlotte Doyle *by Avi*

Key Takeaways

- Children do not come into this world understanding gender stereotypes, but they are influenced by them from the moment—and sometimes even before—they are born.

- Girls often face unfair expectations and inaccurate assumptions about their potential, but moms play an important role in helping them defy sexist expectations.

▰ Marketers and retailers are complicit in reinforcing these stereotypes—"girliness" is big business! Understanding this is key to helping your daughter filter out harmful media messages.

"Girls only wear dresses. Pink dresses."
"When I grow up, I'm going to be a famous model."
"Math is for boys and reading is for girls."

All three comments are examples of what I have heard dozens of times on the playground, in the classroom, and in many other public and private spaces. My own daughter made the third comment when she was about eight years old. At the time, I was a member of the undergraduate admissions committee at MIT. She had not gotten that idea from me! I've heard many versions of the self-fulfilling prophesy "girls aren't good at math and science" during my educational career. When girls sell themselves short, we all lose out, but it doesn't have to be this way.

Where Do Stereotypes Come From?

Children see no limitations to their possibilities—that is, until adults point them out. Sometimes this means adults making undermining comments directly to girls (for example, "Little girls don't play with footballs/climb trees/collect bugs") but more often adults do this through the television shows, movies, books, advertising, and magazines that they create and distribute. That parents allow media into their homes is not blameworthy. After all, we live in a technological and connected world, often for the better.

Placing age-appropriate limitations on media consumption by kids is always a good idea, but short of going off to live in a cave, even the most vigilant mother cannot inoculate her daughter against exposure to stereotypes and sexism. We often lose sight of the fact that media is ambient in our culture, and stereotypes are everywhere. Setting the expectation that all negative messages can be kept at bay is akin to asking mothers who live in high-pollution areas not to let their daughters breathe the air. The more productive tack is for mothers to drag the problem out into the sunlight so their daughters can see it for what it really is.

What Are Some Examples of Common Stereotypes About Girls?

- ▰ Girls like pink.
- ▰ Girls want to be princesses.
- ▰ Girls love to shop.
- ▰ Girls are boy crazy.
- ▰ Girls are obsessed with their appearance.
- ▰ Girls are not good at math and science.
- ▰ Girls are quiet and well-behaved.
- ▰ Girls are passive and helpless.
- ▰ Girls want to be wives and mothers when they grow up.

How Do Stereotypes and Sexism Work?

While some of the above generalizations are true for some girls, what makes them stereotypes is that they indiscriminately ascribe assumed characteristics about an entire group—in this case, the female gender—to individuals. They say to girls, "This is how you are all supposed to be." They leave no room for exceptions, and there are *many* kinds of girls! Stereotypes like these are very limiting to girls and the women they become. They can result in the flattening of ambitions, especially as girls grow older and incorporate these narrow generalizations into their own identities.

> "The stereotype about girls that worries me the most for my daughter is that she must be gentle and patient, making others happy before herself. I'd like to see her comfortable in saying no, setting limits, prioritizing her own well-being and growth. I ask her all the time, 'What do you want?' And as she heads into the teen years, that question seems to be harder for her to answer."

When Do Stereotypes and Sexism Start and How Do They Play Out?

Gender stereotypes and sexism are a pervasive part of our culture, and they begin at—and, thanks to ultrasounds, often *before*—birth. Walk into any store that caters to babies or children and you can't help but notice how the toys, clothing, and sometimes even the books are organized. A sea of pink lets you know you have found the section designated for girls. Blue, and most of the other colors of the rainbow, now live in the boys' aisle. This is a relatively new development. It was not like this when many of today's moms over age thirty were girls. Here's the thing: culture has a hard time seeing itself. For younger mothers in their twenties, there may be no collective memory of the days before this exaggerated gendering of childhood, so the current culture appears normal to them. Ask yourself whether children's stores look *very* different than when you were a child. And have you observed the creep of pink fishing rods, tool kits, Bic pens, handguns, and other color-coded items for grown women? Our gender has been pinkwashed!

Recently I was thinking about my relationship with Disney as a child and young mother—before the days when I could not go to the supermarket without seeing some four-year-old dressed as Belle. As a child, I watched some of the movies and read some of the books. The Disney brand accounted for perhaps 3 percent of my possessions, and appeared just as infrequently in my playtime.

When I was pregnant with Charlotte in 1991, I was so unconcerned about Disney's market share of my and my unborn baby's lives that when the time came for me to carry on my father's tradition of painting murals in the nursery, I chose to paint Snow White and the Seven Dwarfs on one of the nursery walls. At the time I did not know if I would have a boy or a girl, and it didn't matter. There were three other murals in the room, and none of them depicted princesses. I was not worried about the message Snow White might send to my child about the domestic role of women or the necessity of being rescued by a man. That Snow White mural was just a mural, nothing more. In 1991 there was no army of princesses descending upon my daughter's childhood. Her horizon was deep and wide, and there was room for a princess. It did not define Charlotte or her femininity or her play.

My, how things have changed. Today, Disney is an enormously powerful and influential media conglomerate, and the Disney princess brand is one of its most successful marketing tools. Unsurprisingly, everything Disney does is aimed toward maximizing profits. The executives behind the princess franchise do not care whether girls are empowered or disempowered; they simply want to broaden their customer base however they can. At the deepest level, I resent that a for-profit company has had such a far-reaching and lasting impact on children all over the world, redefining "girl" as "princess." Girlhood has been *branded*. Perhaps from this example, marketers and retailers have discovered how to double their profits by gender-segmenting everything, including "pinkifying" a huge chunk of the girl market.

It is often the children who are the harshest enforcers of the gender rules, and this behavior can begin as early as preschool. Among many young girls, if you are not wearing a dress or wearing the color pink or wearing a Disney princess outfit, you might not even *be* a girl. With such literal thinking, gender identity is very concrete in children younger than six, and indeed, society reinforces for them that these standards are very, very important.

Young children learn about gender roles through socialization, especially by observing their parents' relationship. Gender differences are in great part cultural constructs of a society or community, and differ widely across the country and around the world. Until they are older (perhaps ten or eleven) and can think more abstractly, kids interpret these roles as fixed, not fluid, and they often seek the comforting structure of stereotyped roles to help them understand how to perform their gender properly.

"The whole idea of girls as princesses is disturbing to me. I explained to my daughter that the problem with wanting to grow up to be a princess is that it doesn't involve you; it involves who you marry. It doesn't involve an accomplishment, learning anything, or doing anything. We talked a bit, and then she decided she was going to be a firefighter and a police officer, because then she could help people!"

What Messages About Females Do Girls Receive and What Drives This Messaging?

Girls, the media tells them, are there to be looked at. The outsides of their heads seem to be valued above what's inside. All the "You're so pretty!" and "What a gorgeous dress!" comments—unless combined with comments like "You're so smart!" and "What are you reading?"—send girls a *very* clear message about what is important. Unsurprisingly, they seek the approval of others by providing what they believe others want from them. This is a wonderful human adaptation—that children care about pleasing adults and doing what is "right." But the problem we have today is that the gendering of childhood is so greed-based that the culture around girlhood has become one in which femininity is greatly exaggerated. Worse, the traits one might want for one's daughter—such as healthy risk-taking, active physical play, and emphasis on intelligence—have been categorized as boy attributes simply because of their presence in the boy aisles and absence in the girl aisles. For every science kit on the boy aisle, there is a manicure kit on the girl aisle. This matters. The message may be subtle and indirect at times, but it is there—and it has consequences. As a school administrator, I often found myself having to ask parents to please send their daughters to school in play clothes and shoes they could run and jump in because the fancy dresses and sparkly shoes had the effect of keeping girls sedentary and focused on their appearance at recess.

As girls grow older, they take their cues about who they should be (often indistinguishable from how they should look) from fashion magazines, billboards, television, movies, music, and the Internet, just to name a few sources. They absorb stereotypes about women as sexual objects, as supporting characters in the lives of men, as suited for some roles but not others. How can we short-circuit that process?

Using Books, Movies, and Other Media to Push Back Against Female Stereotypes

Literature plays a major role in both constructing and deconstructing gender roles. Books can transmit cultural mores to children. Gender bias exists in the text, illustrations, and themes of many children's books, and these messages are often detrimental to girls. Most readers naturally identify with the characters of their own gender, so this acts as subtle conditioning.

Most children's literature and movies are boy-centric. Female characters are often portrayed in stereotypical ways. However, by carefully selecting empowering girl-centric books for your club to read (as well as movies to view), you can counter many of the prevailing stereotypes about girls and women, and allow girls to see themselves positively in what they read and watch.

Girl-centric literature and movies often depict female protagonists as independent, adventurous, confident problem-solvers, and provide an extremely helpful countermessage to the images of femininity presented by other books, movies, and society at large. In your club discussions, you can talk about how these issues manifest themselves both in the stories and in real life. Connecting the world within the fiction to the real-life world of school, family, neighborhood, and community helps girls integrate these healthy messages into daily life.

▶ RECOMMENDED BOOK

The True Confessions of Charlotte Doyle by Avi (age 10+)

In this fast-paced Newbery Award winner, Charlotte Doyle is a typical, well-mannered girl of wealthy upbringing in the year 1832. After attending school in England, she must return home to her family in America. The two-month ship voyage she takes presents her with substantial challenges and dangers usually encountered only by men, forcing her to abandon many of her preconceived ideas about the "proper place" for girls and to completely reevaluate her role within her family and society. One might call the book a gender bender—somewhat along the lines of *Kidnapped, Mutiny on the Bounty,* or *Treasure Island,* but centered around the experience of a female protagonist. There are many exciting twists, with several mysteries woven throughout the plot. I read this book years ago and had forgotten a lot of it, but when I sat down to read it again, I polished it off in one long afternoon, unable to put it down!

Of great interest to me as I read the book was the concept of the traditional female identity based upon the "ladylike" qualities of beauty and proper attire, meticulous attention to cleanliness and appearance at all times, and obedience to men. Throughout this book, that gendered ideal is repeatedly held up and examined in ways that both fit the context of a book set in 1832 *and* that remain relevant today. In a modern culture that still stereotypes girls and women as being defined by their outside, this book shows the reader what is *inside* a thirteen-year-old girl who can no longer afford to keep up appearances in either sense of the term. Charlotte becomes a character of great complexity who has much more going on inside her than her outward appearance would lead you to believe at the start of the book, when Charlotte journals the words quoted at the beginning of this chapter (page 45).

This is one of those riveting page-turners that girls will not be able to put down. The protagonist draws readers into her life aboard ship and it's hard not to feel every wave, every wind, and every moment of joy, fear, courage, disappointment, confusion, and enlightenment that Charlotte feels herself. Daughters need not have experienced their own swashbuckling adventures to be able to talk about times in their own lives when they have been forced out of their comfort zones and triumphed!

DISCUSSION QUESTIONS

1. When Charlotte first boards the *Seahawk*, how does she feel about her surroundings?

   Prompts

   - What is her room like? Other parts of the ship?

   - How do these things affect her ability to stay clean, attend to her appearance, maintain clean changes of clothes, rest comfortably, and eat well?

   - Have any of you faced similar circumstances? If so, what were they, and how were they managed?

2. How do Charlotte's feelings about the rugged life aboard ship change over time?

   Prompts

   - When Charlotte joins the crew, why does she write, "And there I was, joyous, new-made, liberated from a prison I'd thought was my proper place"?

- What does Charlotte exchange for this liberation, and what does she receive in return?

- When Charlotte is accused of murder and placed in the brig, she runs her fingers through her "hacked" short hair and wonders if it has been days or years since her time back in England. What do you think she is feeling and thinking about?

3. When Charlotte's adventure is over and she returns home to her family in Rhode Island, how does she feel about this return to her former comforts? What about her role as a young lady?

Prompts

- When Charlotte changes into the one clean outfit she saves for her departure from the ship, why does she say she feels "pinched and confined" in her clothes?

- Why does Charlotte have mixed emotions when the ship pulls into port and she sees her parents, brother, and sister waiting for her on the dock?

4. Both Charlotte's father and Captain Jaggery attempt to exert great control over Charlotte's behavior and appearance. How are these men similar? How are they different?

Prompts

- After being led along by the ship's crew, Charlotte writes, "What could I do? All my life I had been trained to obey, educated to accept." What is her conflict about?

- Both of these men talk several times each about "the natural order of the world" as it relates to the established roles of girls and women. What do they each mean? Is this still true today?

5. When Charlotte is offered an opportunity to avoid being hung for murder, the captain tells her that in exchange for her life she must help restore order by removing her sailor's clothing of pants and a shirt and putting on her pretty dress, stockings, bonnet, and gloves. He says, "Resume your place and station." Charlotte refuses. What is this power struggle about?

6. During Charlotte's trial for murder, there is much angry talk about girls who are "unusual" versus those who are "unnatural." What does this mean?

Prompts

- What do you think about Charlotte picking up unladylike habits from the crew, such as swearing and spitting? What does Charlotte mean when she writes that swearing made her feel "exhilaration"?

- When Captain Jaggery is disgusted by what he deems "unnatural" about Charlotte—even before the trial—but which Charlotte deems simply "unusual" for a girl, how does he attempt to shame her?

- Do you see any ways in which girls are shamed today when they do not act "feminine" enough?

7. In which ways is Charlotte manipulated by men to keep her afraid of leaving her proper place as a female? What role does her physical appearance play?

Prompts

- At the beginning of the story, Captain Jaggery labels Charlotte "pretty," and tells her that a pretty woman can "keep the crew in a civilized state." What does that mean? How does she feel about the captain's flattery?

- At the end of the book, when he is angry, he yells at her. One of the words he calls her is "ugly." How do you think Charlotte feels when she hears this?

- When Charlotte wants to join the crew, one sailor says contemptuously, "You're a girl," and then another sailor adds, "a *pretty* girl." How does Charlotte feel when her beauty is used to demean and control her?

- Are there any times you can think of today when being pretty is not an advantage to a girl? What about times when it *is* an advantage?

FUN ACTIVITY

Go to a history museum where there are displays of female clothing from the 1800s. Compare it to modern clothing for girls and women. Ask the girls what would be fun about wearing the old-fashioned clothes versus what would be difficult about wearing them. Talk about your favorite and least favorite things about yesterday's fashions and today's.

What About the Math/Science Stereotype in Particular?

Stereotypes persist that girls have less ability or interest in math and science, and that they will be unpopular among their peers if they excel in them. Studies show that girls begin to purposely lower their performance in these subjects in order to meet the reduced expectations for them. Peer pressure, especially in middle school, drives girls further away from the sciences. This is especially true of African American and Latina girls, who face the double jeopardy of race and gender stereotypes. Studies also show that teachers subtly endorse all of these messages by helping girls too much in math and science, while more often pushing boys to solve problems on their own. And then there are all the female teachers along the way who say, "I'm not good at math, but . . ." Ouch.

Yet even before any of these school-related factors can kick in, our toy

"I spoke to my girls—one an engineering major at Georgia Tech and the other an applied mathematics major at Cal. Both are geeky and beautiful—you can be both. Yes to fashion and beauty; both feel strongly about its importance especially when presenting yourself in the workforce. Advice from two STEMs! We discussed many gender stereotypes that just aren't accurate in their social circles."

and clothing retailers let girls know that these subjects are very hard for them. JC Penney's I'M TOO PRETTY TO DO HOMEWORK, SO MY BROTHER DOES IT FOR ME T-shirt . . . Teen Talk Barbie saying, "Math class is tough!" . . . Lands' End girls' backpacks with the slogan AS TOUGH AS LONG DIVISION . . . Blue baby onesies that read SMART LIKE DADDY and pink ones that read PRETTY LIKE MOMMY: these are but a few of the items that are commonly peddled to children, especially girls, creating a backlash among parents who do not want their girls sold out in this way. It all starts *very* young.

I interviewed Stuart Schmill, dean of admissions at MIT, about what he believes can be done to counteract the stereotypes and sexism inherent in the STEM fields (science, technology, engineering, and math), and how to encourage more girls to pursue STEM subjects.

"Stereotypes linger long past the generation in which things have changed," Schmill says. "A generation from now, I think we'll be in a better place." He explains that it is possible to help girls feel comfortable pursuing math and science before they can be "infected" by negative messages from society and peers. Some of the solutions lie in how we as adults present the STEM subjects, and to some degree the acronym itself may be part of the problem.

"We need to stop using that term. It can be off-putting to girls who feel they are being forced to make an either/or choice between the sciences and other subjects they love. It makes it sound as if there is a separate world where the math and science kids—mostly boys—go. Girls need to see that these subjects are *integrated* with the humanities. Reading, writing, and speaking are crucial to the communication of scientific ideas, and to solving real-world problems, for example the problem of global climate change."

Schmill believes that if girls are encouraged by parents and teachers to believe they have skills equal to boys, if they can see that math and science can be combined with other subjects in an interdisciplinary way, if science can be viewed as fun rather than cloaked in sterile acronyms, and if girls can be shown that scientific outcomes are exciting—and making the world a better place—girls will be more likely to rise above the stereotypes and achieve their potential, increasing the odds they will enter scientific professions.

Recently deceased astronaut Sally Ride double-majored in English and physics at Stanford University, illustrating Schmill's point that the humanities and sciences are not mutually exclusive. I believe the biggest problem with the math/science stereotype is that it begins to affect girls so early that it is hard to get out in front of it. Clearly, girls are capable of excelling. The jokey, sexist climate of girls being too pretty to do homework and finding long division tough may make some adults laugh when they see these slogans plastered across girls' clothing and accessories, but it's not funny. It is undermining girls in a serious way.

As an example of this, be sure to watch the European Union's disastrous attempt to make a video ("Science: It's a Girl Thing!" in the media recommendations at the end of this chapter) promoting science to girls in a uniquely girly and sexy way, and then watch the video response by Dr. Meghan Gray about why this is *not* an appropriate way to "market" science to girls. We have a long way to go, and we're not going to get there in stilettos!

Reading this next book is a good way to explore this stereotype within a mother-daughter book club:

▶ RECOMMENDED BOOK

Hannah, Divided by Adele Griffin (age 8+)

Thirteen-year-old Hannah Bennett is growing up on a dairy farm in Depression-era Pennsylvania when her outstanding math talent captures the attention of a wealthy philanthropist in Philadelphia. Mrs. Sweet offers to take Hannah into her home while she is tutored for a prestigious math exam that could earn her a scholarship. Only Hannah's grandfather recognizes Hannah's potential. Hannah's parents do not want her to leave the farm, and do not believe there is any good reason for her to do so. Even Hannah's teacher disapproves, saying, "math is more practical for boys."

Hannah's passion for math is not the only unusual thing about her. She is unable to read, and also has certain "peculiarities," such as counting and tapping, that make her stand out and at times attract teasing. Her family and friends all worry that she will never fit in at a posh girls' school in Philadelphia. Encouraged by her grandfather, who is the head of the family, Hannah takes the risk and leaves behind all she has ever known to attempt to show the world that she—a girl—*can* win a math scholarship! This is a story of a girl who is not only pursuing her passion, but also dealing with a variety of unexpected challenges. Issues of female friendship, bullying, classism, and the struggle of being different and learning differently are all explored in this charming book about the costs and rewards of chasing your dreams when others cannot understand them.

Our mother-daughter book club read *Hannah, Divided*, and one of the most fun things about it was the 1934 setting. We all loved being immersed in Depression-era slang, the descriptions of the fashions of the day, discussions about old-time movies and movie stars, tales of "Baby Face" Nelson and other notorious criminals who captured the imaginations of average citizens, and reminders of the hardships of daily life that are often easily forgotten. All of the characters have struggles, but find ways to grow and persevere with their senses of humor intact.

DISCUSSION QUESTIONS

1. When Hannah's father says at the beginning of the book, "I don't myself see much point to girls learning fancy math," how does that set the stage for the rest of the story that follows?

   Prompts

   - Who else does not believe that Hannah should pursue her love of math? Why?

   - What are some of the stereotypes the book presents about mathematicians and scientists?

   - Who defends Hannah's dreams at the beginning? Who defends them by the end of the book?

   - Have any of you faced any stereotypes when you were pursuing an interest that others did not support? What did you do?

2. Who are Hannah's role models? Who inspires her to reach her potential?

   Prompts

   - Discuss: Granddad, Mr. Cole, Dr. Clayton, Mrs. Sweet, Hepp, Joe, and "Madame Curie, Pythagoras, and Mae West."

   - What do Hannah's famous chosen heroes say about her? How does she think about them to give herself encouragement?

▰ What does Dr. Clayton mean when he talks to her about pushing doors open?

▰ Do you think it is easier for girls today who want to study math and science and enter those careers? Are there ways in which it is still hard?

3. In addition to her unusual love of math, what else is "peculiar" about Hannah?

Prompts

▰ What things does Hannah do when she is anxious?

▰ What does she do when she feels superstitious?

▰ How do her friends, family, and teachers feel about these behaviors? They all have different reactions. See if you can remember what they were.

▰ Do you ever count, tap, blink, jump rope, say rhymes, place your belongings in certain places in a certain order, or do any of the other things Hannah does in this book?

▰ What are other things people do when they are anxious? How do Hannah's behaviors and habits hurt her? How do they help her?

▰ What does it mean when the author writes, "Counting was a bolt of hot, bright lightning in her brain"?

▰ We all have things about us that are different. Does anyone want to say what makes *you* peculiar?

4. Hannah is a very different kind of girl in many ways. How does this affect her friendships?

Prompts

▰ Think about Hannah's female friends from home and the new girls in her Philadelphia school. How do each set of friends feel about her competing for the math scholarship? How do they feel about her as a person?

▰ How do both sets of friends change during the course of the book?

- Why is Hannah sometimes bullied? Who bullies her? How does she respond?

- Who seems to be Hannah's truest friend? What is unique about their friendship?

- Why does Hannah admit to Joe that she can't read?

- How does she feel about her nickname "milkmaid" at the beginning of the book? What about at the end?

- What does Lillian say about herself to Hannah that lets Hannah know that other girls also get teased about things they can't control? How does that confession make Hannah feel?

5. Why is the title of the book a pun? In what ways is Hannah divided?

Prompts

- How do you feel about the ending of the book? Are there ways in which it was unsatisfying? Why? If you like it, why?

- If the book had ended with an answer to the question everyone is wondering about—Does Hannah pass the exam and get the scholarship?—would that have improved the story?

- When the story ends, is Hannah still divided?

- Do any of you ever feel divided? How?

FUN ACTIVITY

Share stories in your club about what you do that others might consider "peculiar" when you feel nervous or superstitious. (I used to step over cracks in the sidewalk, hold my breath as I passed cemeteries, and mentally count dots on acoustic ceiling tiles, *always* having to end on an even number.) Talk about why you think so many people perform these kinds of rituals. You might be surprised by how many people have them!

What Happens as Little Girls Who Have Consumed Many Stereotyped Messages Approach Puberty?

Somehow, what started out as a clever corporate strategy for making money by feeding girls a steady diet of hyperfeminine toys, clothes, games, books, and movies has resulted in an entire little-girl culture that now revolves around princesses and all things pink and sparkly. Offering that rare, penetrating glimpse into the obvious, toy companies now conduct their very own in-house studies that show that (surprise!) girls "innately" want the very things that have been spoon-fed to them since birth. What a shocker. But to many mothers, it all seems so normal. Why would anyone have a problem with it? It is so *sweet*, so *cute*, so *harmless*. And after all, it's *just a phase anyway*.

But what can feel like an age of innocence and a temporary happily-ever-after before the onset of the teenage years—especially to moms who are consciously avoiding sexed-up dolls like Bratz, Winx Club, and Monster High—is actually a Trojan horse. Many of the pretty pink princesses become adolescents who obsess about their looks in a different, more concerning way. The marketers continue their laser-like focus on girls' appearance until girls begin to stereotype *themselves* as they compete for the attention of boys and seek continued praise for their looks.

This carries over to behaviors such as girls dumbing themselves down in class, saying "I'm no good at math" even when they are, wearing suggestive clothing, and obsessing over their weight, hair, nails and makeup. Some girls stumble off this merry-go-round relatively unscathed, yet others will become teens and eventually mothers who are overly fixated on beauty, constantly fretting about their appearance, and ultimately passing that legacy down to their own daughters. If girls do not receive feedback from adults they trust that they are more than how they look, they are at risk of not meeting their potential, or worse, of developing a poor self-image that may lead to other emotional problems during their childhood and later in life.

Don't most mothers want their daughters to grow up in a world that takes them seriously? Wouldn't it be great if moms could somehow take back some of the power that corporations like Disney and Mattel have taken from their daughters and return it to them? This can all feel like a vicious cycle that is impossible to break. Good news: it's not!

How Can Mothers Help at This Stage?

Mothers can have an extremely beneficial effect on how girls see themselves despite all of these continually reinforced stereotypes. The model of femininity they personally provide for their daughters is crucial. The tricky part is that mothers, as females, have also been affected by our culture, and many struggle with the same issues as their daughters. That is why the first two steps for mothers are to (1) try to become more aware of how their own beliefs and behaviors have been influenced by media and popular culture, and (2) observe how their daughters absorb everything they see, from celebrity magazines in the grocery store checkout to their mothers' own wardrobe and food choices. No one ever said that being a role model is easy, but like it or not, mothers have signed on for the part!

I interviewed Peggy Orenstein, author of the *New York Times* best-seller *Cinderella Ate My Daughter: Dispatches from the Front Lines of the New Girlie-Girl Culture,* about the changes she has observed over the past ten years in how our culture defines femininity and how it has redefined the notion of empowerment for girls.

"Girl power used to be about ability over appearance," Orenstein explains. "Now the message given to girls is that appearance is not only *a* source of empowerment, but *the* source. It's all about beauty and, of course, being a consumer of beauty products. Female identity is increasingly based upon that, and it is the backdrop for raising daughters. Not all girls who go through a looks-obsessed pretty-princess phase when they are young transition to a more sexualized and self-objectifying phase as they approach adolescence, but society does create a vulnerability for this behavior in girls."

When I asked her how moms could push back against this new, very disempowering version of empowerment, Orenstein had lots of helpful tips, from limiting media exposure to "fighting fun with fun" by not just saying no, but by finding girl-positive things to say yes to.

"The birthday party goody bags with makeup in them will always find a way into your house," quips Orenstein. "So ultimately it's about what *else* you can show them about femininity. How do mothers prioritize the role of physical appearance in their own lives? What are mothers verbalizing about their own bodies and faces? Good modeling needs to happen at home, but mother-daughter book clubs are another great place for it, and for giving girls *truly* empowering, enjoyable experiences in place of the necessary nos."

Moms can come to understand the insidious nature of stereotypes and learn to process how stereotypes affect their daughters. Media literacy is a skill that children can develop as early as preschool. You can teach media literacy to girls by discussing girl-centric literature, movies, and other media in your club.

By helping daughters develop a variety of interests and abilities, and by helping them observe stereotypes and inequities in their social environment, mothers can raise awareness in girls so that they begin to think critically for themselves, a skill that will serve them well throughout their lives. It all begins with the teachable moments in daily life. While writing this chapter, I e-mailed Charlotte at college to ask her if she remembered any teachable moments between us that helped her feel better about herself as a girl, and this is what she e-mailed back:

> I remember a time when I somehow thought I couldn't be pretty because I didn't have blonde hair and blue eyes, so not only did I think only those features were pretty, but I also believed that as a girl, I should be pretty and I was lacking because I wasn't (due to having darker features). But you told me that wasn't true and explained it was just what was most valued by our culture and the media, and that beauty was subjective and came in many forms. You also pointed out a friend of mine who was blonde and blue-eyed but still wasn't pretty by conventional standards to show that there wasn't something objective about those characteristics that automatically made a girl pretty.

Where did Charlotte's idea come from that fair coloring was the epitome of beauty? It surely did not come from one experience, one observation, one movie, or one doll. I have no recollection of this particular conversation, but that just goes to show you that our daughters are paying attention even when, for us, it is just an ordinary day of parenting.

Taken individually and out of context, harmful marketing can look quite benign. Anything can be a one-off. It is easy to be skeptical about the damage done by one sexy blonde doll, one sexist T-shirt slogan, or one pink vacuum cleaner toy. What really matters is the *collective* effect the many gender-stereotyped products have over time, and the messages girls take in consciously or subconsciously every day. Some mothers say that their daughters are just innately very girly. There is nothing wrong with being feminine! In fact, if mothers were to attempt to fight every manifestation of exaggerated femininity, not only would this be doomed to failure, but it might also have the unintended consequence of making girls feel criticized or self-conscious.

That said, there is an old Chinese proverb: "If you want to know what the water is like, don't ask the fish." Moms can allow daughters to freely express their inner girl while understanding that how they do so is partly "innate" and partly a response to the specific zeitgeist of girlhood in which all girls now swim. Moms can provide balance and offer choices that are sometimes missing in the larger culture.

RECOMMENDED MOVIE

Bend It Like Beckham (PG-13, but considered suitable by "mom reviewers" for girls as young as ten)

Jess Bhamra is an eighteen-year-old Indian girl from a traditional Sikh family living in London. She's been playing soccer in the public parks with boys for years when an English girl her age, Jules, spots her talent and recruits her to play for an all-female team that is professionally coached and competes nationally and internationally. The expected East-meets-West culture clash ensues, but with many unexpected twists. Both girls struggle within their families to be who they are—athletic, driven girls who are not interested in being the very feminine, boy-obsessed, "typical" girl of each of their cultures, respectively. They are competitive, goal-oriented, and keen to be seen as different—but just as worthy—kinds of girls. They in no way fit the "princess" stereotype—either the Disney variety or any other—and they resent that this is expected of them by their families, friends, and society at large.

Charlotte and I loved this movie when it came out. It is a fascinating exploration of the intersection of gender, race, and culture. Be prepared to want to talk about this movie for hours! There are so many substantive conversations a mother-daughter book club could have about this movie beyond questions about stereotypes and sexism, including but not limited to: race, sexual orientation, mother-daughter relationships, female competition, beauty, the definition of femininity, and what it means to pursue nontraditional female goals in a man's world. This movie's a winner.

DISCUSSION QUESTIONS

1. *Bend It Like Beckham* involves many instances of deception, miscommunication, and misunderstanding. Name some of them. What are the sources of these conflicts?

   Prompts

   ▰ How important are the following factors in shaping a girl's identity: mothers, fathers, siblings, friends, relatives, society, religion, family traditions, ethnic culture, and any others you can think of?

   ▰ When there is discrepancy between a girl's goals for herself and the goals and roles thrust upon her by others, how might this tension play out?

   ▰ What does the mother of Jess's sister's fiancé mean when she says to Jess's parents, "Children are a map of their parents' character"? Do you agree or disagree?

2. Why are Jess's and Jules's mothers disappointed in them? What examples of this do you see in the movie?

   Prompts

   ▰ How important is it to most mothers that their daughters resemble them in their appearance, behavior, and interests?

   ▰ Why is this so important to some mothers?

   ▰ Do you or any other daughters and mothers have tension like this?

   ▰ What role should mothers have—or not have—in molding their daughters to their own version of femininity and their own vision of the female gender role?

   ▰ How can mothers and daughters communicate better than the ones in the movie around difficult issues like this one?

3. At the end of the movie, why does Jess's father allow her to accept the scholarship at Santa Clara University?

Prompts

- How does he change over the course of the movie in the way he views and parents Jess?

- What is the importance of his past history as a cricket player?

- Do you feel the father's decision at the end was realistic—in the context of the movie and in real life? Why or why not?

4. What do you think of today's "princess culture?"

Prompts

- Discuss the term first and see if you can agree on what it means.

- In what ways are you—moms and daughters—like princesses? In what ways are you different?

- Moms and girls: Is princess culture a good thing, a bad thing, or something in the middle?

- Moms: How has the role of princesses in girlhood changed since you were a child? How is it the same?

- Can a girl be a princess *and* a competitive athlete? How about a princess and a scientist?

- When is it helpful and when is it harmful for girls to immerse themselves in the hyperfeminine princess culture?

- What messages—positive or negative—do girls and women send when they perform this version of being female? How is it broadening? How is it limiting?

FUN ACTIVITY

Go see a women's professional soccer (WPS) match if there is a team close to where you live. If not, take in a game at a nearby college that fields a women's team. Cheer on these amazing athletes!

Reflection from Charlotte

All of the books and movies recommended in this chapter portray girls and women as dynamic and independent characters. In *The Golden Compass*, for example, Lyra resists growing up and obeying adults and avoids "acting like a girl." She's a really independent character on her own terms, even though she does not face direct gender stereotypes in the book. She demonstrates courage and critical thinking skills as she evolves as a strong female protagonist. There were countless female characters like this with whom I identified and about whom I loved reading when I was young.

When I got older, I started wondering why I liked the particular kinds of characters I liked. Now I believe that in order to understand what makes a female character unique, you sometimes have to think about her choices deeply and compare them to the choices of other people in the book and the expectations of her society. Gender and gender-based stereotypes won't always be at the root of all the problems female characters face, or the foundation upon which their strong personalities are built. It's great when this is the case, but I also think it's important that resilient female characters go beyond challenging gender stereotypes and be their own people in all aspects of life, even when gender is not involved in a specific challenge they're facing. After all, real people who lead their lives in this way are the ones I've always respected and been inspired by the most.

I have possibly learned more about my world through reading than I have through experiencing it. Having fictional and real-life female role models to show girls all that they are capable of as women and as people is an invaluable gift for them, one that I was very lucky to have in my own mother-daughter book club.

RECOMMENDED BOOKS

TITLE	AUTHOR	AGE RANGE	MOVIE ADAPTATION?
A Wrinkle in Time	Madeleine L'Engle	10+	Yes
Breadcrumbs	Anne Ursu	10+	
Hannah, Divided	Adele Griffin	8+	
Inkheart	Cornelia Funke	9+	Yes
Sidekicks	Jack D. Ferraiolo	12+	
The Golden Compass	Philip Pullman	12+	Yes
The Scorpio Races	Maggie Stiefvater	13+	
To Kill a Mockingbird	Harper Lee	13+	Yes
True Confessions of Charlotte Doyle	Avi	10+	
Wonder	R. J. Palacio	10+	

RECOMMENDED MOVIES

TITLE	MPAA RATING
Bend It Like Beckham	PG-13
Brave	PG
Kiki's Delivery Service	G
The Lion, the Witch & the Wardrobe (miniseries)	NR
The Secret World of Arrietty	G

RECOMMENDED MEDIA

Use an Internet search engine to locate these videos on YouTube, Vimeo, or other video hosting sites.

"Science: It's a Girl Thing!"

"Science: It's a Girl Thing—FAIL?"

"Born That Way?" Deborah Siegel TED Talk

"Riley's Rant: Why Do Girls Have To Buy Pink Toys & Princesses?"

"Toy Ads and Learning Gender"

"Gender and Disney"

"How Gender Stereotypes Influence Emerging Career Aspirations"

"Arthur S14 E2-1: The Agent of Change"

Saturday Night Live's "Chess for Girls"

"Rachel Simmons: The Curse of the Good Girl"

The Sexualization of Girlhood

YOU *CAN* BYPASS IT!

—⟶ ⟵—

"Why would anyone say this stuff about themselves on the Internet? It's crazy!"

—*from* The Future of Us
by Jay Asher and Carolyn Mackler

Key Takeaways

- "Sexualization," as applied to girls, means that they are viewed and presented as sexual beings, but do not feel authentic sexuality themselves.

- Our society now markets products and services to young girls that reinforce sexiness as an appropriate and desired characteristic for them to strive toward, beginning the process of objectifying girls at increasingly younger ages.

- Mother-daughter book clubs provide a safe haven where girls can enjoy their childhoods without being rushed to grow up too fast, and a place where they are respected for their full potential as human beings.

As mothers, we love our daughters and want to do everything possible to raise them to be happy, healthy, well-adjusted women. We are not always supported in these efforts, and at times it can even feel as if our culture is out to sabotage our daughters' childhoods by trying to speed them up, pushing girls in directions that are directly opposed to the values we are trying to instill. Halloween is approaching as I write this chapter, and the costumes out there for girls are a perfect illustration of this push toward sexualization. But it's not just Halloween. You hear it all the time: girls are too sexy, too soon.

Why and how does our culture push girls to grow up so fast? How can mothers guide their daughters toward better choices in the face of relentless marketing and peer pressure that tells girls their value lies in their sexiness? How is the sexualization of girls related to objectification—and self-objectification—of girls and women? What conflicts might mothers have within their own relationships with media and sexiness that interfere with their ability to coach their daughters toward healthier behavior? How can mothers learn to recognize "age compression"—the trickle-down of adult sexuality into kid's clothing, literature, films, music, and other aspects of pop culture—and successfully circumvent the known negative emotional effects of sexualization on girls? All of these questions can be answered, and without reinforcing the unfortunate stereotype of moms as puritanical, pearl-clutching prudes! All it takes are open eyes.

Mothers need to be able to impart a healthy understanding of female sexuality to their daughters. This can be anything from easy to awkward to downright difficult. With support, more mothers will be able to do this, while also helping girls develop the self-confidence and strength of character to be their authentic selves rather than the sexualized caricature of femininity being promoted to them by fashion magazines, billboards, television, movies, music lyrics, and yes, even Halloween costume merchants.

What, Exactly, *Is* Sexualization?

While this term is common among media analysts, it is not generally well understood by parents. The American Psychological Association (APA) is so concerned about the sexualization of girls that in 2007 it created a task force to study it and to define it. The APA explains that a person is sexualized when any of the following occurs:

- a person's value comes only from his or her sexual appeal or sexual behavior, to the exclusion of other characteristics

- a person is held to a standard that equates physical attractiveness (narrowly defined) with being sexy

- a person is sexually objectified—that is, made into a thing for others' sexual use, rather than seen as a person with the capacity for independent action and decision making

- sexuality is inappropriately imposed upon a person

Sexualization is the opposite of healthy sexuality, and these two things should never be confused. When moms thoroughly understand the difference, it is easier for them to guide their daughters well.

The Early Years

When girls are young, they often come to us with many questions, curious about their bodies and sexuality. It can be tricky to answer their questions, and sometimes we sidestep them or even directly state that these are not appropriate topics for conversation. This can eventually cause some girls to stop coming to their mothers for answers and to get their information elsewhere. Girls sense our fear or embarrassment and are confused by it. When we can't get past our own hang-ups to give our daughters the information they need and the connections with us as females that they crave, they can feel alienated. Then, when they are older, that important bond we hope to have with our daughters may be missing and difficult to establish.

I have very few memories of these sorts of conversations with my own mother—not because we didn't have them, because I know we did—but because I was not growing up in the same kind of sexually charged pop culture that is the wallpaper of today's girlhood, with all of the attendant risks that come with sexualization. At eleven or twelve, I had no idea what "hot" meant, apart from temperature, and I certainly had no concept that little girls could be or act sexy. There was no collective gaze at girls as sexual beings the way there is today, nor was there any collective perception among girls that they were sexy.

Charlotte had plenty of questions, and at times expressed confusion about the mixed messages she was getting from her parents, her friends, and television. It seemed I had to constantly reiterate our values and help her deconstruct, for example, everything about young female singers in music videos that suddenly had very little to do with singing! I remember joking to a colleague one day that I felt certain I would eventually be forced to move to Greenland and dress Charlotte from head to toe in seal fur. In my less panicked moments—which were most of them—I knew it would all be fine. I just had some work to do, and needed to find allies. I found them in many places, and our mother-daughter book club was one of them.

What Are Some Examples of How Girls Are Sexualized?

There are many ways that you can see girls being sexualized, but let's just consider a few:

- clothing
- Halloween costumes
- photographic and video imagery
- dolls and toys
- female characters in books, movies, and television shows
- certain salon services

It is hard to avoid seeing sexualized girls' clothing, whether for dress-up or everyday wear. "Fashionable" has become synonymous with "sexy" for girls, and the natural desire many girls have to be stylish now has a very narrow definition. Child-sized thongs, padded training bras, string bikinis, micro miniskirts, T-shirts and panties with suggestive slogans, kitten heels, and even girls' lingerie can be found from one end of the mall to the other. These items have a cultural association with seduction, and this is at the root of many mothers' vague (or not so vague) feelings of unease when they see them.

Of course, when these items become deliberately packaged as "fashion" by the clothing manufacturers—who understand that they can make a lot of money by offering girls the allure of looking older—it is easy to become desensitized to seeing girls dressed in these items. Seductive clothing simply does not belong on little girls—on Halloween or at any other time. Although grown women have every right to dress as they please, they should be aware that their daughters are watching closely, and are apt to desire the type of clothing worn by their mothers. Sexualized clothing gets in the way of girls experiencing their own bodies as children. It also garners reactions from other people that contribute to an anxiety girls feel but do not understand.

Women and girls should not be shamed for how they dress. While it is important that girls be informed and empowered to make good choices when it comes to their appearances, it is not their responsibility to control or prevent misogyny through the selection of their own attire. That said, decisions need to be informed, and this is something I discussed with Jean Kilbourne, coauthor with Diane Levin of *So Sexy So Soon: The New Sexualized Childhood and What Parents Can Do to Protect Their Kids.* Kilbourne is not only a highly esteemed author, but also a veteran speaker and filmmaker who is internationally recognized for her work on the images of women in advertising. She acknowledges how hard it can be for moms to find appropriate clothing for their daughters once they reach a certain age, but notes that nonsexualized clothing *can* be found. The bigger problem may be how to get girls to accept it without feeling that it makes them look too different than their peers.

A way to lessen this problem is for mothers to join with other like-minded mothers and mutually agree not to purchase these types of items for their daughters. Mother-daughter book clubs can tackle the problem together by discussing it and agreeing to reject products being marketed to girls that are not age appropriate.

I asked Kilbourne how mothers could explain to young daughters *why* they should not dress "sexy." "In an ideal world, children should be able to dress

"Hopefully we can avoid the clothing wars by helping her develop so many interests that she has no desire to be involved in that silliness. Based on the sheer volume of 'reading' she does with us at age one, things are looking bright there!"

however they want," Kilbourne explains, "but in this world, when young girls dress provocatively, it sends signals they do not really mean to send. It attracts attention young girls really don't want—from older men, and so forth. It can be dangerous." Mothers can find a way to get this message across to their daughters using subtle, age-appropriate language.

We also discussed the issue of mothers—adult women—having every right to make the choice to dress in overtly sexy clothes. However, they must not expect a different choice from their daughters if they do. "Do as I say, not as I do" almost never works.

RECOMMENDED BOOK

The Penderwicks: A Summer Tale of Four Sisters, Two Rabbits, and a Very Interesting Boy by Jeanne Birdsall (age 8+)

There are not a lot of books and movies that address the topic of the sexualization of girls—at least, not many that are appropriate for younger girls to read/watch. One way around that problem is to encourage girls to read books and watch movies that show girls who are definitively *not* sexualized, and come at it that way. *The Penderwicks: A Summer Tale of Four Sisters, Two Rabbits, and a Very Interesting Boy* is one such book. If you enjoy it, there are two more books that follow it in the series.

Jeanne Birdsall won the National Book Award in 2005 for her funny, charming story of four motherless girls who spend a summer with their widowed father on an estate in the Berkshire Mountains of western Massachusetts called Arundel. The owner of the estate, Mrs. Tifton, is not fond of the carefree Penderwick sisters and their messy lives. She is obsessed with her magnificent gardens. Her sensitive, musical son Jeffrey Tifton is doomed to go to military school, but the girls are determined to rescue him from that fate.

This book has been compared to others that were perhaps childhood favorites of today's moms, such as *Little Women* and *All-of-a-Kind Family*. The misadventures of the four sisters (and their pets) as they do what kids do—disobey adults, run away, and get into trouble, for example—are lighthearted in one way, but deeper in another. The girls are all strong characters with much better things to do than try to grow up fast or look sexy. They are thoroughly enjoying their childhoods, and they are *girls*, not tweens.

I personally loved this book. It felt like the books of my childhood, and was refreshingly devoid of vampires, string bikinis, or any of the other devices so many writers of kids' books today employ to try to give their stories an "edge." Nostalgia: it ain't what it used to be! Well, maybe this time . . .

DISCUSSION QUESTIONS

1. At the very beginning of the book, you learn that Mrs. Penderwick died of cancer shortly after the birth of Batty. How might the lives of the four girls have been different if she had lived? Why do you think so many books, movies, and fairy tales involve characters who have lost their mothers?

2. What do you think about the relationship between the sisters? Do you think they are close? Do they have any rivalry? Do you know any sisters like the Penderwicks?

3. Which sister do you like the best and why?

4. Which sister do you feel is most like you and why?

5. Describe Rosalind, age twelve.

   Prompts

   - Does she seem like a typical twelve-year-old? Why or why not?
   - How do you think her character would be different if her mother were still alive?

6. Describe Skye, age eleven.

   Prompts

   - What role does her temper have in her experiences?
   - How is she shown to be a strong girl who defies female stereotypes?

7. Describe Jane, age ten.

   Prompts

   ▰ Does she remind you of one of the March sisters from *Little Women?*

   ▰ How do her creativity and imagination set her apart from her other sisters?

8. Describe Batty, age four.

   Prompts

   ▰ Why is she always getting into trouble?

   ▰ How do you think her life is different from her three older sisters because she is the only one who has no memories of her mother?

9. How are the Penderwick sisters like girls today? How are they different? Talk about the girls in the context of sexualization. How do you think their lives as children—and one day, as women—are better without the pressure to be beautiful, thin, and sexy first and foremost?

FUN ACTIVITY

Jane Penderwick is the ultimate bibliophile, which means that she loves books and they play a large role in her life. In *The Penderwicks*, Jane makes many references to literature and the various characters in the books she has read, and quotes from them. She believes that a great book is one you can read over and over again and never tire of it. Discuss the books you feel this way about—the ones that would be considered great by Jane's definition. Assign someone to write them all down, and then share the list of must-reads you have created together.

Trickle Down ... Drip, Drip, Drip

Magazines, television, movies, and the Internet often depict women, and now girls, in sexy clothing with come-hither facial expressions and body language. Everything from cars to orange juice can be sold this way. On television and in movies, strong female roles are increasing, but too often women are still passive, sexy, decorative window dressing, or arm candy for the male protagonists. When they do have lines, they are too often saying that things are "hot," or for younger girls, "sassy."

The same theme pervades the toys and dolls marketed to girls:

- dolls with plump, pouty lips, doe-eyes, and heavy makeup, often frighteningly thin bodies, posed on inwardly turned legs in stiletto heels, wearing clothing often associated with prostitutes (hello, Bratz and Monster High!)

- makeup for preschoolers (*actual* makeup, not face-painting kits)

- salon-themed kits

- toys, board games, and other items that now come in needlessly pinkified for-girls versions that reinforce the importance of girly-girl culture which, almost without exception, is about the focus on physical appearance, shopping and/or consumption, gossip, and boys

There is an important distinction to be made between a little girl dressing up in her mother's black cocktail dress/oversized high heels/lacy bra, and corporations producing these items *in children's sizes* and lining the aisles of Target with them. Girls now purchase, use, and wear these items not as pretend or dress-up clothes, but on a daily basis.

It is also now considered mother-daughter bonding time for moms to take very young girls to the salon with them for makeovers, manicures, pedicures, hair highlighting or straightening, or brow waxing (and other waxing—don't get me started!). Going to spas or beauty salons once in a while, as one activity among many, is harmless and fun. Doing it often sends this message: *This is how we spend special time together: working on our appearance, making ourselves sexier, and getting hooked early on expensive products and services that we believe help us become "better" females.* A mother-daughter hike in the woods on a crisp autumn day delivers a much better message!

Sexualization Is Not Empowerment— Empowerment Is Empowerment

Has anyone noticed the tug-of-war going on with young girls today, in which they are taught to be confident and believe they can do anything, and also taught that beautiful and sexy are the most important things they can be? It's a bit maddening and, shall we say, *disempowering*. Where does this come from, this tension between focusing on the outside and focusing on the inside? There is no easy answer, but let's consider a good illustration of the schizoid way society has of communicating to girls that they should be opposite things at the same time. Let's look more carefully at the princess craze.

Little girls are in love with the Disney princesses. We are told they teach the important female virtues of kindness, generosity, and friendship (and that we need not worry about things like independence, ambition, or adventurousness). But if you look at how they are drawn, and how those illustrations have evolved since the 1930s, you see something you didn't consciously expect—their busts get bigger and their waists get impossibly smaller. Girls who move on from the princesses to other mainstream dolls such as Barbie and Bratz then see the same sexualized body types, but even thinner, and with sexy clothing, makeup, and attitude.

Older girls, no longer playing with dolls, become the newest group of barely pubescent Facebook users posting scantily clad pictures of themselves looking flirtatiously into the camera, wide-eyed, pouty-mouthed, and as if they had to take one hundred photos to come up with one that exudes the perfect mixture of seduction and nonchalance. It's sometimes called "the duck-faced selfie," and girls themselves seem to have at least some awareness of the self-parody. We've somehow gotten to the place where the documentation of our lives has become more important than living them, and for many tweens and teens, social media *is* life. How do girls go from Ariel obsession to this quest for Facebook "likes" for being hot in the span of five or six years? Easy: because the message to girls from the princess phase to the self-objectification phase is that beauty and sexiness equal empowerment. You will be loved and desired and the master of your own destiny if you look a certain way. It's a fairy tale.

This is false empowerment. Real empowerment comes when a girl understands her value to herself and others *apart from* her ability to attract the male gaze. It means that a girl can make decisions about sexual expression that are evaluated against a certain standard: whether those decisions strengthen or weaken her faith in her own value. It is not empowering to put one's body parts on public display to attract attention. That is dehumanizing. Furthermore, it is dangerous, because when society sees girls as merely a collection of female body parts, and girls view themselves that way, they are more vulnerable to sexual abuse. It is easier to commit violence against someone when you do not see her as a whole person.

It is great to feel sexy when you are old enough. But sexy is a *part* of being female, not the end-all, be-all. And sexiness should not be a part of childhood for girls at all. That is called sexualization. The freedom to claim one's own authentic sexuality, beyond the pressing desire to be desired, requires freedom *from* sexualization. Moms must teach daughters that their sexuality belongs to *them* and is not something to be delivered to, performed for, or owned by someone else. At the right age, sexuality can bring joy, emotional intimacy, and fulfillment, but today's girls are growing up believing that it only has value if it can be displayed, shown off, or proven. Moms can play a crucial role in helping girls understand that the pressure they feel to be sexy is hurting them, and that they have many other positive qualities that will one day be attractive to boys and men, but most importantly, to themselves.

> "As a mother I feel like I'm facing an uphill battle on so many fronts. I think I have made the right decision in talking to my daughters and not supporting companies or products that are detrimental to their self-image . . . but then there's me. It's hard not to feel like a hypocrite when the things I don't want for my two daughters I've fallen into myself."

RECOMMENDED BOOK

The Future of Us by Jay Asher and Carolyn Mackler (age 12+)

Who remembers those CD-ROMs you'd get in the mail from AOL in the mid-'90s, giving you one hundred free hours of this new thing called the Internet? Those were the days of dial-up, "You've got mail," and ridiculously slow downloads. This is the setting for *The Future of Us,* featuring two best-friend protagonists, Emma and Josh. When Emma logs on to AOL for the first time, she somehow stumbles through a wormhole to the future, where she discovers something called Facebook and has no idea what status update, poke, or friend request mean. She soon realizes she can glimpse her own future as a thirty-one-year-old woman, as well as the futures of her high school friends. Soon, the teenagers start to understand "ripples"—the things they say and do in daily life that have observable effects on what they see in their future lives on Facebook. Josh sees a happily married adult version of himself, while Emma sees an adulthood she is desperate to change. Along the way, Josh and Emma realize that it is better to live in the present, especially because the future they decide they want is with each other, not the spouses they see on Facebook.

This was a really fun book and a relatively easy read. Mothers will especially love all the '90s technology and pop culture references that won't be completely understood by daughters. I recommend this book in this chapter because the characters, while typical sixteen- to eighteen-year-old high schoolers, have romantic relationships with each other without the ubiquitous sexualization found in so much of today's YA literature. Yes, kids make out, and yes, they focus on who has pretty hair or who drives the nicest car, but the book has a lot more depth than that. Emma and Josh care about their futures and about each other in the way we all wish our teenage children could—as friends first, without Emma feeling the need to objectify herself, and with Josh demonstrating profound respect for girls and greater interest in who they are inside rather than how "hot" they are. Girls will likely read this book and be entertained primarily by the plot, but in book club discussion, character development will be just as interesting a topic!

DISCUSSION QUESTIONS

1. If you could look into your future the way Josh and Emma do, would you? Why or why not?

2. Surfing the Internet and using social media like Facebook is much different today than when Josh and Emma use it. How is it different? Are these differences good or bad or something in between?

Prompts

- ▸ How fast was the Internet then compared to now?
- ▸ How many types of social media are there now?
- ▸ How much time do kids spend using it today?
- ▸ How have mobile, handheld technologies changed the power of social media?
- ▸ Think of any other differences you can and discuss.

3. Social media is widely used by kids (and adults) today to bully each other. That had barely begun when this story takes place. What seems different about the lives of Emma, Josh and their friends compared to the lives of kids today in terms of how social media is used? What did kids do with their time in the mid-'90s before technology was such a big thing?

4. In an entire book about Facebook, the posting of sexy pictures is never mentioned. Why do you think that is?

5. How do most of the kids feel about Sydney Mills? How is Josh similar and how is he different?

6. When Emma discovers what Cody is really like, what does she do? Do you think it was easy for her? Do you think most girls today have Emma's self-awareness and courage?

7. Talk about the relationship between Emma and Josh, from the time they are young children and neighbors to the time they finally get together as a couple at the end of the book. How often are romantic relationships in high school grounded in this much friendship and shared history? What are the advantages of basing a relationship on friendship?

8. How does the absence of sexualization—even in the presence of sexual experimentation—affect your perceptions of the female characters and the agency they have in their own lives? What about the males? How does "hook-up culture" work today in terms of how well kids know each other in daily life? How does sexualized imagery in marketing and social media play a role in kids' relationships?

9. Has this book changed anything about how you think about your life today? In the future?

FUN ACTIVITY

Imagine that you are all able to see your futures, fifteen years from now, through some social media wormhole, just like Josh and Emma do. Share your "status updates" with each other as if you are all Facebook friends in your mutual adult futures. "Comment" on each other's updates. Have fun with it!

How Did This Happen? Things Have Changed!

Where did the line go? You know, the line between girlhood and womanhood that kept girls safe and kept adults aware of their responsibilities toward them? The erosion of this line, the blurring of this boundary, has serious consequences for girls and for any society. For example, little girls wearing sexy "fashions" do not understand how they are perceived, but adults in public spaces do.

It is not hard to understand why girls, especially by the time they enter middle school, put so much energy into looking hot. They believe it leads to popularity and the advantages high social status brings in school. Both boys and girls strive to be popular—it is natural—but only girls experience pressure to be sexy as a requirement of popularity or a path to it.

No wonder so many girls are always thinking about how their bodies, faces, and hair look while they are doing other things. One of the burdens of self-objectification for girls is this constant preoccupation with how others might be viewing them. They imagine and internalize what boys might think about how their bodies look in their clothes or how their lips look in high gloss—and they do this while walking down the hall, studying, playing sports, and so on. If that energy were directed *into* academics, sports, and extracurricular activities rather than detracting from their performance in those areas, girls would feel a lot better about themselves. They would also feel less competition with other girls to be the hottest, which might lead to a reduction in bullying and an increase in camaraderie among girls.

Perhaps if, during the princess phase, parents helped girls care less about being the fairest in the land, those girls would not care so much about being the hottest in the land when they get older. The root problem is looks-obsession and the idea that a girl's appearance is what gives her intrinsic value. If more adults said, "Wow, you're a good runner," instead of "Wow, what a beautiful princess," girls might adopt a healthier focus while they are young. They could fall back upon that foundation when they are older and in need of other sources of gratification and success in order to have strong self-esteem during adolescence.

What's the Big Deal? Why Does It Matter if Girls Are Sexualized? Won't They Outgrow It?

We started with the American Psychological Association's definition of sexualization. Its studies, as well as studies by many other experts, show that there are consequences to a sexualized girlhood, including:

- anxiety and depression
- body hatred and eating disorders
- vulnerability to sexual harassment and assault
- earlier and riskier sexual behavior
- relationship problems with boys and men
- difficulty developing a healthy and enjoyable sex life in adulthood
- low self-esteem
- poorer school performance
- dropping out of sports
- turning away from math, science, engineering, and technology

Sexualization and self-objectification are not passing phases that leave no trace. They also are not inevitable! There are many ways that mothers can help their girls bypass sexualization.

Saying No to Sexualization

What should you do when items you prefer your daughter not receive still come into your house as well-meaning gifts from friends and fam-

> "The expensive birthday parties and the many other activities we load our kids down with is a whole other topic. But I had a lot of good conversations with my daughter in the car, with the radio ads and news as good catalysts for some important ones. I sometimes called the car a 'confessional on wheels,' and in retrospect it was one of my ears to the ground as a parent."

ily? I asked Melissa Atkins Wardy—owner of Pigtail Pals & Ballcap Buddies and author of *Redefining Girly: How Parents Can Fight the Stereotyping and Sexualizing of Girlhood, from Birth to Tween*—that very question.

"People often make requests of relatives and friends. We ask them not to smoke in our house, or perhaps to take their shoes off. We don't consider this insulting, and most adults don't take it that way. It is about respect," says Wardy. "So why is it any different when it comes to our children? It is OK to say, 'No thank you. We don't accept gifts that do not empower our daughter. We try to focus on toys and clothes that don't make her grow up too fast.' If you have a daughter with a nut allergy, you naturally request that people do not give her food with nuts in it. This is similar—it is about protecting the physical and emotional health of girls."

Wardy went on to point out that we also teach our children to say no—to drugs, to sex at a young age, to getting in the car with someone who has been drinking, to proverbial candy from strangers. It is equally important to teach them to say no to sexualized media and products and to instill in them "body agency," which is the understanding that they have autonomy over their own bodies and how they are touched. When girls are young, this agency helps them to recognize or speak up about inappropriate touches. When they are older, it helps them make healthy decisions about sexual activity rather than be pressured into situations for which they are not ready. Moms need to set this example for their daughters. When they speak up on behalf of their girls and politely refuse sexualized toys and clothes, they are modeling an important skill: being able to say no to things that are harmful and learning to set boundaries and limits.

What Else Can Moms Do?

When mothers model healthy femininity and help their daughters make good choices, girls learn that there are lots of ways to feel great about themselves besides cultivating sex appeal. You can begin communicating with your daughter when she is as young as three or four about your family's values, about the negative effects of media and marketing, and about the many ways of being a girl and feeling good about being a girl. The teaching of media literacy—explaining to girls the ways in which they are being targeted to buy and consume sexualized products and perform sexiness as an indicator of their membership among the female gender—can begin when girls are in preschool. The earlier communication begins and the more it is nurtured, the more likely your preteen and teen daughters will be listening—and talking—when there is something important to discuss.

Here are some more tips for raising girls to bypass sexualization:

- Question, question, question. Stay tuned into your own child's comfort level with this approach, and moderate accordingly. Ask your daughter what she thinks of the clothing she sees girls wearing at the mall, the uniformly pink toys and sexy dolls on the girl aisle at Toys "R" Us, the roles of females in television shows and popular movies, the dance moves she sees on music videos or at a friend's dance recital, the ultra skinny models she sees in magazines, and so on. There is no scarcity of material out there to use as a conversation starter!

- Explicitly teach older girls that sexualization is *commercial* and *greed-based*. Explain that companies actually make money by exploiting girls' vulnerabilities about how they look and the need to feel desired, which is why your family does not reward those companies with your dollars.

- Listen to your own inner voice of unease. When you see a product intended for girls that makes you uncomfortable, don't push that feeling aside—figure out *why* you feel uncomfortable, and use that insight as guidance for whether or not it is appropriate for your daughter.

- Provide healthy alternatives—toys, dolls, clothes, movies, and books—that slow childhood down. It can be hard to find these items in large, mainstream shopping venues, but there are many small shops and online businesses set up by mothers that provide other moms with nonsexualized items for girls. Some are listed at the end of this book. Have the courage not to conform.

- Moms are very busy today, but the ways in which they keep busy with their daughters should be examined. If you are spending all of your time driving your daughter to soccer practice, music lessons, and many other activities—but not talking to her about the culture all around her—you may be providing her one kind of enrichment but depriving her of something more important. What do our girls *really* need? They need adult protection, guidance, and limits. They also need mothers with whom they can really talk. It does not always happen spontaneously, but is something that can be methodically encouraged and prioritized in a busy life.

- Reduce media consumption, but do not eliminate it entirely. Girls need less exposure to all of the craptastic messaging out there, but they do need to understand the world in which they live. Interact with your daughter about what she is seeing and experiencing, and help her process it. Mothers who try to shield their daughters completely often find that plenty of sexualized imagery seeps through anyway, because it is ambient in our culture. Then, for girls who have mothers who try to shut it all down without talking about it—or while constantly preaching about it—that media becomes the forbidden fruit.

- Moms can feel powerless when they see their daughters adopting sexualized attitudes and behaviors. Seek support from other moms, friends, relatives, your school or religious community, or your mother-daughter book club. Creating a small community of like-minded parents is helpful in all kinds of ways.

Modeling a healthy body image, having the ability to be physically active without worrying about hair getting messed up or nail polish getting chipped, and the expression of femininity *apart* from sexuality are among the messages a mother can give her daughter that will make her stronger, better able to resist peer pressure, and more likely to sidestep sexualized media.

> "As a nanny I saw a lot of this body insecurity in the little one I looked after. She was only six and a half and she told me that she didn't feel pretty because she didn't have breasts and that she didn't have white skin. (Both of her parents are from India.) When I was her age, I didn't want bigger breasts, I wanted a bigger backyard!"

RECOMMENDED TV SERIES

Toddlers & Tiaras (NR, pick any episode)

The irony was not lost on me when I spent a snowy International Women's Day writing a review and discussion guide about heavily made-up four-year-olds with spray tans, hair weaves, acrylic nails, fake teeth, and $1,000 dresses. That's leaving aside the towering rhinestone tiaras that could break a small child's neck. You've got to give it to reality TV: it may be a vapid, lowest-common-denominator magnifying glass that focuses laser-like attention on the people who least deserve it, but no matter how far the elevator drops, you can't avoid learning something. Sometimes I think about my mother's generation and wonder if they are bewildered that the Good Ship Lollipop now transports the shockingly bratty Honey Boo Boo and her go-go juice into our nation's family rooms. That has to be a mind-bender.

Toddlers & Tiaras episodes are essentially interchangeable, so watch one randomly. In every show, several small girls vacillate between incredible narcissism and gut-wrenching insecurity as they prepare for and compete in child beauty pageants, often begging their mothers to let them quit, but always being reassured by their mothers that they actually *love* being in pageants. It's all fun and games until someone gets eyelash glue in their eye. But the little girls almost always buck up and get out on stage shaking their booties, smiling, waving, and blowing kisses despite whatever melt-down they have just been bribed out of.

These episodes are unrated, but suitable for girls of all ages, and I can't think of any other television show or movie that demonstrates the sexualization of girlhood better than *Toddlers & Tiaras*. Try not to squeeze your eyes shut while watching little human beings reduced to gyrating bling. No matter how cringe-worthy the episodes, this weird little world needs to be seen, because it is the ultimate exaggerated microcosm of the real one.

DISCUSSION QUESTIONS

1. What do you think about beauty pageants for little girls? Do you think they are all good, all bad, or something in between? What concerns you about them? What do you like?

2. Beauty pageants are competitions. What are the girls (and mothers) competing to win? What factors determine who wins? What message does this send?

3. How do you feel about the mothers?

   Prompts

   - Are they harming their daughters? Do you consider the girls exploited or abused? Why or why not?

   - What do the mothers personally get out of putting their daughters in pageants?

   - When the mothers are shown backstage having "catfights," what stereotype does this reinforce?

   - What reasons do the mothers give for putting their daughters in pageants? Do you agree or disagree with their reasoning?

   - What do you think the average viewer thinks about these mothers? Are *they* exploited in any way?

   - What roles do the dads play?

4. There is an expression that people cannot look away from train wrecks. Do you think that applies to the viewers of this show? What does that say about our culture of celebrity voyeurism?

5. Discuss the sexualization of girls in today's media culture, and in real life. How much crossover is there between what you see on screen versus out in public? What amount of sexualization do you think is OK for you/your daughter?

FUN ACTIVITY

Watch Shirley Temple's "Animal Crackers in My Soup" online.

Shirley Temple was a child star in the 1930s. For many, she represented charisma, talent, wholesomeness, and many other virtues that young girls of the day admired. Instead of watching Miley Cyrus or Taylor Swift, the girls of her generation watched a girl of their own age sing and tap dance her way across a series of television and movie sets, charming adults and children alike. After viewing this short video of Shirley performing one of her biggest hits, compare it to what you just saw on *Toddlers & Tiaras*. What has changed for girl stars, and what remains the same? If you have a friend or relative who was a child in the 1930s, ask him or her to share memories with you about Shirley Temple. Do you think Shirley would be popular today? Why or why not?

Reflection from Charlotte

When I think back on my middle school years, I feel that there was much more bullying and social pressure within the groups of girls who wore the sexy clothes, because if you were going to hang out together, you all had to have the same look to compete for boys' attention. So girls trying to fit in were constantly comparing themselves to other girls who were considered popular. They didn't bother people like my friends and me; they picked on each other more. That's how the whole mean girls thing played out in my middle school.

I've often thought about why it was that I escaped the social pressure to be sexy and popular, and I know that part of it was that I was utterly uninterested in that kind of stress. But also, my childhood was probably fairly different from the childhoods of a lot of girls growing up then and certainly today. I had fewer electronic devices, and my time watching television and playing games on the computer was limited. I therefore read a great deal, wrote stories that I acted out with toys and stuffed animals, and played outside and with friends. Our book club was a way that I shared reading with friends in a group of other mothers and daughters like my mom and me, and that was always a safe place where we got to be just kids.

Because my exposure to media as a small child was also limited, I didn't become aware of the sexualization of females until I was a little older and able to analyze it and discuss it with my mom whenever she pointed it out to me. Although messages and pressure from the media seem to reach much younger girls today, I think it's still definitely possible for moms to guide their daughters away from harmful trends such as sexualization. My mom always said it was not her role to be my friend, but to be my mom, and we can be friends now, but when I was little, she really did not give in to what everyone else was doing. I respect that a lot more now than I did then!

RECOMMENDED BOOKS

TITLE	AUTHOR	AGE RANGE	MOVIE ADAPTATION?
Fever Crumb	Philip Reeve	10+	
The Hunger Games	Suzanne Collins	12+	Yes
Matilda	Roald Dahl	8+	Yes
One Day and One Amazing Morning on Orange Street	Joanne Rocklin	8+	
Saffy's Angel	Hilary McKay	8+	
The Future of Us	Jay Asher and Carolyn Mackler	12+	
The Lemonade War	Jacqueline Davies	9+	
The Penderwicks: A Summer Tale of Four Sisters, Two Rabbits, and a Very Interesting Boy	Jeanne Birdsall	8+	
Various series	Steve Augarde	8+	
When Life Gives You OJ	Erica S. Perl	9+	

RECOMMENDED MOVIES AND TV

TITLE	MPAA RATING
American Girl movies	G
Little House on the Prairie movies	G
Lolita (1962)	NR
Memoirs of a Geisha	PG-13
Toddlers & Tiaras	NR

RECOMMENDED MEDIA

Use an Internet search engine to locate these videos on YouTube, Vimeo, or other video hosting sites.

Jean Kilbourne's Videos

"Caroline Heldman: The Sexy Lie" (TED Talk)

Dove's "Onslaught"

"Sexualization of Girls in the Media—SPARK Summit"

"Tropes vs. Women"

"Cover Girl Culture"

"Sexualisation of Young Children"

"Sext Up Kids"

Lyn Mikel Brown: Taking Back Girl Power (TED Talk)

"Middle School Girls Talk About the Sexualization of Middle School Girls"

"Mommy, Do You Think I'm Fat?"

TEACHING GIRLS TO DEFINE THEMSELVES FROM THE INSIDE OUT

—⬦ ⬦—

"Why do girls always feel like they have to apologize for giving an opinion or taking up space in the world? Have you ever noticed that?" Nicole asked. "You go on websites and some girl leaves a post, and if it's longer than three sentences or she's expressing her thoughts about some topic, she usually ends with 'Sorry for the rant' or 'That may be dumb, but that's what I think.'"
—*from* Beauty Queens *by Libba Bray*

Key Takeaways

- ▶ Beauty and thinness have become obsessions for many girls, crowding out their ability to develop a variety of deeper and more important personal characteristics.

- ▶ A mother's relationship to her own physical appearance and its upkeep is as influential on her daughter's self-esteem as the beauty industry's efforts to groom girls as lifelong consumers of their products.

⯈ By reading girl-empowering books and watching movies that
depict girls as being much more than pretty objects, mothers
can show girls healthy alternatives and can guide them toward
goals that transcend this fixation on appearance.

Tavi Gevinson was having a hard time finding positive female teenage
role models, so, at age thirteen, she created the very popular *Rookie*
magazine, where girls could come together online to share writing, photography, videos, and other material contributed both by readers and the
publication's staff. (Be sure to check out Gevinson's TED talk in the media
recommendation section at the end of this chapter.) A longtime admirer of
this young girl, I was especially tickled when she appeared recently on *The
Colbert Report*. Stephen Colbert, brilliant comedian that he is, interviewed
her and asked, "Your magazine actually has positive images for girls and
positive messages for girls. But if girls feel good about themselves, how are
we going to sell them things they don't need?" I often say that really good
satire is the purest form of truth.

In many places around the world, women struggle for safety, education,
equality, and basic human rights. I can't help but notice that in developed
countries such as the United States, girls and women are prone to engage
in a different kind of struggle, one that is more internal. It is a "first-world
problem" of relative affluence and freedom from the kinds of physical
labor and abuse that occupy the waking hours of women in many other
countries. Here in the United States, where we are all awash in pop culture
and consumerism, there seems to be much collective navel gazing over
issues of personal image.

Physical appearance is important to men and women, boys and girls,
all around the globe. Cultural ideals about facial features and weight vary
greatly, as do the amounts of time and money people choose to spend on
the cultivation of physical beauty. In wealthy societies like ours, where
females feel intense pressure to attract male admiration, and where the
beauty industry has been marketing to them since they were in diapers,
many girls grow up believing that they must spend a lot of money on
makeup and other beauty products and services, as well as a lot of time
every day applying and using them. There are companies that could not
profit, let alone exist, if they did not instill insecurities in women and girls
about their appearances, because the beauty products and services they

sell are intended to fix perceived flaws. By that logic, the more "flaws," the better. Insecurity is very lucrative.

As treadmills go, this one is particularly difficult to dismount. When you live in a culture that holds up a certain facial and body archetype that is nearly impossible for the average girl or woman to achieve, and when there is a media complex constantly disseminating that image such that this ideal becomes even more of an imperative to those who believe they must somehow attain it, they become willing to engage in increasingly unhealthy behaviors—physically, emotionally, and financially—in pursuit of a mirage.

When you turn on the television, whether you are watching a sitcom, a reality show, a movie, or even the evening news, you see a very narrow segment of the female gender. When you open a magazine or drive down the highway, passing billboards along the way, you see a carefully selected and often digitally altered paradigm of very young, almost exclusively Western beauty. Flawless faces atop extremely thin bodies are equated with popularity, happiness, and success. This leads typical girls and women to grow even more concerned with becoming thinner and thinner, and to correct any facial features that they believe are not pretty enough. This feedback loop can result in great expenditures of money, time, energy, and emotion over the course of a lifetime.

"I live in a wealthy community where many preteen girls get weekly manicures, hair coloring, and plastic surgery by sixteen. It's a tough crowd! I avoid the spa gifts for this very reason, though I think the periodic mani-pedi can be a fun gift. I don't want my girl getting hooked on a spa life but I do want her to appreciate the concept of self-care. It's a fine line!"

Personally, I am rather annoyed by it all. I don't want people to think I can't be bothered with "keeping myself up," and I don't want to go all Women's Studies 101 on anyone, *but I've got stuff to do,* so I hope the carefully considered and minimal amount of attention to my appearance isn't robbing anyone of their God-given right to see me with eye shadow and lipstick, rocking some skinny jeans. I like my comfy "mom jeans" and I get more writing done in them. I realize that being pretty and hot is relentlessly promoted as any woman's greatest contribution to everyone else's aesthetic landscape, but I've got better things to do.

Confession time, folks: I did *not* have a grip on this as a teenager. I remember spending an exhaustive amount of time on my hair and makeup. I would not leave the house without my beauty routine fully completed. Summers were most challenging in the hot, humid weather down south. I would spend more than forty-five minutes blow drying and ironing my hair to get it Marcia Brady straight, only to step out of the air conditioning, or, God forbid, into any body of water, and have it return to its naturally curly state. Swimming was an exercise in keeping my hair out of the water and never getting the relief of submerging my head unless I was willing to have curly hair *and* wear waterproof mascara.

When I think about the years I spent this way, I feel wiped out emotionally. I keenly recall the anxiety of worrying that I was not beautiful, or simply that my eyeliner was smudged and I didn't know it. I blamed my lack of a boyfriend on my failure to be pretty enough. I remember thinking I could get more sleep or have more time for various other things I enjoyed if I did not "have" to spend so much time fixing myself up. I absolutely resented it, but I was absolutely *enslaved* by it. When I think back on all the time I spent fretting in front of a mirror, I am seriously angry with my younger self. *Grrrr.* This is one of the reasons I feel so strongly about helping today's girls stop acting like heat-seeking missiles for the male gaze, because really, that *is* what this is about. I call BS on everyone who says "I do this for myself."

Do I think girls and women should never wear makeup or style their hair? Of course not! It's fun and makes you feel good if done in moderation and without terror. But if the thought of going to the grocery store without looking perfect gives you an anxiety attack, it might be useful to examine why that is. Look around: boys and men are not experiencing this—they have much more time and money at their disposal that the beauty industry does not consume like a vampire.

I remember once hearing that if smokers saved all of the money they spent on cigarettes in their lifetimes, they could buy cars or pay full college tuitions. I wonder what girls and women could do with the money spent on beauty products, diet books, weight-loss classes, and salon services— even just a portion of it. I wonder how much more confident and truly successful girls and women could be if they somehow felt better about themselves on the inside, which would make them more comfortable with themselves on the outside. What would it take to help today's girls not step on the beauty treadmill in the first place?

RECOMMENDED BOOK

Real Beauty: 101 Ways to Feel Great About You by Therese Kauchak (age 8+)

Published by American Girl Library, *Real Beauty: 101 Ways to Feel Great About You* is a very short, interactive book (involving reading, writing, and activities) that helps girls feel good about themselves during the preteen and early teen years. It is inexpensive, but you will need to purchase it because your daughter will write in it. It gives many tips about healthy eating, exercise, body image, dealing with bullies, changes during puberty, relationships, and so forth. The information is presented in an upbeat, easy-to-read manner and is suitable for girls to read on their own or with their mothers. There are lots of fun checklists and other creative ways for girls to process their observations and experiences at this age, and to develop greater confidence and self-esteem.

We all intrinsically know where "real beauty" comes from. This book will help daughters focus on the things that are more than skin deep.

DISCUSSION QUESTIONS

1. Why do you think it is hard for girls to accept compliments? Why do girls so often ask "Do I look OK?"

2. Do you have friends who talk a lot about their weight and dieting? How does it make you feel? The book suggests changing the subject. How might you try to do that?

3. Why do you think some girls don't get enough exercise? If a friend of yours were feeling self-conscious about exercise in some way, how could you help?

4. The book talks a lot about looking good versus feeling good. Are there some times in your own life when it is hard to do what feels good at the expense of what looks good?

5. Think about the quote, "Wearing tiny T-shirts and itty-bitty shorts might get you attention—but people might not see the *real you*." Are there any types of attention that you don't want to have? What do you think stops girls from dressing and behaving in ways that show others who they really are?

6. Think about these two situations: (1) You are looking at a fashion magazine and observing body shapes and sizes, and (2) you are in a public place like the mall or the airport and observing body shapes and sizes. How are these situations different? Why? What does this tell you about real life?

7. Think about the quote "Insulting others insults your own spirit." What do you think that means?

8. How did you feel at the end of the book? Which parts did you find most useful?

FUN ACTIVITY

To the degree girls are comfortable, take turns sharing some of the responses written in the book. Is there anything you think the book missed? Create your own activity for the book that addresses something else you wish had been in there. Make it fun and engaging for your "readers!"

How Should Mothers Think About Beauty— Their Own and Their Daughters'?

Beauty is a cultural construct. It changes over time, and varies from place to place. In some cultures, such as ours in America, beauty also has a shelf life. It is best to understand and plan for that fact, even if you personally believe that beauty is ageless. Once women reach forty in this country, they virtually disappear from media. Some resort to drastic measures to appear younger than their chronological age in order to remain relevant and avoid this anticipated erasure. I will never forget my fortieth birthday. I locked myself in my office at work and cried. I didn't see that brief, twenty-four-hour midlife crisis coming. By the end of the day it had passed, but like most women, I am resentful that the older I get, the less our culture seems to value me.

"Erotic capital," a term I find quite distasteful, comes from the book *Erotic Capital: The Power of Attraction in the Boardroom and the Bedroom* by Catherine Hakim. It refers to a woman's ability to professionally and personally trade upon her sex appeal. Erotic capital dissipates quickly, leaving women to rely upon other skills and qualities later in life—things that they may or may not have developed if they relied on sex appeal to open doors for them. It is therefore obviously advantageous to teach girls that at some point their looks will fade, and that their identities, if wrapped up in their appearance, will be challenged. From the earliest days, girls need eggs in lots of baskets.

The term "beauty myth," borrowed from the book by Naomi Wolf of the same title, suggests that as women increase their social power and make gains toward equality with men, they are expected to adhere even more rigidly to external standards of physical beauty. Wolf argues that this is less about beauty than it is about conformity. Whatever they are doing, women must first and foremost look attractive. This is my favorite quote from that book, and by favorite I mean most vexing: "A cultural fixation on female thinness is not an obsession about female beauty but an obsession about female obedience." Let that sink in for a moment.

Mothers often experience conflict between their own relationship with beauty and body image and what they want for their daughters. They truly want their girls to feel good about themselves on the inside. And they want their girls to say no to the many products advertised to them, for them to feel they do not need routine salon services or frequent check-ins with their bathroom scales. On the other hand, mothers want their daughters to be popular, to fit in, and to be considered attractive. Sometimes, they enjoy the compliments from others on their daughter's appearance, as if it affirms their own value in some way. But such comments can be damaging if mothers are unaware of the ways in which they inadvertently contribute to their daughter's body consciousness.

I interviewed Dr. Robyn Silverman, child development specialist and author of *Good Girls Don't Get Fat: How Weight Obsession Is Messing Up Our*

Girls and How We Can Help Them Thrive Despite It, about how mothers can compliment their daughters in ways that increase their self-esteem, and their body image in particular.

"Sometimes mothers compliment their daughter's appearance while simultaneously disparaging their own. For example, a mom might say to her daughter, 'I wish I still looked like you. Look at that beautiful, flat tummy you have.' What this communicates to the daughter is that her mother does not like her own body, and that the changes that come with age or weight gain or pregnancy are very undesirable," Silverman explains. "Daughters look *to* their mothers as role models, but also are often told they look *like* their mothers, and so they are listening carefully to how mothers critique their own looks."

Silverman then outlines a helpful strategy that mothers can use from the time their daughters are very young through their teen years. "We need to say what's beautiful about us—*both* of us, mother and daughter. Define beauty as being both inside and out, with inside being most important. Beauty is kindness, thoughtfulness, healthiness, and many other things that apply equally to all females, young and old. So for example, say to your daughter, 'I love my legs because they let me do yoga. Why do *you* love your legs?' A young girl might say, 'Because they help me run and jump,' and you can affirm that by explaining that our bodies are beautiful because of all the things they let us *do.*"

Silverman emphasizes that this is a manner of communicating our values, and that although it might feel contrived at first, it will become natural to talk in these positive ways with girls. It is important to be purposeful about encouraging healthy body image because the media is such a powerful negative force in the lives of girls today. Moms need to talk, question, and reinforce what is healthy in strategic ways while daughters are growing up. Silverman finishes with a personal comment about her own daughter: "While everyone else is calling her Princess, I call her Super Girl!"

This reminds me of a great quote by the actress Kate Winslet: "As a child, I never heard one woman say to me, 'I love my body.' Not my mother, my elder sister, my best friend. No one woman has ever said, 'I am so proud of my body,' so I make sure to say it to [my daughter] Mia, because a positive physical outlook has to start at an early age."

No woman ever said this to me, and I never said this to Charlotte. I'm thinking about whether it's too late. I hope it's not.

As mothers, if we believe that greater happiness and success always accrue to the thinnest, most beautiful women—which is sometimes the case, at least superficially and temporarily—then we may pass this idea to our daughters whether we like it or not, especially if we are at a stage in life where it has become increasingly difficult to hold onto the advantages conveyed by physical appearance for ourselves. As mothers get older, some of us find ourselves spending even more time and money—and going to more extreme measures—trying to remain thin, pretty, and youthful. All the while, our daughters are watching. When mothers are observably unhappy with their appearance, it shows girls that if their first and possibly most important female role model in life is constantly looking in the mirror and finding imperfections, then they should do the same. And they do.

> "To quote the brilliant character Charles Wallace from the *Wrinkle in Time* series by Madeline L'Engle, 'Mother isn't the least bit pretty. She is beautiful.' My thoughts: Pretty is skin deep. Beauty is from the soul."

Teaching Balance: Finding Middle Ground Between Beauty Obsession and the Occasional Pedicure!

Is it possible, or even desirable, to raise girls with no regard for beauty—their own or others'? I don't think so. It is natural to want to feel desirable, to take pride in one's grooming and self-expression, to want to look stylish and put together at work or school, and to want to be attractive to potential romantic partners. As with most things in life, *balance* is what is important. There is nothing wrong with wanting to feel feminine, to occasionally go to a salon to be pampered, to wear makeup, or to exercise and eat a balanced diet to maintain a healthy weight. These things are pleasurable and socially acceptable, and there is nothing wrong with enjoying them. The problems arise when girls and women become preoccupied with their appearance, thinking and talking of little else. We all know some people who are like this, and even if they are human beings of substance and depth, no one sees it; all they see is superficial behavior.

On the other hand, if the topic of physical appearance were completely ignored by mothers around their girls while they were simultaneously exposed to the thousands of beauty-related advertisements they see and hear each year, those girls might feel disconnected from their mothers, confused, and might even wonder if they are unattractive, trying to find an explanation for the silence.

Striking an ideal balance on the topic of beauty may be difficult, but with thought and deliberation, moms can show girls that it is nice to be pretty or have a slim physique, but that intelligence and other traits and talents are a different kind of beauty that get you further in life and last a lot longer. Girls can be pretty *and* smart; attractive *and* compassionate; have a pleasing figure *and* be ambitious. Girls can do and be many things simultaneously, but this requires the strength to define personal goals that are distinct from—and of greater importance than—the goal of looking attractive for other people.

What about girls who are not and will never be considered conventionally attractive, no matter how much effort they bring to the endeavor? They may need even more guidance as children because they should not be left to feel they are failing at the one thing to which so many of their peers collectively aspire and set up as a pathway to group social acceptance. *Who* they are *must* become their beauty, and mothers who convey this type of self-love will one day be thanked for doing so.

I always saw Charlotte as genuinely pretty and still do, but she has never viewed herself that way. She has, however, expressed appreciation for my focus on the *inside* of her head, and for not pressuring her too much about the outside. I know I did do that a little, because I'm human and wanted her to see her own beauty. But mostly, I tried my best to give her the kind of attention *she* wanted. Since she always had the not-buying-it attitude when I praised her looks, I tried to take the hint and adjust course, succeeding and failing in bits and pieces as most moms do.

For girls who are not Caucasian, there is additional pressure—to have lighter skin or hair, and to have more classically Caucasian facial features and other bodily characteristics that align with what is racially and ethnically represented as beautiful in the media. There is always a holy grail of beauty that is in one way or many ways out of reach for girls and women of all races, shapes, and sizes. It will never be obtained, even by females overwhelmingly considered beautiful, because perfection is denied to all of us.

If I could only emphasize one point about the beauty myth, it would be this: *Girls and women do not owe prettiness or thinness to onlookers.* Being beautiful and skinny is not a requirement of being female. We have a hyped-up culture of celebrity worship that can undermine the full emotional and intellectual development of girls, sacrificing them to the quest for something that is fleeting and only skin deep. This is one of the biggest ways that females give away their power.

RECOMMENDED BOOK

Beauty Queens by Libba Bray (age 12+)

Part *Lord of the Flies*, part *America's Next Top Model*, and part *Gilligan's Island*, Libba Bray's fast-paced, tongue-in-cheek send-up of American girl culture, reality TV, and a beauty industry run amok is some of the smartest social commentary I've ever read in the YA fiction genre. Fifty contestants in the Miss Teen Dream Pageant are in a plane crash and find themselves surviving, *Lost*-style, on a desert island without makeup or cameras, and also without food, water, or shelter. Their surreal adventures as they cope with their own human foibles without hair spray or the Internet are actually an interesting counterpoint to the descent into savagery seen among the boys in *Lord of the Flies*. For these beauty-obsessed mean girls, being cut off from civilization gives them freedom from societal pressures. As a result, they actually find themselves and come of age in a remote location where their appearance is no longer the core of who they are.

Is it satire? Is it parody? Is it over the top? Yes, yes, and yes! It's also hilarious, biting, in-your-face storytelling about the sexualization of girls, the beauty myth, gender stereotypes, and many of the other things being discussed in *Her Next Chapter*. Take the message seriously, but don't take the book seriously. Let it make you think and talk. There isn't much out there like this book. It gets five stars from me for actually taking on—in a clever, albeit deliberately heavy-handed way—our corporate consumer culture and the way we casually accept the specific ways that it targets girls.

The best thing about this book? It addresses real issues while being irreverent and funny. Thumbs up!

DISCUSSION QUESTIONS

1. When the girls are first stranded on the island, they seem to size each other up, as if the pageant were still about to happen and were more important than the immediate emergency of survival. Do girls (and women) do this to each other as a matter of course? Who do you think are more competitive: men or women? Or are the ways in which they compete different?

2. On the "Miss Teen Dream Fun Fact Pages!" you get to know each character and how she sees herself. Who is your favorite and why? With whom do you most identify? Are there any you really dislike?

3. Do you see any connections between society's beauty standards for girls and society's behavioral standards for girls? What about for boys? Do you or your girlfriends feel pressure to act in a certain way when you're at school? Do you think boys feel a similar pressure?

4. Think about this quote from the book: "when it came to love, the message for girls seemed to be this: Don't. Don't go after what you want. Wait. Wait to be chosen, as if only in the eye of another could one truly find value." (Moms: There's a lot to talk about here.) What does it mean for girls that their primary role is to attract sexual attention and then wait? What kinds of behaviors does this double standard encourage in both boys and girls? How is this different in the human species than among most animals? Why do you think it is different for humans?

5. What do you think about the girls outlawing the word "sorry" on the island? How do girls and boys use this word differently? Do you and your friends use it a lot? Should you?

6. Another great quote: "Maybe girls need an island to find themselves. Maybe they need a place where no one's watching them so they can be who they really are… They were no longer performing. Waiting. Hoping." What does this mean? Why do some girls seem to act so differently for boys? Is it healthy? Do boys act differently for girls? How?

7. Do you remember the quote about what girls are reduced to in front of boys? They are described as "giggling, lash-batting, hair-playing idiots."

Pretty harsh! Have you noticed this in your school? Why is this behavior so entrenched for some girls?

8. When Mary Lou let herself get angry, she wondered, "Why do girls have to be all pure and innocent and good? Why don't guys have to be?" Why do you think? Do you let yourself show anger when you are angry? Do you think girls are taught to keep these sorts of emotions inside? What about boys? Are there emotions girls are encouraged to express that boys aren't?

9. In the end, the girls do survive and get rescued, and they make their own choices about staying or going. They have changed while on the island. Do you think those changes will be permanent? After reading this book, have you gained any new insights into girls' relationships to beauty?

FUN ACTIVITY

In the book *Beauty Queens*, the girls put on a convention called a "Girl Con." Think about the workshops they create. Which ones would you have liked to attend? Are there any panels you feel you could have been on? Now, as a mother-daughter book club, pretend you are hosting your own Girl Con. Make up the workshops and play it out! (Moms: your job is to help guide this activity toward both what the girls want *and* what you think is empowering!)

Body Image and Weight: Shifting the Focus from Numbers to Nutrition

We have all had the experience of seeing paintings of nude women from a long-ago era when visible hipbones, "thigh gaps," and collarbones were not considered attractive. Today's cultural ideal in terms of the female form seems to get thinner and thinner every year, as if, on some level, the message to women is *take up less space, disappear.* I want girls and women to take up *more* space . . . with their voices, their ambitions, and yes, their physical bodies. Women's bodies—and girls' bodies, too—are constantly scrutinized. No one escapes it, not even female Olympic athletes who can be the best in the world at their sport but are still interviewed, photographed, and written about in terms of their conformity to accepted beauty standards.

Celebrities are often described as being too heavy or too skinny—and sometimes both at the same time! There is no perfect weight—no magic number on the scale—that will release them from being under this microscope. There is also no checkout aisle at the grocery store where young girls do not see this dynamic splashed across half a dozen magazine covers right at eye level. In magazines, on the screen, and in the real world, female clothing styles have become uniformly body hugging. No one escapes notice and assessment when dressed this way, and it is difficult for females to release themselves from dissecting their every line, curve, or bulge in the mirror and considering how others will judge their bodies.

We also have an obesity epidemic in this country that has raised legitimate concerns about fast food, school lunches, and sedentary American lifestyles (among other issues). It is reasonable to worry about this and to feel action is needed to help both adults and children live healthier lives. Unfortunately, an unintended backlash of our media campaign to combat childhood obesity is that more young girls than ever have become highly body conscious at very young ages. They believe they are fat; they are bullied and told directly that they are fat; they sometimes diet excessively and develop eating disorders—often when they are *not* medically overweight. What constitutes "fat" these days is everything from medically obese to almost but not quite skeletal. That's a zone where *most* girls fall.

Puberty is an especially delicate time for girls because their bodies begin to fill out as they become women. Preteens gain weight around their hips and buttocks and develop breasts. I talked with Marci Warhaft-Nadler, body-image advocate and author of *The Body Image Survival Guide for Parents: Helping Toddlers, Tweens, and Teens Thrive,* about the relationship between puberty and body image issues in girls. Warhaft-Nadler says that puberty begins earlier in girls than it did even a generation ago, so concern with body image is beginning earlier as well. This is a common time for eating disorders to manifest in girls, because the healthy signs of entering womanhood are often mistaken for getting fat. This particular topic is rarely discussed in sex education classes in school, so girls might not learn that these are *normal* changes in their bodies unless their mothers explain it.

"If a mother is worried about her daughter's weight gain at this age, she should make an appointment with the pediatrician to find out if there really is a problem. If there is, she can get advice on the best ways to address it. But most of the time, this is normal, healthy weight gain," Warhaft-Nadler explains. "When mothers compare their daughters to their friends' daughters, that can lead to a wrong conclusion about their own child's weight. Puberty and genetics take some time to play out. Worrying prematurely, or placing young girls on diets, can backfire. For moms who worry about their own weight, it can be particularly stressful seeing daughters gain weight, but it is always best to seek professional advice and not project concerns onto girls who are very sensitive about their bodies."

Eating disorders are on the rise in all age groups—below age ten, during the teen years, and even during middle age and beyond, the last of which is a relatively new phenomenon reflective of a generation of older women desperate to retain a youthful appearance. Eating disorders often develop in girls and women (and sometimes boys and men) who feel many things are out of their control, and by regulating their food intake, they have a way of exercising control over something in their lives.

How can moms help their daughters feel good about their bodies? For starters, take the emphasis off the bathroom scale and place it on healthy lifestyle choices, such as eating nutritious foods, encouraging outdoor play, limiting sedentary computer and video game time, encouraging participation in sports, and finding active things to do together as a family. Reduce the amount of messages coming into your home that are inclined to focus girls on body image—this means replace the fashion and celebrity gossip magazines on the coffee table with better options, swap out reality shows about dieting for better programming, and stop criticizing your own body and weight in front of your daughter. Instead, talk about what is good about your body (it is strong, it brought your child into the world, etc.). You can still exercise and eat less-caloric foods, but don't make it a discussion topic around the house.

As a family, shift the focus from weight to health, from inactivity to activity, and from everyone's outsides to their insides—there will be much more to feel good about!

"Forty Is the New Twenty" and Other Baby Boomerisms That Undermine Graceful Aging

I can't remember when I first heard someone say this or any of the other versions substituting different numbers, but I do remember Charlotte being a teenager, hearing this and quipping, "So does that make twenty

"My mom is an aesthetician and is completely obsessed with having young-looking skin. She's in her late fifties but looks like she's in her forties. That's fine and all, but my whole life, she has spent a half hour in the morning and again at night applying serums, chemical peels, moisturizers, and anything else you can think of. I wish that time had been spent with me or my sister. I don't think it's worth it. I have already decided to age gracefully and naturally. Besides, silver and white hair is gorgeous, in my opinion. Laugh lines are amazing. Aging is a natural, wonderful part of life. I wish society would stop portraying it as something so horrifying."

the new zero?" She was irritated. So was I! To myself I often think, *what is up with the boomers and their refusal to age with dignity?* I never say it out loud—it could get me killed. So here's my concern: if the age you are can't be embraced or even tolerated without creating desperate, embarrassing slogans to apologize for it and reframe it, how can one look *forward* in life rather than backward, let alone set a positive example for girls and young women? If you are forty and feel twenty, great! It is the impulse to verbally disparage the aging process and set yourself apart from it that sabotages impressionable girls. They learn very early that getting older is the worst thing that can possibly happen to a woman. I wish this were not the case, but that ship has sailed.

So what can be done? Truthfully, it *is* hard getting older as a woman in America, and it deserves a little strategic thinking. I turned fifty while writing this book. Look away now if you don't want to see me throwing my integrity in the trash, because I'd be lying if I didn't admit I felt depressed—for a day or two. I looked in the mirror and said to myself, "It's official, Lori: you are now completely invisible in society!" Then I pulled back my slightly graying hair and got back to work doing what I love. Why? Because fifty is fifty and it's OK. And because I want Charlotte to see that.

Movies, magazines, and even most other women your age will not tell you this, but girls need human examples of healthy aging. They need mothers who are not shopping at the same clothing stores as them, don't try to fit into and share their daughters' clothes, do not complain about fading beauty and fight it tooth and nail, and don't scramble to look younger as young girls scramble to look older. Mothers and daughters have different roles and different stages on which to live their respective and simultaneous lives. It's natural for their appearances to reflect that.

More Tips for Raising Girls with Positive Body Image

- When your daughter is young, do not use food as a punishment/reward system, because that gives it too much significance.

- Talk about what women and girls look like in the media. Discuss the epidemic of Photoshopping and explain that the images of beautiful women are not even real. Supermodel Cindy Crawford was once quoted as saying, "I wish I looked like Cindy Crawford." Observe women and girls of different body types out in the real world, and discuss with your daughter that we do not need to starve ourselves and do not need to be rail thin to be attractive. Show them examples of healthy women of all shapes and sizes.

- Compliment your daughter on who she is more than on how she looks.

- Be cautious about complimenting other women and girls on beauty and weight loss in front of your daughter, and be sure she hears you compliment them on things unrelated to appearance.

- Avoid purchasing clothes for your young daughter that make her look like a teenager and that focuses her and others on her body. Find stylish but age-appropriate outfits that let her be a child.

- Help your daughter develop hobbies and talents so she will have a sense of pride in her accomplishments. The girls most vulnerable to looks-obsession are the ones without an extracurricular passion. There is very little difference in the self-esteem of a girl with five strong passions/talents and a girl with only one, but there is a significant difference in the self-esteem of a girl with one deep passion and a girl with none.

RECOMMENDED MOVIE

Hairspray (2007, PG)

What I love about *Hairspray* is that it teaches a number of important lessons without trying too hard—and in a production that is lively and fun, contagiously so. The story centers on Tracy Turnblad, an overweight teen who longs to audition for *The Corny Collins Show*, a teen dance show broadcast from a local TV station in Baltimore. The show is racially segregated, and there is plenty to discuss here for clubs wishing to analyze this aspect of the movie. It also features uniformly thin, pretty girls, and Tracy's compelling desire to star on the show despite her appearance challenges the notion that heavy girls "know their place." Tracy knows her place is wherever the hip kids are singing and dancing, because her talent speaks for itself. She is utterly lacking in self-consciousness. How often do our girls today see female characters in movies who are—let's name it: fat *and* happy? That is what really captivated me. Tracy never acts like a *fat* girl. She just acts like a girl.

The comedy is marvelous. John Travolta dons a fat suit and a lot of makeup to play Tracy's mom with gender-bending hilarity, and Christopher Walken scores yet another brilliantly quirky role as Tracy's dad. Both are supportive of Tracy as she challenges and overcomes weight bias and joins forces with the show's African American characters as they march and practice civil disobedience to end "Negro Day" on the dance show. The issues of body-image perception and civil rights are prevalent throughout the musical, but never heavy-handed. This one's a lot of fun!

DISCUSSION QUESTIONS

1. During the first scene of the movie, when Tracy is singing through the streets of Baltimore, did anything surprise you?

   Prompts

   ▦ Does Nikki Blonsky, who plays Tracy, look like the actresses you usually see these days in movies?

- Does her dancing ability seem expected or unexpected given her weight?

- Do you often see portrayals of overweight girls who are happy and confident?

2. John Waters, the writer and director of the original *Hairspray* movie on which this is based, likes to focus on society's misfits and nonconformists. Who in the movie seems to fit into these categories? Do they seem marginalized by themselves or by others?

3. Are Tracy's parents good parents? Why or why not?

Prompts

- How does each of her parents react to her desire to be on *The Corny Collins Show*?

- Why does her mother fear for her?

- How do they support her over the course of the film?

4. Compare Tracy's family life with her friend Penny's. Which would you prefer and why?

5. Is the relationship between Tracy and Link believable in the film? Is it believable in real life?

Prompts

- Do good-looking guys ever go out with girls who look like Tracy in real life? What about good-looking girls—do they go out with less attractive guys?

- In movies, what do you notice about the relative attractiveness of couples?

- Do you think movies reflect culture or do you think movies drive culture?

6. Is there anything you've ever wanted to do that you felt was unattainable because of your physical appearance, race, or another factor? How did you handle it?

7. Do you think it is harder, less hard, or equally hard to be a girl who is overweight today as opposed to a generation ago? What about several generations ago? Do cultural ideals for female beauty vary over time and across cultures?

8. Why does Tracy seem to have high self-esteem? What bullying does she encounter? If she were a girl in your school, do you think her social life would be the same as in the movie or different?

9. In the last musical number of the film, we hear the lyrics "we've come a long way, but we've still got a long way to go." What does the song refer to? In what ways do you think today's society still has a long way to go?

FUN ACTIVITY

The Corny Collins Show in *Hairspray* was actually modeled on a real teen dance show called *The Buddy Dean Show*, which aired in Baltimore from 1957 to 1964. It ultimately went off the air because it refused to integrate black and white dancers. Here are two short clips from the original *Buddy Dean Show* that you can watch together as a club and talk about.

"Dancin' the Madison on The Buddy Dean Show"

"Buddy Dean clip—Potato Chips!"

Reflection from Charlotte

I recently read a news article about a fourteen-year-old girl who was bullied about her appearance. Kids at school teased her because her ears were big, and they had done so since she was in first grade. Eventually the bullying got so bad that she asked her mother if she could have surgery to pin back her ears. Her mother couldn't afford it, but the girl was given free plastic surgery by an organization that provides financial assistance for children with facial deformities. She had initially planned to change only her ears, but then she also decided to have more work done on her nose and chin as well so that she could become even prettier. After the surgery, kids stopped bullying her, and she was happy with her decision.

Did the parents make the right decision? Why or why not? I think this story is a good one to discuss in mother-daughter book clubs in conjunction with the *Uglies* series. These young adult novels by Scott Westerfeld depict a futuristic society in which teens are required to undergo significant plastic surgery to become pretty and "perfect." I was reminded of these books (which are recommended at the end of this chapter) when I read the story about this girl who was bullied, and I found the dystopian setting of the series to be entirely believable based on American popular culture today. In addition to the disturbing parallels between Westerfeld's fictional world and our own, I am fascinated by the fact that it was envisioned by a male author rather than a female. Most critiques of the ways in which our media culture harms women come, understandably, from women themselves. However, these books present the view of a man who sees what many women do, and who wants to show young readers the dangers of what is happening here and now for teenage girls.

RECOMMENDED BOOKS

TITLE	AUTHOR	AGE RANGE	MOVIE ADAPTATION?
Another Way to Dance	Martha Southgate	12+	
Beauty Queens	Libba Bray	12+	
Charlotte's Web	E. B. White	8+	Yes
If a Tree Falls at Lunch Period	Gennifer Choldenko	12+	
The Kiesha'ra series	Amelia Atwater-Rhodes	12+	Yes
Real Beauty: 101 Ways to Feel Great About You	Therese Kauchak	8+	
The Second Life of Abigail Walker	Frances O'Roark Dowell	8+	
The Uglies series	Scott Westerfeld	12+	
When You Reach Me	Rebecca Stead	8+	
Wintergirls	Laurie Halse Anderson	13+	

RECOMMENDED MOVIES

TITLE	MPAA RATING
Girl Model	NR
Good Hair	NR
Hairspray (2007)	PG
Miss Congeniality	PG-13
Mulan	G

RECOMMENDED MEDIA

Use an Internet search engine to locate these videos on YouTube, Vimeo, or other video hosting sites.

"Keep Her in the Game"

NIKE's "Voices"

"Dove Real Beauty Sketches"

"Dark Girls"

The Illusionists videos

Kattie Makkai "Will I Be Pretty?"

Julia Bluhm and Izzy Labbe of SPARK Summit (TED Talk)

"Tavi Gevinson: A Teen Just Trying to Figure It Out" (TED Talk)

"The Evolution of Beauty"

"Teens Take On *Teen Vogue*"

7

Dealing with the "Mean Girls"

HOW TO TALK ABOUT GIRL-ON-GIRL BULLYING, AND HOW TO RAISE WOMEN TO BE ALLIES

"She laughed when there was no joke. She danced when there was no music. She had no friends, yet she was the friendliest person in school.

In her answers in class, she often spoke of sea horses and stars, but she did not know what a football was . . .

She was elusive. She was today. She was tomorrow. She was the faintest scent of a cactus flower, the flitting shadow of an elf owl. We did not know what to make of her. In our minds we tried to pin her to a corkboard like a butterfly, but the pin merely went through and away she flew."
—from Stargirl *by Jerry Spinelli*

Key Takeaways

- Girls bully in a different way than boys—called "relational aggression." They tend to use relationships to manipulate other girls and sabotage their ability to gain social acceptance.

- ▶ The "mean girls" phenomenon now starts much earlier than in the past, and is often related to enforcing peer conformity to popular culture representations of femininity.

- ▶ In the world of adult women, there is a lot of conversation about why it seems that women often undercut each other rather than support each other. A mother-daughter book club gives mothers an opportunity to show girls what adult female allies look like.

Once upon a time, bullying took place on playgrounds, on school buses, and in hallways. At the end of the day, both the bully and the bullied went home. There is no such "home" anymore—at least in terms of a safe retreat—because social media bullies can attack their victims online at any hour of the day. Bullies today have so much more power than when I was a girl. My generation's bullying was akin to BB guns, but the Internet is more like an AK-47. Cyberbullies who squeeze the trigger feel very powerful, and they are often quite disconnected from the consequences of their actions.

Bullying has always been a problem, for children of both genders. The metaphor of the playground as jungle has persisted until quite recently. Fortunately, heightened adult awareness of the real and serious suffering endured by bullied kids is fostering positive social change. Extreme and tragic consequences such as suicide have sparked a wide-scale effort on the part of adult professionals, parents, and schools to resist the idea that bullying is an inevitable and rather Darwinian part of childhood. Instead, many people have reframed bullying as a social problem—one that can be solved if enough energy is brought to it. It's about time.

Whether or not the incidence of bullying can truly be decreased, it would be irresponsible to continue ignoring it. Our children need us. They need us to set good examples, to support them emotionally, and to intervene as needed. Because this book is about girls and women, I want to keep a tight focus on the bullying culture among girls and women. For all of the women out there who wonder why it seems that women do things such as undermine other women in the workplace; prefer male bosses; vote for male political candidates instead of female candidates simply because the male ones seem vaguely "better"; gossip about and tear down their friends; criticize other women's choices about work and motherhood; and so on, it is important to understand that many behaviors, preferences, and beliefs begin in childhood. Girl-on-girl bullying will never go away, but will recede for those girls who learn that they are stronger together than apart.

Among women, we need less competition and more camaraderie. If we are to raise girls to be allies when they grow up, it must begin when they are young, and a mother-daughter book club is a fantastic place to explore female friendships and discuss the dynamics of the type of bullying unique to girls: relational bullying. Unlike boys, who often bully in less sophisticated and more physically intimidating ways, girls use language and relationships to bully in relational ways. For example, girls may ignore or exclude other girls, "triangulate," spread rumors, create powerful cliques, and isolate certain girls by telling their peers not to be friends with them.

Girls seem to use cyberbullying more often than boys, possibly because it is under the radar and is a more effective way of spreading rumors and engaging in the usual relational forms of aggression, but on a larger scale for a larger audience. For hundreds of years, girls have passed notes in class. Now they send texts, and forward them around. When female bullies use their relationships to manipulate others, injure feelings, and sabotage other girls' abilities to gain social acceptance, they are sometimes referred to as mean girls.

"My nine-year-old daughter is on Instagram. I thought this was a ridiculous idea, but it turns out most of her friends and classmates are on as well. . . . . When I look through her feed every day, I can't believe how many pictures these little girls post of themselves, all of them with these common themes—duck face, shock (hand over mouth), or fake sleeping. I don't know why I find this so, well, disturbing, but I do. I've talked with my daughter and she agrees that it's a little odd how many of her friends do this, but she certainly sees nothing wrong with it. She's put a few of herself on there; in one she zombified her face, and has made a few other photo manipulations, like sunglasses or a mustache. I think it's the focus these little girls put on their face and being pretty/cute/clever in the picture that I find upsetting."

Is the Onset of Bullying Behavior Coming Sooner?

If you talk to teachers about this, most will tell you that bullying used to begin around fifth or sixth grade and pervade the middle school years; it now appears much earlier, in elementary school and even preschool. Of course, when children are this young, they may see what they are doing as "funny" or a game, without fully realizing the ramifications or understanding the ethics involved.

I have had the interesting experience of working with preschool-aged children in three settings, spread out across time, in each of the past three decades. One of the biggest changes I have observed in early socialization is that boys and girls play in a far more segregated fashion now than they did thirty years ago, with toys that are color-coded and increasingly gender-specific.

Rigidly separate boy/girl play used to begin during or just before kindergarten, around age five, the age at which it had long been considered developmentally typical. Now, preschool girls and boys gravitate to "girl toys" and "boy toys" at ages two or three, observing the cues they get from TV commercials and toy packaging. The children with interests that cross over into what has been recently categorized as being "for" the other gender—many of the unisex toys we all played with, together, as boys and girls growing up—are vulnerable to bullying by other children for stepping outside these gender boxes. When children see others of their own gender bullied for not conforming, it reinforces their own desire to conform, rather than risk censure by their peers.

Thus it begins, with gender-segregated toys and play spaces and single-gender play. The girls who are most socially attuned to the play of others and most concerned with those girls who do not stick to playing in prescribed "girl" ways are often the ones who set the social rules for the girls in their class—and who point out the rule breakers. I notice these girls often become the "queen bees" when they are older, enforcing peer conformity to popular culture representations of femininity through relational bullying.

I have also noticed that those children who are most accepting of differences in others—including individual play preferences—are the kids with greater fluidity in their friendships, those who can move in and out of different social groups and find things in common with different types of children.

But it's not just kids. Too many adults—as parents, as teachers, as media and product designers, as retail store owners, as marketers—are complicit in setting kids up to treat each other more harshly when they designate toys and games and behaviors as "for boys" or "for girls" rather than "for children."

I interviewed Carrie Goldman, author of *Bullied: What Every Parent, Teacher, and Kid Needs to Know About Ending the Cycle of Fear*, about what adults can do to help children resist conforming to the restrictive gender roles they see in the media and elsewhere. Goldman points out that when parents, teachers, and other adults inadvertently foster this gender segmentation in children's early years—in the toys they buy, suggest, or discourage; in the way they set up play spaces; and in the explicit and implicit messages they give children about who they can play with—gendered behavior starts earlier and becomes more extreme. The teachable moment that adults can seize is to proactively encourage children to play across gender lines—with members of the opposite sex and with all kinds of toys, both gender-neutral ones and those targeted toward one gender or the other. This can actually shift the whole social dynamic in positive ways at a time when young children's brains are developing rapidly but are still fluid and adaptable.

Goldman also explains the power of mothers to shape the ways in which girls interact with peers in childhood and throughout their lives. "Mothers really can raise girls who are less likely to bully or be bullied by finding ways to stay emotionally connected to their daughters. By communicating openly and fostering empathy and emotional intelligence, moms can add a layer of protection that we often see is missing in both bullies and victimized children. Also, when mothers can be physically present in their daughters' social lives, they can see for themselves who their daughters' friends are and how the social dynamics work. For example, a mom can lead a Girl Scout troop, volunteer in the lunchroom, chaperone field trips, or just be the parent who has an open-door policy at home and welcomes her daughter's friends to gather there," Goldman says.

When I asked Goldman if she had any advice for mother-daughter book clubs, she gave this terrific tip, and I wish I'd thought of it for our own club years ago! I pass it along for yours: "Allow the girls to have five or ten minutes together in private at the beginning of a meeting to discuss among themselves any concerns or questions they have about the book they just read, or something happening in their own lives, that they want to bring up in the meeting but would like to bring up anonymously, as a group. One girl can speak for the group if she is willing, or the question can be written on a piece of paper and placed in a jar. This allows the girls the feeling of safety in numbers when they wish to bring up a discussion that none of them are willing to voice on her own." Brilliant, right? Because mother-daughter book clubs should be all about facilitating difficult conversations in ways that make girls feel safe, heard, and validated but not embarrassed. When it comes to painful and potentially loaded topics like bullying, this type of clever device to aide open dialogue is invaluable.

► RECOMMENDED BOOK

The Secret Language of Girls by Frances O'Roark Dowell (age 8+)

The triangle is one of the strongest and therefore most important shapes when it comes to engineering, but the opposite is true when it comes to friendships, as most girls and women experience at some point in their lives. *The Secret Language of Girls* begins with a plot that revolves around the protagonist, Kate; her best friend, Marylin; and a new girl in the neighborhood, Flannery, who comes between them. As the book progresses, the girls all move into their own rotating and evolving social spheres, which intersect in interesting ways as the girls encounter middle school and the inevitable shifting sands of friendship.

This book does a great job of showing how these social dynamics work and how bullying arises as kids figure out who they are and where they fit, trying on different identities and experiencing the inevitable growing pains that accompany this developmental stage of childhood, where girls are on the cusp of adolescence and becoming young women. Written for children in elementary school, it encourages younger girls to begin processing their social worlds and whatever friendship struggles they may be having already, with an eye toward what lies a few years down the road. The characters and plot are unusually wholesome and pleasantly lacking the edginess of typical YA lit on the topics of bullying, popularity, and social striving. There is much to discuss here as a mother-daughter book club.

DISCUSSION QUESTIONS

1. Of Kate, Marylin, and Flannery, who do you think is most similar to you? Have you felt like more than one of these characters at different times or in different social situations?

2. Have you ever been a part of a friendship triangle? What caused their triangle to collapse in the book? Did yours?

3. Think about this quote: "At the very beginning of spring, weeks before anyone even knew Paisley Clark existed, everything about sixth grade changed. It was as if a mysterious force had taken over. The sixth grade had gotten shuffled like a deck of cards and been dealt into entirely new groups. At lunchtime kids walked to their tables as though an invisible hand were guiding them to where they were supposed to be. The weird thing to Kate was that no one ever tried to switch tables or join a new group. Everyone just seemed to accept the decisions the mysterious force had made." What does this mean to you?

Prompts

- Give some examples of how the "deck" got reshuffled. Is this metaphor of a card deck a good one? Why?

- Why does Kate call it a "mysterious force," and what do you think it is?

- Why is the school lunchroom such a common and powerful setting within kids' books and movies?

4. There seem to be a lot of unstable adult relationships in this book. Why do you think the author wove in so many adult characters who are divorced or divorcing, or in some other way going through major transitions in their lives?

5. Throughout the book, the author uses idiom, slang, and cultural references that can seem a bit old-fashioned. It was written in 2004, not in the distant past. Does the book feel any less relevant to today's culture when she does this? What does this use of language *add* to the book?

Prompts

- How is childhood depicted? Are the role of play, imagination, reading, and other aspects of growing up as described in this book different from yours?

- Talk about the girls and the mothers in this book and how they all interact around things such as makeup, boyfriends, watching TV, and so on. Are the girls growing up fast, slow, or just right? Are they sexualized?

- While some situations in the book may feel out of step with today's girlhood, what is timeless about the story?

6. Toward the end of the book, Paisley asks, "Why don't you come sit over here? We can make room for everyone," followed by, "There's room for everyone. Plenty of room," as she pulls more chairs around the lunchroom table. What is unique about the character of Paisley? What does she really mean when she says this?

7. What is "the secret language of girls"? Talk about how you have experienced it in your own lives.

FUN ACTIVITY

Remember the descriptions of "slam books" in *The Secret Language of Girls*? Talk together as moms and daughters about what those books are, as well as similar digital versions on the Internet (such as Facebook and college "confessionals"). Discuss how hurtful they can be, whether they bring out the mean in mean girls, and the social purpose they seem to serve. Now, make your own version of a slam book for your mother-daughter book club. Pass it around, but only allow positive comments. After everyone has read the finished book, talk about how it felt when used in this affirming way.

How Does Early Gender Policing Play Into Girl-on-Girl Bullying in Later Grades?

Many psychologists point out that there is a considerable disadvantage to gendered play in the early years. It encourages children to put more energy into seeking out and naming the ways in which the opposite gender is different, rather than what they have in common. For example, when girls say, "Boys are dirty. I like to keep my pretty dress clean," they are inadvertently doing the following:

- criticizing boys in order to strengthen female identity and bonding
- reinforcing gender conformity
- associating active play and dirt with boys
- associating cleanliness, beauty, and sedentary behavior with girls
- starting down the road of looks obsession and aversion to physical exercise
- suggesting that boys are from Mars and girls are from Venus and never the twain shall meet
- giving boys the message that they are not wanted as friends

Boys do this too, in their own way. To some degree this has always happened between children as they form their gender identities, and it is developmentally normal. Young children who make comments like the one above are certainly not cognizant of all those bullet points! They are just being kids. However, they are being kids in a way that is now increasingly reinforced by society. The problem is with how exaggerated this behavior has become and how much earlier it now starts. There used to be a longer period of time when boys and girls played together, shared gender-neutral toys, and felt free to use toys often associated with the opposite gender. This facilitated boys and girls getting to know each other as human beings and as potential friends before the tween and teen years, when many would begin to view each other as potential romantic partners.

For older girls—accustomed to defining themselves according to the new hyperfeminine representation of what it is to be a girl—other girls now become automatic sources of competition. All those toys and movies and books and magazines that told girls it was all about beauty and attracting boys created girls who now look around at their female peer group and suddenly see a whole lot of competitors for fairest in the land. Here's where the discussion of mean girls comes in.

The mean girls phenomenon is an early manifestation of females riding herd on other females, often about various aspects of *being* female, and often reinforcing a false notion of scarcity. Since there are not enough alpha boys to go around for everyone, it's every girl for herself. Girls bully girls about being "sluts," being uncool, being unattractive—all of which are really about adhering to gender norms, places within the social hierarchy, and commodification of beauty.

Gender conformity is essential for social acceptance, and girls who express themselves in more fluid ways, or even in predominantly "male" ways, are often targeted. Sexual orientation is scrutinized, and girls who are suspected of being lesbians, or even simply "tomboys"—a word I dislike, because there are many ways of being a girl, but one whose meaning is easily recognizable—are at an increased risk of being bullied as compared to girls who toe the line when it comes to performing femininity as they "should." Part of that "should," however, requires girls to be desirable to boys but not promiscuous. They must be sexy but not too sexual. They must not be "sluts."

> "I was bullied by girls in middle and high school. By the time I was eleven I was 5'8" with a C cup bra. This brought many snide remarks and rumors my way until I was old enough to realize why I was excluded. Having had this experience I do struggle with body image, but I feel it has actually liberated me from caring how other people, especially women, feel about my body. In the long run it gave me tools to actually pick friends who had the same values and priorities as me. It's also given me a great basis for how I am going to prepare my daughter, who already shows my Amazonian genes, to navigate the trickier stages of friendship."

One of the reasons there is so much more anxiety among girls today is that there are so *many* rules, it's hard to keep them all straight. Once again, the media culture for females sets the framework. When girls define themselves and assess their own worth against a measuring stick provided by a society that seems to value their femininity above their humanity, there is a tendency for girls (and later, women) to turn against each other. We must teach girls that the notion of the zero-sum game—at which some girls *must* lose for others to "win"—hurts them all.

How Does the Bullying Culture Among Girls Play Out in the World of Women?

I interviewed Rachel Simmons, author of *Odd Girl Out: The Hidden Culture of Aggression in Girls*, about the link between relational bullying among girls, and the competitive, critical behavior that can sometimes be observed among adult women at times when one would expect and hope for camaraderie and collaboration. Although some of this competition, especially in the workplace, can be attributed to actual as opposed to imagined scarcity (such as too few promotions available for women who must compete for them), much of it is a carryover of things learned in childhood.

"What girls learn in their early relationships with each other and their family establishes a template for how they will act toward each other throughout their lives. If they learn not to share their feelings directly but instead to roll their eyes or go silent or gossip to another girl, this pattern will be set. If girls are not taught healthy alternatives, then this behavior migrates with them as they get older," Simmons says. "Girl bullying is not just the drama of a particular moment. Teach girls that there is a better way, or this is how they will always navigate the world."

Whenever I see women sabotage each other, I feel especially sad. Today's women often do not possess the sense of solidarity I hope for, and see as necessary, in a world where gender equality has not yet been reached. When I read articles by female journalists criticizing Hillary Clinton's hairstyle or "tired" appearance, it hurts my heart. When female reporters ask female politicians how they will manage both their job and their family responsibilities, but don't ask that same question of male politicians, I can't help but wonder, *Do these women understand that they are fanning the flames of the Mommy Wars, and would they like the same to be done to them?* The double standards are everywhere, and they are not perpetuated in an all-male echo chamber. For women seeking professional success outside the home—and for stay-at-home moms as well—they are held accountable by many other women for making sure they remain highly invested in their physical appearance, all while they are doing whatever else it is they are doing. This is not much different than schoolgirls bullying each other about clothes and hair and make-up in math class. What gets lost in this equation, sadly, is math.

Women often criticize other women's choices as a way of validating their own. This idea that there is one best way to be a woman or to be a mother is preposterous. Imposing that conformity as a way of winning approval from like-minded women (and perhaps, ultimately, from men), hurts all women, and turns grown-up life into a new version of high school. Notice how men escape this drama. They do not typically pass judgment on how other men divide their time between work and home. Nor do they talk or write about how other men sacrifice their looks while participating in their careers and family life.

Because I have always been very kid-focused in my career, it took me well into my thirties to truly observe, experience, and pay attention to the ways grown women sometimes bully each other. This bullying may happen between colleagues, friends, neighbors, relatives, or even women who are barely acquainted, and it perpetuates the stereotype that women are "catty" and somehow innately dislike other women.

Why do women do this to each other? Haven't we worked hard for decades to be able to make our own choices and be respected for them? We need to explicitly communicate to our daughters that we value kindness and camaraderie among girls *and* women, and we need to walk the walk in our own adult lives as well. Because who is watching? Right. The children.

How Can Mothers Talk About Girl-on-Girl Bullying and Raise Girls Who Are More Likely to Be Allies Than Competitors—in Childhood and Beyond?

I have always felt that the wounds received by one's child cut more deeply than any received personally. We all know parents who ache for their bullied children to the point of nausea and headaches or worse. And we know parents who feel intense shame when their children bully. We also know ones who *don't*. I distinctly remember a conversation I had with the mother of one of Charlotte's classmates in elementary school. Her daughter was a classic mean girl at a very young age, and I talked to this mother about a few incidents that had occurred on the playground. She responded very calmly and directly, explaining that popularity is very important for girls, and she wanted her daughter to be in the popular group. According to this mother, it was unfortunate but necessary that certain behaviors such as exclusion and teasing would happen. She looked at me and asked, "Didn't you want to be popular too when you were a girl? I know *I* did!" I have often wondered how many mothers think this way and simply have a better filter.

Which feels worse: when your daughter is hurt by mean girls, or when your daughter *is* a mean girl? Do most girls try on both pairs of shoes during childhood, or do they tend to end up wearing one pair or the other? And what about the role of the bystander? Many professionals believe that intervening at the bystander level is the most effective way of preventing or stopping bullying, because bystanders are enablers but are often quietly disturbed by what they witness. Today there is more general parental awareness about bullying, greater anxiety about our children's experiences at school and online, and an increasing connection of parents to their own childhoods as well as the examples they set for their children as adults.

I was a bullied and unpopular child who still feels the stretch and pull of some of those scars to this day. Charlotte largely managed to avoid being bullied, with one minor incident in seventh grade. She remembers being occasionally unkind to other children as a very young girl whose social skills were lagging, but she never bullied others during her own later elementary, middle, or high school years. I, on the other hand, remember one time when I joined in with bullies in middle school, and I am ashamed of my behavior even now. As moms, we can all think back on our childhoods and remember whether we were bullies, victims, or bystanders. We may have taken turns in all three roles, as many kids do.

Mothers and other adult role models have an important job in teaching daughters to be kind, tolerant, and compassionate human beings. There are lots of helpful books about bullying, some of which are listed at the back of this book in the resources section. Teachers, counselors, therapists, and other professionals can give parents sound advice when their children are being bullied or are the bullies themselves.

RECOMMENDED BOOK

Stargirl by Jerry Spinelli (age 12+)

Stargirl is one of my favorite books for girls this age! I remember when Charlotte was reading it at about age twelve, and I picked it up and couldn't put it down. This book is as eccentric and enchanting as its protagonist,

Susan "Stargirl" Caraway. Her unconventional life and worldview are at first mesmerizing to her classmates, but things backfire on her after she tries to conform, betraying her true self. There seems to be an element of magical realism in this book, although I've never heard or read anyone else express this same observation. The character of Stargirl is perhaps a metaphor for the inner tension all adolescents feel to some extent between going along with the crowd and daring to be unique.

This book addresses many important issues, such as individuality, bullying, bravery, diversity, and acceptance. Stargirl is unlike most girls we know in real life because she does not care what anyone else thinks of her—not of how she dresses, or dances, or sings. At first her classmates don't know what to make of her, and she is so fun and interesting that she becomes immediately popular in her new school without even trying. Her antics are so unpredictable and deeply, deeply *kind* that everyone loves her, which makes some of the classically popular girls begin to shun her. When her boyfriend, Leo (the narrator), suggests she shift gears and become more like other kids—more "normal"—she starts going by her real name, Susan, starts dressing like the other girls, and starts engaging in more typical activities to try to fit in. None of that works. So she reverts to her original, true personality, which is then met with mixed reactions by her classmates. The ending of the book is stunning, but I won't give it away.

I've never read a book with a stronger message of nonconformity and staying true to who you are than *Stargirl*. It's a very different book. I've talked to many people who loved it, and a few who hated it, but hardly anyone who felt anything in between!

DISCUSSION QUESTIONS

1. What do you think Leo means when he says, "It was a rebellion she led, a rebellion *for* rather than against. For ourselves. For the dormant frogs we had been for so long"?

2. How important to Stargirl is being liked? What about Leo? How important is it to *you* to be liked?

3. Oscar Wilde said, "The only thing worse than being talked about is not being talked about." Do you think Leo would agree with that? How

does Stargirl feel when she is shunned? She ignores it, but do you think it hurts her? Have you ever been shunned? If so, how did you feel?

4. One of the beautiful things about Stargirl is how much she cares about bad things happening to other people, yet she seems unaware or unaffected when bad things happen to her. Do you know any girls like this? If so, how are they treated by other kids?

5. When Stargirl tries to be more normal in an effort to fit in, it doesn't work. Have you ever tried to reinvent yourself? Do you know anyone else who has? Is it easy or hard?

6. What do you think about Leo and Stargirl's relationship as boyfriend and girlfriend? How did you feel when he chose to go along with his friends instead of supporting Stargirl? How did you feel about Leo at the very end of the book?

7. Why do you think Hillari disliked Stargirl more than anyone else? Have you ever been this disliked, or disliked anyone this much?

8. Has this book changed you in any way?

FUN ACTIVITY

When I was working in schools, I heard a story about a teacher in New York who was teaching her class about bullying and gave them the following exercise to perform:

1. Take a piece of paper and crumple it up. Stomp on it and really mess it up, but do not rip it.

2. Unfold the paper, smooth it out, and look at how scarred and dirty it is.

3. Tell it you're sorry.

4. Now, even though you've said you are sorry and tried to fix the paper, look at all the scars still left behind. Those scars will never go away, no matter how hard you try to fix it. That is what happens when a child bullies another child. There may be remorse and even forgiveness, but the scars remain forever.

"My eldest daughter was bullied in preschool. We practiced what she could say and did a kind of assertiveness training and now that she is in kindergarten she will stand up to anyone and isn't afraid to say 'no' or 'stop' or the like. I felt silly doing the assertiveness practice with her but it really did work. If someone tries to snatch what she is doing or push her over, etc., she will turn and tell them, 'No, I'm playing with X now but you can play with it later.'"

Here are some more tips mothers can use in daily life, within the mother-daughter relationship, to encourage girls to be good friends, to seek help when needed, and to become the kind of women who do not tear other women down but rather build them up:

- Try not to gossip about or criticize other women in front of your daughter. Model camaraderie with female friends, relatives, and coworkers as much as possible, and verbalize the importance of being allies with other women.

- This may sound trite, but start talking about the Golden Rule as soon as your daughter can begin to understand it (age three or four) and never stop talking about it, especially when your daughter is in middle school. For example, when it comes to gossip, explain to older girls that friends who gossip *to* them also often gossip *about* them.

- Check in with your daughter often about her social life. Let her know from a young age that you will be doing this because you love her and will always be there to help her. Have this be a common conversation in your home so that it does not feel random or awkward.

- Talk to your daughter about your own childhood. Tell her stories about times you were bullied, or were the bully, or were a bystander. Share similar stories from adulthood. This will show her that you are able to articulate the difficult kinds of social dynamics that you are encouraging her to articulate. It will also open a two-way dialogue about both of your lives as females so that your daughter does not think you are only prying or telling her what to do.

▰ Your mother-daughter book club is the perfect setting to show girls how moms can work together. It is also a great place to discuss female bullying and friendship—among both children and adults—in our culture and to bring it into the open in a safe environment.

Bullying, especially the particular type of bullying girls do, tends to fly under the radar. Even in the protected environment of our mother-daughter book club, there was a time when bullying was happening right under the moms' noses. Anticipate that bullying *will* be a part of your daughter's life in one way or another and discuss with her, and with all of the girls and moms, what your values are when it comes to this kind of cruelty, and how it might be addressed. Gather everyone's ideas, and establish this conversation early on, so that no elephant enters the room. The bullying elephant is a big one, and once there among you, it is very hard to name and get rid of it gracefully.

RECOMMENDED MOVIE

Odd Girl Out (TV-14 for language and a suicide attempt, but I would recommend this for kids as young as eleven or twelve because there is no violence or sex, and the content is important and very difficult to find in movies with a G or PG rating)

Based on the book by Rachel Simmons, *Odd Girl Out* primarily revolves around three popular girls: Stacy, Nikki, and the protagonist Vanessa. Queen Bee Stacy likes a boy who likes Vanessa instead of her, and thus the trouble begins. Systematically, Stacy and Nikki, with the help of other popular kids, bully Vanessa to the point where she becomes depressed and takes an overdose of sleeping pills. The movie depicts the various forms of relational aggression typically used by female bullies—everything from whispering, laughing, and name calling to spreading rumors and cyberbullying. The scenes in the cafeteria in which the girls decide who can sit where speak to the timelessness of this kind of bullying. Before there were laptops and smartphones, there was the school lunchroom, and many mothers will be able to identify with the dynamics at play there. In the world of many girls, it is the place where empires rise and fall.

The movie does a good job of exploring mother-daughter relationships as well as mother-to-mother relationships in the context of an ongoing bullying situation. Very few of us—girls or adult women—completely escape all of the forms of drama depicted in the movie, and as mothers, most of us will see ourselves in one character or another. I've talked to many mothers of young girls who say they absolutely dread the day that their daughter will be in middle school, and many fear greatly that their daughters will suffer as they did. I recommend this movie because it directly addresses these fears on a number of levels, and the end of the movie shows how Vanessa eventually stands up for herself and figures out who her true allies are. Is this a "fun" movie? No, not really. But it is cathartic. I now look back on my middle and high school years with a greater understanding of what was playing out, and this is the kind of knowledge mothers need to guide their daughters through any rough waters they may encounter.

DISCUSSION QUESTIONS

1. What is the misunderstanding that happens early in the movie between Vanessa and Stacy? Why do you think it escalates the way it does? Have you ever experienced a misunderstanding with friends that took this kind of turn?

2. What are some of the methods of bullying you observed in the film? Do you think boys bully each other in similar or different ways? Have you ever witnessed or experienced any of this type of "mean girl" behavior?

3. Think about the specific names Vanessa is called and the specific animated graphics with which she was bullied online. Why are those particular names and online forms of harassment so often used by girls, toward girls?

Prompts

■ What types of bullying are intended to shame a girl about her sexuality?

> What types of bullying are intended to shame a girl about her appearance?

> What "rules" are enforced by this shaming?

4. Talk about the various scenes in the school cafeteria. How do the popular girls control this space? How does control of that space extend to the rest of their social lives? Have you ever experienced or witnessed lunch table harassment or isolation?

5. In one cafeteria scene, Vanessa is exiled to a different table, and finds herself in a conversation with Emily. When Emily says, "They don't have anything that I want," what does she mean? At the very end of the movie, when Vanessa says to Stacy, "You have nothing that I want," what does this signify?

6. When Vanessa first talks to her mother about what is happening at school, her mother says, "I'm sure it will pass. This just happens sometimes with girlfriends." By the end of the movie, how have her mother's feelings changed? Why does she push Vanessa to remain friends with Stacy?

7. What are some things you notice about the relationship between Vanessa and her mother, and Stacy and her mother? How can a mother best help her daughter who is being bullied or who is bullying others? What role can the book club play?

FUN ACTIVITY

I found this game on PE Central (www.PECentral.org).

Get a deck of cards. Deal one card, face down, to each person. Explain the following:

> You are to not look at your card or tell anyone else what your card is.

> Place the card on your forehead, facing out.

> Begin to mingle with each other but treat everyone based on the "face value" of their card. For example, low cards (two to

five) don't get much attention or are avoided, mid-range cards (six to ten) are treated with respect but not overly lauded, and royal cards (jack, queen, king, ace) are the best of the deck—those cards are the ones you try to hang out with, treat well, and even kiss up to.

Everyone should mingle for several minutes, treating others based on their card's value. After a few minutes, divide into groups based on how you feel you have been treated: low cards, mid-range, and royalty. Discuss how it doesn't take very long to figure out what "group" you belong to based on how people treat you. Talk about why you felt like you belonged in that group and how people made you feel.

Now, take the cards off your foreheads and check to see if you are correct in guessing your "value." Discuss how bullying stops when people stop doing it. It *has* to be a personal and individual choice to make it stop; everyone deserves to be treated as royalty.

Reflection from Charlotte

I have observed many forms of online bullying that I believe are particular to this day and age, as opposed to more generic social pecking orders that have existed among adolescents in our culture forever. When I began to explore sites such as Facebook, Tumblr, and forums for topics that interested me, I saw teenagers bully each other on those sites just as cruelly as they do in real life, if not more so, because of the option in some cases to be anonymous, which tends to engender a sense of invincibility in bullies.

Mother-daughter book clubs can be a safe space for girls to learn about and discuss personal, political, and societal issues without fear of reprisal. Book clubs can also be a place to talk about experiences with bullying, both face-to-face and online. The more you read, the more open you become toward other people and different ways of living. My own experience in our

(cont'd on the next page)

mother-daughter book club was very much entwined with standing against all forms of bullying and behaviors that hurt people, particularly adolescents who are developing their identities as they learn about the world.

RECOMMENDED BOOKS

TITLE	AUTHOR	AGE RANGE	MOVIE ADAPTATION?
Confessions of a Former Bully	Trudy Ludwig	8+	
Flip-Flop Girl	Katherine Paterson	8+	
Rules	Cynthia Lord	12+	
Stargirl	Jerry Spinelli	12+	
The Girls	Amy Goldman Koss	10+	
The Help	Kathryn Stockett	13+	Yes
The Hundred Dresses	Eleanor Estes	8+	
The Secret Language of Girls	Frances O'Roark Dowell	8+	
The Skin I'm In	Sharon G. Flake	12+	
Travel Chix series	Angela Sage Larsen	12+	

RECOMMENDED MOVIES

TITLE	MPAA RATING
A League of Their Own	PG
Mean Girls	PG-13
Odd Girl Out	PG-13
The Powerpuff Girls Movie	PG
The Sisterhood of the Traveling Pants	PG

RECOMMENDED MEDIA

Use an Internet search engine to locate these videos on YouTube, Vimeo, or other video hosting sites.

Episode of What Would You Do? on Girl Bullying

Rachel Simmons "BFF 2.0" Videos

"Girl to Girl Bullying: Why Girls Bully and How to Stop It"

"Girl Scouts Bullying Prevention"

"Amanda Todd's Story: Struggling, Bullying, Suicide, Self-Harm"

"Little Girls Can Be Mean"

"The Cyber Bullying Virus"

"Thandie Newton: Embracing Otherness, Embracing Myself" (TED Talk)

"Bully in the Clique" series

"Best PSA Ever"

8

Keeping Girls Safe

ENCOURAGING HEALTHY RELATIONSHIPS AND BEHAVIOR

"Voice is not just the sound that comes from your throat, but the feeling that comes from your words."
—from A Northern Light *by Jennifer Donnelly*

Key Takeaways

➤ Throughout time and around the world, girls and women have experienced some degree of threat to their physical and sexual safety from boys and men. Most girls will experience *some* violation of their rights in their lifetime, whether it is sexual harassment at work, catcalling on the street, domestic violence, or rape.

➤ These difficult topics often go undiscussed between mothers and daughters, leaving girls to face these very difficult challenges on their own.

➤ There are many ways mothers can address these issues with their daughters that will equip them to understand from a young age that they have the right to emotional and physical safety, how to handle various difficult situations, how to lower their odds of victimization, and, most important, how to stay connected to mothers and feel comfortable talking to them when talking is critical. Using books and movies as a catalyst for discussion in mother-daughter book clubs provides an easy side door to otherwise tough conversations.

One Saturday, when I was fourteen or fifteen years old, weighing in at maybe eighty-five pounds, I was allowed to go by myself to Lenox Square Mall in Atlanta to shop for some new clothes. I was wearing blue jeans and a yellow Shetland sweater. The freedom to come and go from stores at my own pace was exhilarating. I could spend as much time as I wanted flipping through the clothing racks and trying things on. I could get fast food for lunch. I could sit on benches and people-watch when I was tired.

When I woke up that morning, looking forward to my first solo day at the mall, I never imagined that I would end up scurrying, hiding in stores, and crying behind window displays because grown men were harassing me. But that is exactly what happened—and it only got worse. After fleeing those men, on my way outside to meet my mother to get picked up at the curb, I heard another male voice call out to me. "Hey beautiful!" he said. "What's your name? Come on over here. Let me have a good look at you!" I looked up. It was the popular local weatherman who I'd watched on television my entire childhood. He always smiled into the camera as he forecast the weather in his cheerful, avuncular manner. Everybody loved him.

No one had ever explained to me that if I walked around a mall minding my own business, men might whistle, make kissy noises, or thrust their hips at me. No one ever told me that throughout the country, all over the world, every single day, girls and women face street harassment like this and even worse. I do not know many women whom I have asked about this—and I've asked many—who do not have at least one, and often dozens of stories to tell about being whistled at, catcalled, followed, groped, or publicly berated for not graciously accepting these "compliments."

The simple act of writing this book has made me remember other incidents of harassment throughout my life, everything from the daily catcalling I experienced living in the Fenway Park neighborhood of Boston to being accosted by a cabdriver in front of an eleven-year-old Charlotte in Rome. While we were revising this chapter, Charlotte reminded me that her own induction into the club of women whose bodies are considered up for grabs by men occurred on a fishing trip a few years ago. As she and I and the other passengers were busy fishing, Captain Grab-Ass, as my husband

Geof affectionately nicknamed him, pinched both of our bottoms, but not Geof's, and we didn't talk about it until later on the car ride home. This entitled guy to whom we had paid good money basically strolled along the sides of the boat, grabbing the asses of girls and women who were focused on baiting and casting. In the car, I asked Charlotte if by any chance her butt had been grabbed while onboard, and she exclaimed, "Yes! I thought I'd imagined it or that it was an accident!" Naw! Not an accident! Welcome to the club, dear daughter!

The physical, sexual, and emotional safety of girls cannot be taken for granted. Whether we are talking about street harassment, sexual cyberbullying, online stalking, physical or sexual abuse, rape, dating violence, emotional manipulation, or any other similar topic guaranteed to make mothers anxious and afraid—and even tempted to put this book down—as mothers we know that we must do our best to keep our daughters safe. Not talking about dangerous situations like these leaves girls more vulnerable and more afraid to discuss incidents or ongoing abuses with their mothers. It's true that we can never fully protect them, but we can absolutely put ourselves through our paces trying, and *hoo boy*, we've got to try! Please don't put this book down. We can face this challenge together.

So how can we best keep our girls safe? How can we teach them the skills they need to make good decisions, encourage them to talk to us when they are scared, and prepare them for an adulthood as women for whom their gender will always be a point of vulnerability in some ways, no matter how strong and confident and vocal we have raised them to be? How can we, as mothers, get past our own dread of raising these topics, avoid the procrastination that often results, and find age-appropriate ways to communicate important information to our girls at every age?

Even though it may feel at times that the culture we live in makes our jobs harder than ever before (and I would argue that it does) there are many steps mothers can take to guide their daughters toward safety, appropriate behavior, and healthy relationships.

Let's Start at the Beginning, When It's Easy: Bring Back Cross-Gender Play

As discussed in the last chapter, gender-segregated play has many downsides. In the absence of sufficient opportunities to grow up closely together as playmates, boys and girls tend to see each other as being much more different than they really are. Each sees the other as alien, with alien interests and alien toys and alien colors that are even a little bit threatening to the security of one's own gender identity. For example, most boys avoid pink like the plague, and girls are quick to discern which toys and games that used to be for all children are now considered masculine and therefore off limits or risky to their social capital.

When dating begins, kids today have had less prior experience with boy/girl friendships, so they struggle more to understand one another. This can lead to problems, from boys seeing girls as objects, to girls dumbing themselves down. There are gender stereotypes and media influences to which both boys and girls are more vulnerable because they have spent most of their childhoods in parallel, largely nonintegrated social and cultural worlds.

Stereotyped views can take much deeper root when they go unchallenged by real relationships. As many boys get older, they are more inclined to think of girls as sexual objects if they have not had many true friendships with girls while growing up. At the risk of wandering too near the pornography/free speech precipice, I simply want to suggest that mothers research the connection between men's violent behavior and the consumption of pornography. When a boy views a girl as a collection of body parts to be critiqued and to exist for male pleasure, it is easier for him to act in an abusive fashion toward that girl because her humanity has been undermined by her objectification. This can be tricky to talk about publicly for anyone wanting to keep the dust down, but I'm obviously not particularly concerned about that! Moms, there are ways to privately, intimately guide your daughters without appearing to overreact to the culture, something many contemporary parents fear.

I interviewed Dr. Jennifer Shewmaker, a psychology professor at Abilene Christian University who writes and speaks on the topic of healthy girlhood, about the whys and the hows of facilitating boy/girl friendships. She spoke to me as both a psychologist and the mother of three daughters between the ages of eight and thirteen. "As a mother of girls, I think about this a lot. Girls and boys will one day be women and men who need to get along as more than just romantic partners. They will need to work together, raise children together, walk down the street together, and in so many other ways be comfortable in their relationships. It needs to start young, and this has become somehow less natural than it used to be, but it's not that hard," Shewmaker says.

"Try to have mixed boy/girl playdates. Go to the park. I know I made the conscious decision along with some other moms to make this a priority. I do not want my girls to see boys only as possible boyfriends. I talk to my oldest daughter, who is in eighth grade, about boys who are friends, not just 'boyfriends,' and reframe it that way, so that there is not an exclusive focus on romance. My daughter tells me that the romantic relationships she sees among her peers happen between boys and girls who will readily admit they do not even really know each other. I want my girls to have true friendship in their relationships with boys as children, as adolescents, and as adults," she continues.

When I asked Shewmaker to talk about her observations on gender-segregated play, she had this to say: "Separation by gender starts too early these days. It also makes kids think of their gender first, and as the primary identifier of who they are as people. It comes before anything else that defines who they are. This means that from an early age, their identities have been narrowed down to what society characterizes as masculine and feminine, and the gap begins. It is so limiting to both genders. The way the media portrays relationships between boys and girls is so often romantic, and depicts stereotyped roles. As adults we can help kids not feel so much pressure to be sexual before they are ready. We need to help them be friends first, and we can do that. It's an issue of awareness and does not take that much effort. Many parents instinctively encourage boy/girl friendships, and those that don't could do so if they could be helped to actually see what is happening in society and why the default of separation is not healthy."

I see this problem as much more fixable for one's family than the problem of pop culture and media. Perhaps we cannot get rid of online porn or sexist video games, or stop young boys (and girls) from being influenced by these things. Maybe we can't change the entire media culture overnight. But we *can* encourage and facilitate cross-gender play and friendships for our own daughters, and ask their teachers to do the same.

By simply being aware of the problems that await our tweens and teens, moms can try very hard to find ways to include male playdates and friendships in our girls' lives in a number of ways:

- Be more mindful of the pitfalls of highly gendered birthday parties when children are very young.

- Get together often as families with other families that have sons, especially when girls do not have brothers.

- Encourage girls to engage in activities where boys are more likely to be found (such as nature programs and ice skating).

- Start as early as possible to really push back when our daughters or others say things like, "Girls don't play with boys!" Yes they do, and yes they can. This idea needs to be directly challenged by parents, teachers, and the other adults in a girl's life.

This is one of those times when parents need to be very clear in their own minds that *they* are raising their daughters, not the culture around them. Daughters may balk and say "but all the girls only play with other girls, and I only want to play with girls"—but stand firm on the inclusion of boys as friends to at least some degree, in some avenues, and work at it, beginning as young as possible and persisting through childhood.

How else can parents help?

- They can model egalitarian gender roles at home in their own relationship, and in how they treat children of both genders (for example, in the assignment of chores).

- They can show and discuss that men and boys are friends as well as romantic partners and parents.

- They can point out commonalities in their interests and hobbies.

- They can talk to their daughter's teachers and ask that play and cooperation across genders be actively fostered, and that grouping children needlessly by gender (seating arrangements, group work, organization of play spaces, line formation) be avoided.

- They can explain their goal of promoting boy/girl friendships to grandparents, aunts, uncles, adult friends, and others who spend time with their daughters.

Go forth and challenge the system rather than accept it! This one is low-hanging fruit.

RECOMMENDED BOOK

Turtle in Paradise by Jennifer L. Holm (age 8+)

What a delightful book! I wasn't sure what to expect when I picked it up, but I was quickly absorbed into the world of eleven-year-old Turtle and her new life in Key West, Florida, in the 1930s—before completion of the overseas highway and during the days of hurricanes, hidden pirate treasure, barefoot free-range childhoods, and living off the land, for better or worse. *Turtle in Paradise* is based on the true history and family of the author, and includes many characters and historical events that are authentic to 1935 Key West.

When Turtle's mother takes a job as a housekeeper for a woman in New Jersey who does not like kids, Turtle is sent back to her mother's hometown of Key West, to temporarily live with her aunt. She has difficulty fitting in to a very new and different culture, and it is hot! There are all kinds of new creatures and plants, from scorpions to sponges to alligator pears (avocados). Even the ice cream flavors are strange: sugar apple, sour sop, and tamarind. But the biggest obstacle facing Turtle, besides missing her mother, is adjusting to all the boys with whom she now lives. She has three male first cousins in the house, and there are many other boys on the island who have tight friendships and don't want to let Turtle in. The way she navigates this new social scene will bring a smile to your face—that girl is tenacious! And she is smart, courageous, funny, irreverent, and sure to get under your skin, just as she eventually manages to do with her new friends and relatives.

Although the adult relationships around her each have their unique dysfunctions and reveal some manner of unhealthiness, they stand in sharp contrast to Turtle's own inner strength and confidence about her place in the world as a girl and her ability to triumph. She shows the boys a thing or two, and in so doing, learns that the "hard shell" that earned her the nickname Turtle belies her soft underbelly, which she comes to understand and value by the end of the book. Everyone in Key West has a nickname, and they are all meaningful as well as endearing. Most surprising and enjoyable was the cameo appearance of one of the world's most famous writers, so keep an eye out for him! Hint: Even he had a nickname in Key West, and it was "Papa."

DISCUSSION QUESTIONS

1. One of the earliest pieces of information in the book is that Turtle's mother is not very successful in her relationships with men. Why not?

2. Think about this quote by Turtle: "I blame Hollywood. Mama's watched so many pictures that she believes in happy endings. She's been waiting her whole life to find someone who'll sweep her off her feet and take care of her." Does this quote apply to Hollywood today? Do girls today watch movies with this message? Why does Turtle see this as a problem? How is the way she sees life different?

3. What is unusual about the Diaper Gang? Were you surprised that boys, rather than girls, took care of the babies on the island? What happens when Turtle tries to become a part of the Diaper Gang?

4. How does Turtle navigate her friendships with boys and men? What is admirable about the way she does it? Do most girls today act like Turtle around boys?

   Prompts

   ▸ What does Turtle present as the best thing about her?

   ▸ What does she do that shows she has confidence?

   ▸ How is she different from her mother?

5. What did Turtle learn about herself by the end of the book, after Archie stole her money and fled to Cuba? How does her nickname fit her?

6. Make some predictions about how Turtle will relate to men when she grows up. Do you know any girls or women who are like Turtle? What do you think about them?

FUN ACTIVITY

The book talks about cut-ups. Turtle says, "A cut-up is something these Conch kids do every chance they get. Each kid brings whatever they can find lying around or hanging on a tree—sugar apple, banana, mango, pine-apple, alligator pear, guava, cooked potatoes, and even raw onions. They take a big bowl, cut it all up, and season it with Old Sour, which is made from key lime juice, salt, and hot peppers. Then they pass it around with a fork and everyone takes a bite. It's the strangest fruit salad I've ever had, but it's tasty."

Make your own cut-up for dessert after your book club meeting. Let each member bring one ingredient to the meeting, and with whatever you have, cut it all up and pass it around. Be adventurous! Give yourselves nick-names if you're game. How does it feel to contribute to a community meal? What was fun or difficult about it?

Teaching Girls to Recognize and Avoid Sexual Abuse

Here we go. The sledding is going to get a little bit rougher, but hang on, because we really can take steps to decrease the odds our girls will be victimized.

I'll start with myself. I was the first mom in my peer group to talk to Charlotte about sex. She began asking a lot of questions in second grade. I had always planned to answer her questions simply but directly, and vowed never to sidestep them. I did not want her to pick up any vibes from me that broaching this conversation was not OK. So, when the time came—sooner than I'd expected, but perhaps later than is becoming the case today—I told her first that this was not to be a conversation she repeated on the bus. I did not want to be the source of my friends' children's premature educa-tion about sex. Charlotte was great about it and let her friends and their parents get to it at their own pace, but Charlotte wanted information!

I found I was surprisingly comfortable talking about sex. I believe in using the appropriate terms for anatomical parts, so Charlotte learned the proper names for the parts of her body, as well as male body parts. I didn't even find it that hard to talk about intercourse—at least the baby-making aspect of it, which at that age is all that is asked for or necessary. However, I had a really difficult time talking to her about sexual abuse of children. I wanted Charlotte to be informed and safe, but I did not want her to be scared of sex or men. I recall having the "good touch, bad touch" conversa-tion with her when she was very young, but I skated over it very quickly and superficially, and I regret that. Admittedly, I would give myself a B− on how well I accomplished addressing the topics outlined throughout this chapter, so I really do understand how challenging it is to do a good job of preparing girls to lower their chances of different sorts of victimization. And I need to insert a caveat here: I am well aware of the current global conversation about shifting our language from "Don't get raped" to "Don't rape," and thereby placing the focus where it belongs—on men and boys. However, I do not feel that teaching girls how to lower their odds of abuse is mutually exclusive with advocacy efforts that reframe sexual violence as a men's issue. *It is.* As adults, we do need to start raising boys with explicit expectations for how they treat girls and women, and hopefully one day we will no longer need to talk to girls about avoiding victimization. But we do not yet live in that world, and the parents I know want tools for talking to their daughters about physical and sexual safety, so I give some in this chapter, and most apply to protecting boys as well as girls.

The most important message parents can give kids (boys as well as girls) is that they must tell a parent or another trusted adult if anything happens to them that doesn't feel right. Sexual abuse of children is as much about adults (or older children) misusing power as it is about sex. The key critical message to get across to kids

"From a very early age, I strived to instill in my children a sense of body ownership and body boundaries independent of gendered positioning of vulnerability, generalized fear or, certainly, sexual understanding. (Which is not to say they did not "streak" as toddlers in order to get a good laugh!) Just as important, though, I think, has been very open and easy communication on all fronts with sexuality/relationships treated the same as other issues. They are both in high school now—and my own concern has shifted from close circles to the wider world. Ironically, I find it a bit harder to check in with them now, as most of their comments are designed primarily for ironic bite! But I am hoping the groundwork will hold."

is that their bodies are their own, not to be touched without permission—especially the parts that would be covered up by a bikini bathing suit (a good rule of thumb for girls; underwear for boys).

Children can be taught a few simple guidelines that will help them develop good instincts that will serve them well throughout their lives. Teach children to come to you *no matter what* and tell you anytime an adult or older child:

- talks to them in a way that makes them uncomfortable
- touches them in a way that makes them uncomfortable
- says they must keep something secret, especially from their parents
- causes them to feel confused, because they are being told to do something by an authority figure that doesn't feel right
- bribes them to do something that makes them uncomfortable
- threatens them or their family in any way

Explain to children that there may not be anything wrong with a given situation, but they should err on the side of always coming to you with concerns or questions, *especially* if they have been asked or threatened not to go to you.

When it comes to mothers and daughters, there is a lot of shame still associated with sexuality and sexual abuse. We must break this cycle and begin a lifelong dialogue with our daughters on these topics. If we don't break the cycle of silence, our daughters will grow up to be mothers who do not talk to their own daughters.

But *how* can we talk to them? Here are some more specific tips that flow from the general ones above:

- Bodily autonomy is something not enough children feel, and is a gift all parents should give to them. This means that if your child does not want to be hugged or kissed or tickled or cuddled, don't force it because the implicit message to the child is "Your body belongs to me." Some parents believe that kids need to be "taught" to be affectionate, when in reality it is more natural for some than for others. It can be damaging to the self-esteem of a child who is by nature reserved to be told she is letting you down in this way or is somehow defective.

- Likewise, do not push your child to show affection to other adults if she is reserved. The implicit message here is: "We believe that grown-ups' needs come before children's." This is a hard situation because parents often feel awkward, embarrassed, disappointed, or angry when their kids do not automatically rush to go give Aunt Margaret from Buffalo a hug and kiss or do not want to sit in Grandpa's lap. If you feel this way, remind yourself of what is most important. If need be, explain your views privately to your relatives: kids are people too, and deserve to decide if, when, and how they show affection. Indeed, to send the opposite message to children is dangerous and makes them more vulnerable to predators. Many parents assume that if they judge a relative to be "safe," that is the case, and their child should accept that assessment and act accordingly. Sadly, it is well known that most sexual abuse occurs *within* families, and is often perpetrated by relatives who parents consider "safe." Undermining the bodily autonomy and instincts of children is highly problematic.

- Children sometimes need to be told that it is OK to say no to adults; they mustn't believe they have to do everything an adult tells them to do. This may seem counterintuitive. How common is it to tell children, "Do whatever your teacher tells you to do"? Very! And we mean well! However, the distinction needs to be explained: children should never do things an adult tells them to do *that make them feel physically or sexually uncomfortable.* Any misunderstandings can be sorted out later.

- The concept of privacy is difficult to teach to children, especially when they are young and seem bound and determined to rob you of yours and publicly abandon theirs! But it's important, over time, that you teach kids to knock on doors, shut their own when appropriate (such as bathroom doors), and in general to maintain reasonable boundaries around privacy. This will help them recognize when someone violates their privacy. For families who value being relaxed about privacy, nudity, and so forth, closing doors may not feel right, or may cause self-consciousness. If that is the case, parents can teach their children what private behaviors *are*, and help them practice them outside the home, especially in public places.

A word of caution: while going about all of this teaching, be prepared to don your poker face at a moment's notice! If you encourage kids to talk to you about anything and to tell you whatever is worrying them, they will. And sometimes that will be funny or awkward or alarming. Try not to look embarrassed, panicked, angry, or to break into peals of laughter. If kids sense your discomfort or feel embarrassed or anxious by your reaction, they will be less likely to come to you in the future.

Street Harassment, Cyberbullying, and Stalking Have a Purpose: Understanding Why They Happen and What Can Be Done

When I had my first (and far from my last) experience with street harassment as a young teen, I had no way of processing what seemed so inexplicable to me: *why* did men do this? What did they get out of it? Had it somehow been my fault? Did I not keep my head down enough and my eyes looking forward? Should I have been walking more quickly, with more sense of purpose? Was I not sufficiently aware of my surroundings? Was I wearing something inappropriate? Should I have had my mother or a friend with me and not gone to the mall alone?

Why was I even scrutinizing my own behavior? Shouldn't a girl be able to walk around in a public space in broad daylight unpunished?

Aha. This is the toehold toward understanding what is really going on with street harassment. It's about public spaces: who can use them without fear, who controls them, and how they are legislated. It's all quite simple when properly understood.

Street harassment of women, a form of sexual harassment, exists all over the world and historically has existed since time began. Sexual harassment is when someone deliberately instills fear and discomfort into someone else, through sexually charged or threatening words or gestures. It can lead to sexual assault, from groping to rape, but the type of street harassment most women encounter (verbal harassment) mostly has the effect of making them uncomfortable and putting them "in their place." It is a power dynamic. If a woman or girl changes the route on which she walks from home to school or work, or stops jogging in the neighborhood, or always looks down while getting on and riding the subway because she dreads unwanted attention from men, then men have likely exercised power—they have caused her to alter her routine. Public spaces are the Wild West compared to, say, workspaces. Sexual harassment in the workplace is illegal, somewhat clearly defined, and punishable. That doesn't mean it is easy for women to prove or remedy—just that society does recognize it is wrong, and has sanctions in place for those who harass others, male or female.

The problem on the street, on buses and trains, in subway terminals, malls, and other public spaces is that there seem to be no rules. Technically there are protective laws, and they vary from state to state, but are nearly impossible to enforce. Girls and women will likely face this problem without the help of the legal system or law enforcement.

What about when being catcalled, or whistled at, feels good? Many women and girls do experience this. A male affirms their appearance. Sometimes men who seem completely harmless, as if they are just having fun on a warm summer day, comment on a woman's body or face, say, "Hey baby, looking good," or simply whistle. It can lift one's spirits if delivered without the crude, intimidating language or gestures that can otherwise accompany such comments. That is all very real and understandable. Here's my concern: women spend their entire lives internalizing objectifying messages and learning that their "hotness factor" is super important. So to feel complimented by mild street harassment—and not actually feel harassed by it—is on the one hand really nice, but on the other, something that reinforces the status quo that women are on this earth to be eye candy. That sucks the fun out of it for me, but your mileage may vary!

Because street harassment can be confusing and can feel like good fun *or* like something extremely violating *or* both things at the same time, talking about it with girls when they are young is helpful, especially because the mixed message about street harassment—that it can be terrible for some women and girls, and enjoyable for others—is a great example of how complex our reactions can be to norms that become embedded in societies.

I interviewed Jeff Perera, a community and youth engagement manager for the White Ribbon Campaign, the largest effort worldwide to engage men in helping to end violence against women, as well as the founder of Higher Unlearning, an online space for discussions of manhood and mas-

"I've had multiple experiences during the years of street harassment, whether walking down the street, riding public transit, walking in a park with my dog, being in a public space (i.e., store, library, etc.)—and here's my take on it at fifty-six years old. Why do people think it's OK to say something to another person that you wouldn't want said to your mother, your sister, your daughter or your friend? Why must we accommodate your inability to keep your thoughts from flowing freely and without consideration, from your mouths? I must always be ready, in public, for the potential unpleasant interaction to occur and need to be ready to deal with it, especially when with my daughter and/or my elderly mother. Sadly, it's all too common that other women and men will not intervene or step up to assist others. They don't want to get involved. I'm frankly tired of accommodating others' poor behavior and inability to control themselves in public."

culinity. Perera is a passionate advocate for women's safety and rights, and a devoted speaker and activist who works primarily with men and boys around issues of healthy masculinity.

Perera recounted the story of how he came to find his calling. He was leaving his college campus and walking down the street behind a young female student from his college who was being persistently harassed as she tried to make her way from school to wherever she was going. Perera described all of the "verbal violence" she endured as she walked swiftly down the sidewalk, and the way he took it all in, seeing it for the first time—really seeing—the hassle and violation many women endure in public spaces every day. He kept walking behind her, observing the way people reacted to her, as well as making sure she was OK. Eventually a man stepped in front of her, blocking her path, and shouted, "Yo, baby! Baby! Gimme ten seconds of your time! Five seconds! OK, two seconds! Come on baby!" The woman, with effort, navigated past the man, and Perera impulsively went straight up to him and said, "Brother, respect her, and respect yourself." That's T-shirt or bumper sticker material, isn't it? Perera said the

"I have a friend who was riding her bike home when a car pulled up next to her and the guy in the passenger seat exposed himself to her. Awful. We were about thirteen. I remember speaking to her briefly afterward—she was hysterical and her mother so upset. It changes you in ways that may seem undetectable—but it does change you. I'm not sure if that constitutes street harassment because it seems far worse. I worry for my daughter and hope she can make it through her younger years without this kind of incident."

look on the man's face was comically pained. Clearly he had never been reproached for his behavior before and had no idea how to handle it.

In discussing this anecdote, Perera explained that the burden of street harassment usually falls squarely on the woman, who often feels guilty and ashamed, as well as threatened and scared. There can be dozens of bystanders, yet rarely do any speak up. Perera is trying to change that.

What is needed, here and around the world, is a major cultural shift in the treatment of women. This is certainly true when it comes to the more serious crimes of rape and domestic violence, and in many countries around the world, the culture of harassment and abuse of females is far worse than in the United States. (We'll get to a deeper discussion of this later in the book.)

For now, what can parents do to help their daughters if they encounter street harassment? It is happening to younger and younger girls, and it sometimes happens to girls in middle school or even younger. Some issues to discuss with daughters include:

- When should girls look a harasser in the eye and say, "Leave me alone"? This has been known to make some boys and men very angry and belligerent, and to make others back down. The overall safety (or lack thereof) of the immediate surroundings is important. (For example, a girl alone in a subway car should probably focus on escape rather than confrontation, while a girl in a more crowded place, with friends by her side, might feel empowered to tell a man to stop.)

➤ Male harassers often ask females to "just be nice/smile/say hello/let me talk to you/let me sit with you," and the like. Girls need to be taught that they do not owe "niceness" to anyone who is harassing them.

➤ When should girls go out in public alone? The question itself makes my blood boil. Why should girls and women even have to think this way when boys and men don't? Unfortunately, the reality is that we do, and so we can all discuss how unfair it is, but unless and until the culture changes, there are practical safety considerations to discuss. Parents need to have clear rules with young daughters who are not yet old enough to make these decisions for themselves.

Street harassment is one form of public control and shaming of women; technology provides another. Girls can now be harassed online much more easily and far more publicly than on the street. Some of the more common ways in which girls can be harassed via technology include the following:

➤ Harassment through e-mail, text messages, or social media.

➤ Sexting (encouraging girls to text sexually explicit photos of themselves).

➤ Stalking through social media—using it to keep tabs on a girl's whereabouts (among other things) in an attempt to bully or control her actions.

➤ Humiliation of girls through the posting of sexually explicit photos or videos of them, sometimes called "revenge porn." (Boys must be taught not to do this, and girls must be taught to *never, ever* create or submit to the creation of such photos or videos. It is absolutely, *always* a risky and bad idea.)

➤ Promotion of violence against girls and women in current video gaming culture.

➤ Use of e-mail, text messaging, social media, or Internet commentary to threaten girls and women with physical harm as well as to target those who speak out against this very behavior. It has certainly happened to me.

What is so difficult about our 24-7, technology-driven world is that girls can no longer get away from their harassers and stalkers, even for a moment. For parents and other adults who are trying to help protect them—and teach them to protect themselves—the usual guidelines apply, such as coaching girls from a young age to come to parents when they are afraid or worried. However, part of getting out in front of this problem is an action parents can take that kids will usually strongly resist: namely, curbing their use of interactive technologies. Use of computers and phones after 10:00 PM, for example, should be forbidden. Not only will kids who are unplugged at nighttime get a break from the demands of their online social worlds and any negative things happening there, but they will actually get some sleep!

Hook-Up Culture, Date Rape, and Dating Violence: Raising a Girl Who Does Not Give Up Her Power

If you look carefully, or even not so carefully, at the media and marketing our girls consume everyday—from Victoria's Secret at the mall to the misogynistic lyrics girls sing along with while wearing earbuds while walking through the mall to get to Victoria's Secret—it is no wonder we now have twentysomethings and thirtysomethings saying they thought it would make them feel sexy to have friends with benefits but eventually realized it felt degrading.

We need to ask ourselves, *How did it get to be OK that many twelve-year-old boys consume hardcore porn—on their iPhones, on the bus, under their school desks, and on the computers they are allowed to have in their bedrooms—and learn almost everything they know about sex from that medium?* I'm all for adult freedom of speech, but when it comes before the safety of the most vulnerable members of society—our children—I question it. Loudly. I also question why so many parents abdicate responsibility when it comes to supervising their kids' use of technology. I know it's difficult, and that there are many battles parents can and should skip. However, this is not one of them, no matter how tired or busy we are, and no matter how big a fight our kids put up.

Hook-up culture, date rape, dating violence—why has all of this seemed to escalate? While it's possible teens are being better educated about when and how to seek help in abusive situations, I suspect that another cause of the real or seeming uptick in abusive behavior can be attributed to the ever-widening gender divide that gives boys and men a sense of ownership over female bodies, while simultaneously dehumanizing women and girls. The author Margaret Atwood once said, "Men are afraid that women will laugh at them. Women are afraid that men will kill them." What does this say about masculinity? Femininity? If we can't stop the train, can we help our girls get off it?

Here's some advice for parenting your teen daughter:

- Parents are busy, but kids need us. They crave our time—undivided, offline. If we invest this time in our daughters, they will be more inclined to come to us for help.

- Just as we can coach young children to tell parents if anyone has touched them inappropriately, we can coach older girls to tell us if a date ever makes them uncomfortable or hurts them in any way. We can teach them the early warning signs of an abusive relationship, and give them tips for maintaining healthy boundaries while dating. We must start young, teaching them self-respect and the imperative of demanding respect from boys and men, as well as cultivating ongoing open dialogue with parents. It is beyond the scope of this book to describe all of these warning signs and steps, but there are a number of recommended books on this subject in the resources section.

- Ask daughters basic questions as conversation starters. For example: *How do you want to be treated? When you are with that boy, how do you feel about yourself? Does he ask or expect you to do anything that makes you uncomfortable? Is anything worrying or scaring you?* In no way do I mean to demonize boys. Most boys are kind and respectful. But girls need to be able to recognize when they are not.

- Try to model healthy relationships in your own life, whether with friends or romantic partners. Children will pick up on the dynamics of an unhealthy relationship—especially when domestic violence or verbal abuse is involved—and this may make girls more vulnerable to expecting and/or accepting abuse themselves.

> ▰ Watch for signs that something is wrong in your daughter's life, such as depression, withdrawal, eating disorders, a pattern of "choosing the wrong boys," addiction to drugs or alcohol, problems at school, loss of friendships, and so forth.

There is no going back to a time when girls were depicted in media without being overly sexualized, but our clubs can watch retro television shows such as *Little House on the Prairie*, and read classic books that reflect safe and healthy values for our children. We can talk about how girlhood has changed and how it has stayed the same. In the emotional safety zone of club meetings, where no one feels pressure to look cool or be popular, maybe, for bits of time here and there, girls and moms *can* go back to those days when little girls could just be little girls, back to the values of those days and the camaraderie of parents raising children together. Mothers mentoring daughters by sharing empowering books and movies is a great start.

RECOMMENDED BOOK

A Northern Light by Jennifer Donnelly (age 12+)

If there were a canon of young adult literature, *A Northern Light* would probably be in it. Using the real-life murder of Grace Brown as a historical backdrop, this coming of age novel blends historical and fictional material. The novel takes place in the Adirondack Mountains of New York in 1906, and intertwines the fiction of being a sixteen-year-old girl working at the Glenmore Hotel on Big Moose Lake (where Grace Brown was murdered) with details of the real-life crime. The murder features prominently in the story, which also includes excerpts from authentic love letters between Grace Brown and her lover turned murderer, Chester Gillette (aka "Carl Graham").

This book touches upon so many important themes and pieces of historical information for girls, including domestic violence, unwed motherhood, the insatiable quest for literacy and education by girls, the difficulty in challenging traditional gender expectations and stereotypes, poverty, race, and the early backlash against feminist writing. Mattie Gokey is an unusual heroine. She is bookish yet worldly, and preternaturally self-possessed. There is so much to discuss about this book that bears directly upon the mission of a mother-daughter book club.

DISCUSSION QUESTIONS

1. Mattie loves everything about reading and writing, and this theme runs throughout the book. What different messages does Mattie receive about her writing? When it comes to her love of books, do you think it is impossible for her to pursue her passions without sacrificing the love of another person? Why do conflicts arise?

2. Think about the quote at the very beginning of this chapter: "Voice is not just the sound that comes from your throat, but the feelings that come from your words." What does Miss Wilcox mean when she says it?

3. Why is Mattie not allowed to accept the scholarship she earns to attend Barnard College? Do you think there are still girls today—in the United States and around the world—who do not go to college (or school at all) for these same reasons?

4. How does Mattie's mother die? What does Mattie's brother Lawton think might be the real reason she died? Do you agree with Lawton?

5. What does Mattie promise her mother before she dies? How does she keep that promise, even when she ends up not going to college? Why do you think Mattie's mother extracted this promise?

6. What does Mrs. Wilcox write about and why does she keep writing, even when people dislike or resent her?

7. Why is Grace Brown murdered by her boyfriend?

8. Just before Grace is killed, she asks Mattie to burn some of her love letters. Why does she ask for that favor? What happens when Mattie does not burn them?

9. Discuss the circumstances leading up to Grace's murder. (If you have time, do some research on the Internet on who the real Grace Brown and Chester Gillette were, as well as what happened in the murder trial.) What options did young, unmarried, pregnant women like Grace have in the early 1900s? How is it the same or different for women today? Why do you think domestic violence is so prevalent in general?

10. Why does Mattie decide to leave the hotel and start a new life? How does she make peace with Grace's death?

FUN ACTIVITY

OK, maybe this activity isn't so "fun," but it's eye-opening! The following statistics come from the National Domestic Violence Hotline (www .thehotline.org):

- One in every three teen relationships is violent.
- 36 percent of teens report violence in their relationship.
- One in every three adult relationships is violent.
- 85 percent of reported cases of dating domestic violence are committed by men against women.
- 15 percent of reported cases of dating domestic violence are committed by women against men in heterosexual relationships, women against women in lesbian relationships, and men against men in gay relationships.
- 60 percent of children who grow up in abusive homes will become abusive or be the victim of abuse in the future.
- One out of every three women murdered is killed by a current or former boyfriend or husband.
- Women ages sixteen to twenty-four experience the highest rates of intimate violence.
- 68 percent of young women who experience rape know their rapist either as a boyfriend, friend, or casual acquaintance.

▓ 40 percent of teenage girls ages fourteen to seventeen say they know someone their age who has been physically assaulted by a boyfriend.

Talk about these statistics as a group. Do any of them surprise you? Can you think of any examples in your own lives?

To make this activity more uplifting—if that is possible, or even necessary for this particular topic—discuss how popular music may perpetuate *or* counteract dating violence. What songs can you think of that either condone or criticize violent relationships? What songs have lyrics that promote respectful relationships? Play some of this music and analyze the messages given about power, abuse, and respect in romantic relationships.

RECOMMENDED MOVIE

Reviving Ophelia (NR, but I'd estimate it at PG-13)

One night I was channel surfing and came upon this made-for-TV movie on Lifetime. I started watching it and found that my usual aversion to made-for-television dramas—the poor acting—was less true of this movie than many, and in any case was compensated for by content that seemed unusually well suited to discussion between mothers and daughters. For a movie that deals with dating violence like this one does, it has less sex and violence than a typical Hollywood production, simply because it is made for television. I recommend it because the topic is important and relevant, and it is not easy to find movies about this issue that can safely be shown to middle schoolers.

The movie *Reviving Ophelia* was inspired by Mary Pipher's book by the same name, but is only loosely based upon it. The story revolves around two cousins, Elizabeth and Kelly, whose mothers, Marie and Lee Ann, are sisters. Got that? It's actually easy to follow in the movie. Marie is married, but Lee Ann is raising Kelly as a single mother. When the movie begins, you see the struggles in the mother-daughter relationship between Lee Ann and Kelly, and you see that Kelly is a more "difficult" teen than her cousin Elizabeth, who is a goody-goody by comparison. So you guess that the girl who will be involved in an abusive dating relationship is Kelly, and then you realize you are wrong. From there the movie explores exactly how Elizabeth finds herself with a controlling and violent boyfriend, and why she tolerates and hides her abuse. Kelly plays a pivotal role as Elizabeth's confidante and eventual savior of sorts.

This movie does a wonderful job of showing young girls the warning signs of an abusive relationship, the psychological complexities of these relationships, and the importance of trusting your parents and other friends and loved ones when they try to help you. There is so much to discuss, and this movie makes a difficult conversation easier.

DISCUSSION QUESTIONS

1. Were you surprised by which girl experiences abuse? Why or why not?

   ### Prompts

   - Do you think there are certain kinds of girls who are more likely to be abused? If so, which types and why?

   - Do you have any preconceived ideas about the families of girls who date violent boys?

2. Before we see Mark physically abuse Elizabeth, we see some warning signs. What are they? Have you ever experienced any of them, or had a friend who did?

3. Use some adjectives to describe Mark's temperament and behavior toward Elizabeth. How did it feel to see him behave this way? What role does technology play in their relationship?

4. What is revealed about Mark's life and family that you think might be a factor in his abusiveness? Do you think all abusers have this history? Do you think everyone with this history is destined to abuse others?

5. How does Elizabeth respond when her mother and Kelly try to help her? Do you think this is typical? Why or why not? What would you have done if you were Kelly?

6. Many characters keep secrets in this movie. Who kept secrets for whom, and what were the consequences of those secrets? What secrets would you keep or not keep if you were involved in a similar situation?

7. Why do you think Elizabeth stayed in the relationship with Mark as long as she did?

8. How do you think girls can avoid being in abusive relationships? How can they help other girls who are in them?

FUN ACTIVITY

Go to the Love Is Respect website at www.loveisrespect.org and take one or more of the online quizzes. There are four of them: "Healthy Relationships," "Am I A Good Girlfriend/Boyfriend?," "Do Abusers Change?," and "How Would You Help?". See how you do!

Reflection from Charlotte

I read a lot of young adult fiction as a teen, as many girls do. Some of my favorite novels were the *Harry Potter* series, the *Warriors* series, *A Wrinkle in Time*, *Eragon*, and *Inkheart*. These books inspired me to think about possibilities outside of the world I knew, and to write fantasy and science fiction myself.

If you walk into Barnes & Noble, you'll see that the YA books I used to read are now on shelves *behind* the shelves filled with book covers of teenage girls on the beach in bikinis, in passionate embraces with boys, with their thumbs hooked in their cutoff shorts, and so forth. All those babysitter/nanny/foreign exchange student books are very appealing to ten to fourteen-year-old girls, and grab their attention before they can walk behind those shelves to where the better literature for teens now resides. Many of these so-called popular books have female characters who are conventionally attractive, passive in the face of conflict, preoccupied with romance and boys, and wallowing in angst. In short, they are disempowered. They are also sometimes involved with boys who have complete control

(cont'd on the next page)

within the relationship. *The Twilight Saga* is a good example of this. Such books can lead girls to believe that uncaring, creepy, potentially dangerous, or domineering males are appropriate love interests.

Fortunately, newer books such as *The Hunger Games* and *Code Name Verity* feature empowered girl protagonists, and because these books have done so well, there is reason to hope that the pendulum is swinging back in the right direction! Mother-daughter book clubs can emphasize positive YA literature and help girls in their tweens and early teens choose books that reinforce healthy behavior and ideas. I was greatly influenced by strong female characters when I was younger. They gave me self-confidence and affirmed for me that speaking my mind, respecting myself, and having my own interests apart from a romantic partner are all extremely important qualities for me as a woman.

RECOMMENDED BOOKS

TITLE	AUTHOR	AGE RANGE	MOVIE ADAPTATION?
A Northern Light	Jennifer Donnelly	12+	
Blaze (or Love in the Time of Supervillains)	Laurie Boyle Crompton	13+	
Chains	Laurie Halse Anderson	10+	
Durable Goods	Elizabeth Berg	12+	
If You Come Softly	Jacqueline Woodson	12+	
Same Sun Here	Silas House and Neela Vaswani	10+	
Speak	Laurie Halse Anderson	13+	Yes
The Higher Power of Lucky	Susan Patron	8+	

TITLE	AUTHOR	AGE RANGE	MOVIE ADAPTATION?
Three Times Lucky	Sheila Turnage	10+	
Turtle in Paradise	Jennifer L. Holm	8+	

RECOMMENDED MOVIES

TITLE	MPAA RATING
Flipped	PG
Ella Enchanted	PG
The Man in the Moon	PG-13
Reviving Ophelia	NR
Speak	PG-13

RECOMMENDED MEDIA

Use an Internet search engine to locate these videos on YouTube, Vimeo, or other video hosting sites.

"Tony Porter: A Call to Men" (TED Talk)

"1970s Slinky commercial"

"Is My Teenager in an Abusive Relationship?"

Jackson Katz's "Violence and Silence" (TED Talk)

"Jeff Perera: Words Speak Louder Than Actions" (TED Talk)

"PBS: Teen Sexual Harassment at Work"

"Teen Dating Violence" series

Emily May, founder of Hollaback!, TED Talk on street harassment

Anita Sarkeesian's TED Talk about video-gaming culture and online harassment of women

"Leslie Morgan Steiner: Why Domestic Violence Victims Don't Leave" (TED Talk)

9

Supporting LGBTQ and Gender-Nonconforming Girls and Women

ENCOURAGING INCLUSIVE BOOK CLUBS AND AN INCLUSIVE WORLD

Key Takeaways

- It has always been difficult for girls and boys who do not conform to gender norms, but today's more gender-segregated childhood makes it even harder for these children.

- It is easy to assume heterosexuality as a default, and to be surprised after learning someone is lesbian, gay, bisexual, or transgender. That assumption of heterosexuality gets expressed to kids in many ways, and they can internalize that they do not "fit" expectations of parents or society.

- Mother-daughter book clubs have the power to change the message, to let *all* girls know that love and acceptance is not dependent on the performance of any certain expected female expression or sexual orientation.

If you gather a random group of ten people in one room, odds are that at least one of those people is lesbian, gay, bisexual, transgender, or wondering about their sexual orientation in some way. So why did it not occur to me that this might be the case in my own mother-daughter book club, which had five mother-daughter pairs? Why did I assume everyone was heterosexual? Why didn't I consider that it was possible that someone in our close-knit group might be reading books without characters that represented her own sexual orientation or questions or struggles? As it turned out, one of our members *was* experiencing this at the time—and it was my own daughter.

Charlotte will speak for herself at the end of this chapter. What I want to communicate is that the widespread tendency to assume heterosexuality as a default orientation shortchanges everyone. There are plenty of reasons to address nonheterosexual orientations within your mother-daughter book club and via some of the books and movies you choose. Two of the most compelling reasons are: (1) to ensure that any member of the club who is not heterosexual (or is wondering about it) is not left feeling like the version of the world on the table for

"I teach my eleven-year-old daughter that we treat all people with the same amount of basic human respect. I have encouraged kindness in her every time she showed it. It is not about the 'sex' of it all; she doesn't really think in those terms yet. For her it is about that respect that she knows all people deserve. It is about the beautiful man who used to run the Sunday school program at her church, from the time she was baptized. He was gay. It is about friends and family who are gay, who seem to her no different than friends and family who are straight. They are still people—people she has laughed with, shared memories with, has things in common with. And quite honestly, I wish more people could view the issue through the eyes of a child."

discussion does not entirely include her, and (2) because everyone benefits from exploring and understanding human difference of all kinds.

To the moms: I feel like I let Charlotte down without even realizing it. *Any* of us can have a child who is lesbian, gay, bisexual, or becomes transgender—or who simply wonders about it during childhood or adolescence. Opening the door to dialogue using carefully chosen, age-appropriate books and movies is a good way to demonstrate your acceptance and create a safe place for any member who might be struggling and wants to talk about it. Or not. Communicating your openness and inclusiveness is what matters, putting forth the message that the fabric of society includes them and others like them.

Gender nonconformity describes many people of all ages. And the odds that your club will have someone who does not fit the typical female gender construct is even higher than the odds that you will have an LGBTQ member. So-called tomboys, for instance, are commonplace, yet they are often bullied and marginalized in our hyperfeminine modern girl culture. This chapter will explore the issues of gender nonconformity and sexual orientation in a way that will help moms better understand how to foster inclusion within the club and in the larger world.

RECOMMENDED BOOK

The Story of Ferdinand by Munro Leaf (for adults and kids of all ages!)

The Story of Ferdinand was published in 1936, just before the Spanish Civil War. Because it was widely viewed as pacifist propaganda, it was banned in many countries. Despite its rough start, it became popular around the world, has been translated into more than sixty languages, and won several awards. This book has been beloved by three generations in my family—my father, me and my brothers, and my daughter. I related strongly to Ferdinand as a child and still do. He is more than just a symbol of peace to me; he is also an outsider, bullied for his gentle ways.

Recently my special fondness for this story grew even stronger. I happened upon a list of books about gender transgression, and topping the list was *The Story of Ferdinand*. Talk about an *aha* moment! I suddenly realized that the qualities I had loved about this book as a child, and that Charlotte had loved when I read the book to her when she was a little girl, are that Ferdinand is sweet, loving, and gentle; that he does not want to fight; and that he is not traditionally masculine. In fact, he actively resists gender norms! *The Story of Ferdinand* is possibly the first modern children's book written about a character that did not want to perform his or her gender role. The arc of the story follows a common pattern seen in later books: namely, that a "child" does not fit the expected stereotype, the "parent" is worried, and then the "problem" is solved in happily-ever-after fashion. The plot is resolved with love and the acceptance of difference.

So what if this is a children's picture book? Have fun reading it again as adults and big kids, but through this new lens!

DISCUSSION QUESTIONS

1. How would you describe Ferdinand? How is he like other bulls? In what ways is he different?

2. In what specific way does Ferdinand assert his own identity? What is expected of bulls (male cows), and how does he respond to those expectations? Do you think he shows courage?

3. Is it easier or more difficult to go along with the group and do what others want you to do, or is it easier to be yourself?

4. Ferdinand's mother is worried that Ferdinand might be lonely sitting by himself all day rather than playing with all the other bulls. Do you think Ferdinand is lonely? What else is his mother worried about?

Prompts

- Is Ferdinand a fighter like the other young bulls?
- What does he most love to do?
- Is that something associated with males or females?
- How are males who act like females often viewed? What about females who act like males?
- Do you think it is harder to be a male who is feminine or a female who is masculine—or is it about the same?

5. What do you think of bullfights? What do you think of them as an expression of masculinity?

6. The last two pages of the book read, "And for all I know, he is sitting there still, under his favorite cork tree, smelling the flowers just quietly. He is very happy." What does this mean for you? How important is it to find your own happiness, despite what the world thinks it should look like?

FUN ACTIVITY

How could I not recommend the 1938 cartoon version of *Ferdinand the Bull* by Walt Disney? Released ten years after Disney's first nonsilent film, *Steamboat Willie*, and one year after the original *Snow White and the Seven Dwarfs*, this early example of full-color Disney animation is a delightful blast from the past. You can find it online. Make some popcorn and watch this short, eight-minute cartoon. How is it like Disney movies today? How is it different? Do you think it is true to the book? Talk about your own childhood memories of the character of Ferdinand as mothers and daughters. Do you think children who defy gender expectations today are as happy as Ferdinand?

Challenging the Assumption of Traditional Gender Roles and Gender Performance: Raising Girls with a Broader Definition of "Female"

When I was a child, these are some of the things I saw in daily life:

- books, movies, and TV shows about husbands and wives, boyfriends and girlfriends
- paintings of male/female couples
- wedding books, photo albums, gowns, bride-and-groom cake toppers, and other wedding-related items
- men and women walking down the street holding hands

- ➤ math worksheets with word problems about Susie's mommy and Susie's daddy
- ➤ Barbie and Ken

The list goes on forever.

Today's young girls are more likely to see two men or two women holding hands, more likely to have a friend or relative who is openly gay, and more likely to have a schoolmate who has two moms or two dads. There are even television shows, such as *Glee* and *Modern Family*, that feature gay characters. But when girls walk into a toy store, they see a significantly more gendered, hetero-normative arrangement and selection of toys than I did as a girl. It is not only a problem of limiting the ways to be a girl, as previously discussed. Toys, now grouped by gender, and thus directly prescriptive of gender roles, present a distinctly heterosexual worldview.

In the boy aisle are the toys that show boys they will become men and husbands who work outside the home at a variety of exciting jobs, make important discoveries, run/jump/play, and impact the environment (by fighting, building, solving problems and mysteries, and using superpowers to save the world).

Girls learn the yin to the boys' yang. They see a toy aisle that demonstrates that they will become women and wives who work inside the home, spend a lot of time cultivating their physical appearance, focus on attracting males, are physically sedentary and passive, raise babies, cook, and clean. The two aisles can be taken together to represent the heterosexual couple—the bride and groom, but a decidedly archaic version of it. Obviously, this message is not a healthy one for raising strong, empowered girls. Indeed, it is unhealthy for any child who does not grow up to fulfill traditional heterosexual gender roles.

For the girl who is different, who does not like the trappings that the world rigidly assigns to her gender, or who knows somewhere deep inside that she does not fit into the world that is presented as *all there is*, there is discomfort. There is awkwardness. Or often, there is compliance and a very private, perhaps entirely secret thought process that goes something like this: *I am not like other girls. I am a girl, but I like the things in the boy aisle. But I can't go over there, or I could get teased. People will think I'm weird if I like to play with boy toys. People might bully me if they know I do not want to be a*

"My daughter enjoys rock climbing, martial arts, and Star Wars. And we encouraged all of those (heck, we introduced her to two of them) because they're fun and she showed interest. When she was teased about her Star Wars thermos, I reminded her about *Star Wars* Katie [who was bullied for bringing a *Star Wars* water bottle to school, but who became a national phenomenon for fighting back]. Because she's only six, I also bought her a different thermos. But I always remind her how awesome she is. We have a saying that 'anyone can like anything.'"

princess or a bride when I grow up. What I really want is to be a firefighter. But I can't, and I can't tell anyone. For these children, profound feelings of isolation and loneliness can be commonplace.

This problem can be solved quickly and easily if we as a society so choose. It has already begun to be solved in Europe. There are toy stores across the pond that no longer separate toy aisles by gender. Instead, toys are grouped by type: you have the building toys here, the dress-up costumes there, and the arts & crafts kits around the corner. There are no gendered labels. No gendered signage. No downsides! Boys and girls walk through these stores and to the sections that interest them. What could be simpler? What could be healthier?

When will America follow suit? When will adults realize that this is important? I hope the thinking changes, for the sake of *all* children, especially those who do not fit the mold we have artificially constructed for them, and who are often bullied for it.

I did not know anything about sexual orientations, besides heterosexuality, until I was in middle school. Sure, homosexuality, bisexuality, and other orientations existed to the same degree then as now, but it was much more hidden, and parents usually didn't talk to their children about it. Today's children are more likely than I was to learn about LGBTQ people and families at a younger age. What they learn, and whether they are raised to embrace others with these orientations, depends upon many factors, such as the views of parents, other relatives, teachers, religious institutions, peers, and so forth. As the saying goes, children learn what they live.

I believe that an important part of the mother-daughter book club mission is to foster not merely tolerance but acceptance and celebration of differences of all kinds. Just as reading books or watching movies about other cultures and other races will not change a child's race, exploring LGBTQ issues and the concept of gender nonconformity will not change these fundamental aspects of girls and women either. But discussing the wider spectrum of human experience will help teach daughters that such differences are not to be feared, and that sameness should never be assumed. And if your book club has a gay member like mine did, you may one day find out that engaging in these explorations and discussions quietly or not so quietly helped her. I wish I had known then what I know now.

"Being part of an LGBTQ family, my daughter didn't need much explaining about what LGBTQ families are because it was normal to her. She did, however, need explanations about why she had to defend her own family and why we are sometimes not treated as a family. For instance, my partner is constantly referred to by others as 'special friend,' or 'friend.' Partners don't like to be referred to as 'friends' just because you're uncomfortable admitting that two men or two women are in a relationship. It invalidates the relationship and feelings between two people (which is hypocritical if you're trying to teach your child not to discriminate). Something especially important as kids get older is using the term 'gay' as an insult. Most of the time they don't understand the weight of what they're saying because that word gets thrown around all the time. But when it is used to mean that something is 'stupid' or 'bad,' they are equating someone who identifies as gay as being stupid or bad as well."

Understanding the Bullying of Gender Nonconforming and LGBTQ Youth: Helping Our Daughters Let Other Girls, and Themselves, Be Girls in Their Own Way

"Tomboy." "Sissy." These words have been used for generations as labels for gender transgression, which is when a girl "acts like a boy" or a boy "acts like a girl." A girl past a certain age who likes to climb trees might be called a tomboy. Why? Is tree-climbing not a gender-neutral kid behavior? For some reason, we begin to view it as "unladylike" for girls at an age when it is still perfectly OK for boys to do.

A boy who likes to play with dolls might be called a sissy. Why? Is pretending to care for a baby not a way of practicing parenthood? For some reason we encourage that behavior in girls, but not in boys. And then we talk about wanting men to be more nurturing fathers to their children.

I hate these labels. I use them here because I have no other nonacademic, mainstream vocabulary readers could relate to, and because I believe that beginning to see these words negatively is a good thing. These words are not only descriptive but also prescriptive. They say to a child, "that toy is not for you" or "that activity is not for you." These words are not just limiting, but shaming. Telling a child that her natural joy in something that is otherwise safe, fun, and stimulating is "for" the opposite gender is essentially saying, "Get back in line." I remember an incident that occurred when Charlotte was about four or five years old. It had just rained and she was in the backyard in her rain boots, splashing and looking for worms, having the grandest time. A relative called out to her from the back deck, "Charlotte, get out of that puddle! Little girls don't play in the mud!" Really? Mine did. And I explained that right then and there.

As difficult as it was at times for me to raise a girl who was considered a tomboy, and who provoked comments from others about *me* somehow falling down on the job of teaching her to be more feminine, it was not as hard as I think it is for parents of sons who are considered not masculine enough. It is more socially acceptable to be a girl who gets dirty and likes bugs than to be a boy who likes dolls rather than footballs and does not want to get dirty. For many parents and other adults in the lives of boys who are not traditionally masculine in their interests and behavior, there is real fear. Fear that this boy might be *gay*. Disgust that this boy is like a girl, because being feminine is considered a negative trait for boys growing up in a patriarchal society. There really is nothing worse boys can be called than *like a girl*. As a woman, that offends me!

Times are changing. The world children live in is much more highly gendered than it was when Charlotte was a little girl only fifteen years ago. There is less tolerance for tomboys today than there was in the past. "Sissy" has always had a highly negative connotation that stirred up worries about the entire life of the boy it was applied to, but "tomboy" was often viewed as just a benign phase a girl would outgrow.

Charlotte was not masculine in her behaviors, dress, or interests, nor was she girly. She fell somewhere in the middle. I actually thought that was awesome! A favorite scene from a beloved childhood book, *Charlotte's Web*, featuring my daughter's literary heroine and her namesake, could perhaps sum it up:

WILBUR: I didn't know you could lay eggs.

CHARLOTTE: Oh sure, I'm versatile.

WILBUR: What does "versatile" mean—full of eggs?

CHARLOTTE: Certainly not. "Versatile" means I can change with
     ease from one thing to another. It means I don't have to limit my
     activities to spinning and trapping and stunts like that.

Charlotte the spider was feminine but not uber-girly, and she knew exactly who she was. My Charlotte could be described the same way. I have no recollections of Charlotte being teased at school for not being feminine enough. Then again, the culture around her was not the hyperfeminine one we have today for girls. She would stand out much more today. She would possibly be the child who experiences ambivalence when invited to princess parties or spa parties. She would have to choose whether to go because she wants to be included, or whether to stay home because she doesn't have it in her to spend two or three hours role playing beauty shop and not getting to run around in jeans and just play. She would possibly be teased by her friends for not liking pink, not liking princesses, and not being interested in beauty—as gender nonconforming girls are routinely teased today. Children have always been teased by other children for being different. While boys have typically received harsh sanctions for not being masculine enough, girls used to more or less get a pass for not being girly enough. Not anymore.

I interviewed Michele Sinisgalli-Yulo, founder of Princess Free Zone, Inc., and author of the girl-empowering, antibullying children's book *Super Tool Lula: The Bully-Fighting Super Hero!*, about gender nonconforming girls who need some princess-free space and who need parents who accept them and encourage them to be themselves.

"Gender nonconformity falls along a spectrum, and is not always related to sexual orientation. Children who do not express their gender in traditionally expected ways often feel caught between two worlds. When parents let these kids explore who they are, without pressuring them to conform, they grow up with confidence. They are even sometimes the leaders and the trendsetters among their peers. Some of these children, like my daughter, are amazingly self-possessed but don't even know it! She has to deal with comments made to her in public bathrooms such as, 'Are you a girl?' or 'Oh, so you must be a girl,' and so on, and she has learned, at only seven, to take this in stride, to say, 'Yes, I'm a girl' and be comfortable using her own voice," explains Sinisgalli-Yulo.

I asked Sinisgalli-Yulo how she first came to recognize and accept her daughter's unique gender expression. She says, "I realized my daughter was different, and very much her own person, when she was about age three and put on a knight's costume while the other girls were dressing up as princesses and telling her she could not be a knight if she was a girl. That didn't stop her, and hasn't since. That's why I started Princess Free Zone—because I believe girls like my daughter need to be able to challenge the paradigm and not be sanctioned. But I'll be honest. At first, I did experience a sort of grief. I did not have the kind of little girl I'd imagined I would have when she was born. I had to get used to it. What I've learned is that, as a parent, you have a choice. You can accept your child as she is, let her navigate her world in her own way, and make sure she knows you support her . . . or, you can choose not to do these things, and risk your relationship at some point down the road.

"These kids *have* to assert themselves—it's their identity and they have no choice. It never worked for me to push my daughter toward more classically feminine clothing or behavior—it only made her angry with me, and achieved nothing. I believe that parents should begin supporting their children's gender expression at a young age, before they get to the later grades in school where they are likely to encounter bullying and really,

really need their parents in their corner. My daughter knows I am always there for her, and she respects me for it. My husband and I know we are doing the right thing for her—and for us as a family," she says.

I want to be clear about something: I do not intend to come across as critical of very feminine girls. They have every right to be that way! My concern is with what happens when the dominant culture moves so far in that direction that there is not enough space or tolerance for other kinds of girls. For girls who do not conform to gender expectations, middle and high school can be even rougher than the early years.

Gay and gender nonconforming girls (and boys) are frequently targeted for bullying. Although schools are doing a much better job these days of helping students who are bullied, even the schools with supportive teachers, gay-straight alliances, special assemblies about tolerance, and so forth cannot create climates that are entirely accepting. However, mother-daughter book clubs *can* deliberately create an environment and set of experiences that are inclusive and supportive of girls (and moms) of all sexual orientations and expressions. This is one area where a little proactive parenting goes a long way.

RECOMMENDED MOVIE

Tomboy (NR, but considered suitable by "mom reviewers" for all ages)

Tomboy, a French film with easy-to-follow English subtitles, explores the struggle with gender identity of its ten-year-old protagonist, Laure. Laure and her six-year-old sister, Jeanne, move with their father and pregnant mother to a new neighborhood during summer vacation. Laure, with her short hair and androgynous clothing, is immediately mistaken for a boy by the neighborhood kids, and she impulsively goes along with it, introducing herself as "Mikäel." The summer days are long and the start of school seems far away. Laure is athletic, "boyish" in her mannerisms, and without a trace of pink or princess, unlike little sister Jeanne, who loves girly clothes and ballet and adores her older sister, even though they are very different kinds of girls.

The arc of the story is apparent from the beginning. How long can the lie hold together? What will happen when school starts? The tension I felt as a viewer seems, in retrospect, as much a commentary on my apprehension about how difficult it can be for girls who do not conform to gender roles as it was for the character herself and her collapsing façade.

The film is a story about what it's like to live a lie—in both big ways and small. As Laure deals stoically with the heartbreaking finale she herself has set up, and the unsettling, yet in other ways understandable reaction of her mother to the revelation of the lie, the viewer can't help but experience secondhand the world's intolerance and the dilemma faced by so many children who struggle to reconcile who they are with who they are expected to be. Laure/Mikäel's quest for an authentic self-identity is both beautiful and painful, and on some level this movie changed me.

There is very little material in this film that is inappropriate for children. There is no sex, no drugs, no violence. It is remarkably wholesome in its portrayal of the innocence of childhood. I recommend it for any girls who can read well enough to keep up with the English subtitles, which are happily quite simple and spare, as is the dialogue. It is a gorgeous, moving, and thought-provoking film.

DISCUSSION QUESTIONS

1. When you hear the word "tomboy," what does it mean to you?

2. How does Laure make herself appear more masculine?

   Prompts

   - Describe how she dresses.

   - Describe her physical gestures and mannerisms. Are they different when she's playing with boys than when she's playing with her sister?

   - What steps does she take in the movie to be more like the boys?

3. As sisters and as girls, how are Laure and Jeanne alike and how are they different? Do their parents treat them similarly or differently?

   Prompts

   - Think about their clothes, interests, personalities, and relationships within the family.

4. How do the father, mother, and sister react to Laure's gender expression before they know of her lie? What about after it is revealed?

5. Why does Jeanne help Laure continue the lie when it is almost discovered at the dinner table? What would you have done if you were Jeanne?

6. How did you feel about Laure's mother after the lie is discovered? How are the answers to this question the same or different for mothers and daughters in the book club?

7. How can adults and kids help children with different gender expressions so that their lives might be less of a struggle? What could you do personally?

8. Have you ever pretended to be something you're not? How did it feel?

9. This movie deals with truth, deception, and consequences on several different levels. Do you see Laure's lie about her name and gender to be a metaphor for anything bigger?

Prompts

- What does it mean to say that someone is living a lie?

- Why might someone live a lie? What types of lies do people live?

- How do you think it feels for someone to live a lie? Do you think it is ever justified? Do you think people might rather not have to?

- What roles do culture, media, religion, politics, and other types of belief systems and worldviews play in whether someone lives a lie?

FUN ACTIVITY

What would you do if someone asked you to act like a boy? How would you go about it? What physical mannerisms or facial or vocal gestures would you use? Give it a try if you're comfortable pretending to be an actress like Zoé Héran, who plays Laure/Mikäel in *Tomboy*. How does it feel to take on the identity of the opposite gender, even if only as a brief acting exercise? Was it fun? Awkward? Difficult? Silly? Interesting? Talk about this as a group. How similar or different are boys and girls in their behavior and appearance?

Now talk about how you would feel if society expected you to "act" all the time in a gendered manner that did not feel right to you, or did not respect who you are on the inside, regardless of your biological identity as a girl.

How Parents Can Make a Difference

I talked to Pam Garramone, executive director of the Greater Boston chapter of Parents, Families, and Friends of Lesbians and Gays (PFLAG), about the ways in which we deliberately or inadvertently communicate expectations of heterosexuality to children, and the reasons to challenge the status quo.

"It all starts very young," Garramone explains. "When children are in preschool, you hear parents talk about how adorable it is when a boy and a girl are friends. It is romanticized. Parents will say, 'Oh look, she has a little boyfriend' or 'Maybe they'll get married one day.' Little boys are called lady-killers, and little girls are described as so beautiful their fathers will have to beat the boys off with a stick. It's all very cute and funny. Parents talk about their children's futures in heterosexual marriages with grandchildren coming to visit. Children learn that they get *praise* for acting heterosexual. Kids who know they are gay in middle or high school will sometimes date the opposite gender just to get this praise, but inside it is stressful to them."

I asked what parents could do to change their messaging. Garramone says, "Change the language. Instead of asking a girl, 'Do you like any boys in your class?' ask her 'Do you like anyone in your class?' It's a slight change that makes a difference to a child who is otherwise bombarded by language that expresses assumed heterosexuality."

I told Garramone that I regret not having read any LGBTQ literature as a book club, nor having discussed gender expression or sexual orientation in any way as a club. It might have helped Charlotte simply to see her closest friends and most important female role models addressing the topic and thereby normalizing it and communicating acceptance. Garramone points out that there is also another reason to proactively discuss these issues. While it is true that there might be a girl (or mom) in a mother-daughter book club who is not heterosexual or is wondering about it, it is even more likely that there will be times in the lives of all of the book club members that *someone else* is gay or transgender and perhaps being bullied for it. We all have the opportunity to raise allies—the kids who will stand up for their friends who are called "fag" or "dyke" or "tranny" at school, or who are struggling in other ways and in need of peer support.

According to Garramone, the four factors that most determine how an LGBTQ kid will fare emotionally are:

Parents: Are they negative in how they speak and act regarding LGBTQ people? Or are they silent, which can be read as unsupportive by LGBTQ youth?

Peers: Do they make fun of gay and transgender peers and call them names?

School: Do teachers stop students from gay-bashing? Do they intervene when they hear anti-LGBTQ language such as "that's so gay?"

Religion: Is the family's religion open and accepting of LGBTQ people?

Children and adolescents coming to terms with their gender identities and sexual orientations need support from at least one of the above groups, and preferably more. The kids without support from any of these groups are at highest risk of suicide. If you are concerned about raising kids who are accepting of the sexual orientations and gender expression of others, here are just a few more specific things you can do:

- Help your children understand there are many ways to be a girl or a boy, not just one "right" way, despite what peers and mainstream culture say.

- Encourage teachers to desegregate classrooms that are set up in ways that encourage highly gendered and separate boy/girl play.

- Give all children a broad array of opportunities to express themselves, regardless of gender. Traditionally masculine, feminine, and unisex toys and activities should be made available to all kids without judgment.

- Discuss gender discrimination and bullying, expressing your clear values that it is not OK to harass or tease children who express their gender in ways that do not fit the norm. Room needs to be made for them in the social landscape, which is big enough for everyone.

- Begin discussing sexual orientation at a young age, allowing children to ask questions, and try not to communicate discomfort. (I am *so* glad I did this before I knew there were very important reasons for me, specifically, to do so.)

- Talk about the bystander role. Explain that standing by while another child is bullied is a passive way of condoning it. Help your children plan ways in which they can support peers experiencing gender-related bullying.

- In your relationship with your own child and the children in your book club, be that open and accepting adult that all children need.

- Encourage your child's school to recognize the International Day Against Homophobia (May 17) and Day of Pink (April 10). These are good ways to take a collective stand against the bullying of LGBTQ youth.

One of the things I love about writing this book with twenty-twenty hindsight on my own mistakes is imagining that by describing these missteps, I can spare others from repeating them. There is no better feeling. As moms, we will never get it all right, but our daughters will appreciate all of the ways in which we try to open up the world for them.

RECOMMENDED BOOK

Silhouette of a Sparrow by Molly Beth Griffin (age 12+)

In this beautifully written historical novel set in Prohibition-era Minnesota, sixteen-year-old Garnet must go to live with snobby relatives at a lakeside resort for the summer to escape a polio epidemic in her hometown. It is to be her last hurrah—a summer of fun before her final year of high school, after which she is to get married and settle into being a housewife.

Garnet has a passion for bird watching and dreams of one day going to college and becoming an ornithologist, despite her mother's more traditional plans for her. She creates bird silhouettes in her spare time, and they serve as a unifying motif throughout the book. When Garnet gets a summer job in a hat shop, she meets the beautiful flapper Isabella, and they fall in love and begin a secret relationship.

When the author, Molly Beth Griffin, was asked in an interview why she chose to write a lesbian coming-of-age story, she explained that most books about LGBTQ teens focus on their "coming out" stories, but that this should not be the only type of book out there. The relationship between Garnet and Isabella involves many of the same joys and challenges of teenage love experienced by heterosexual couples, and Griffin wanted to show that. The book also revolves around many important and interesting social and historical issues, including racial inequality, gender inequality, and the economic dynamics of the Gilded Age that led to the Great Depression.

The Roaring Twenties were a complex time. Through the lives of Garnet and Isabella, we see the simultaneous wildness of the era *and* its social constriction as the girls seek to understand—and define—the meaning of femininity and the power of unexpected love.

DISCUSSION QUESTIONS

1. In the 1920s, a woman was expected to get married, start a family, and be, if not happy, at least content with the role of housewife and mother. What important choices does Garnet make that are considered unconventional for women at the time? Do you think young women today are faced with the same choices and struggles, or have things changed?

2. In the scene in which Garnet teaches Isabella to cut out bird silhouettes, she says, "You have to look for the borders between things and trace those dividing lines without thinking that you know what an egret is, or what a cormorant is, or what a grouse is." Could this statement be a metaphor for something else?

Prompts

- How does it relate to Garnet's ambitions for herself?
- What decisions does she make that require this kind of leap of faith?

3. Why is Garnet fascinated with Isabella? An important theme of this novel is the idea that other people can change you. How do Isabella and Garnet find themselves through each other? In your own life, can you think of anyone who changed you in unexpected ways?

4. Garnet says, "I held onto this practice of scientific naming as a small rebellion—a secret whispered between me, the silhouettes, and my bedroom wall." Why does she feel rebellious? What was she rebelling against? How does she view the freedom she admired in birds in relation to her own freedom, or lack thereof?

5. Garnet reflects upon "how many kinds of love there are in the world." Has this story broadened the definition of love for you? Do you think that love transcends gender, race, class, and so on?

6. While on Wawatasso Island with Miss Maple, Garnet comments, "The more I learned, the more I could do to change people's minds, to open their hearts, to be an active force in the world and in my own life, too." Do you ever find yourself thinking this way about your own goals? How could you be a more "active force in the world"?

7. In some ways this book was exquisitely unique, and in others it shares a common plot line found in many books for middle and high school readers: that at some point you must choose between following your family's traditions and following your own dreams (if they are different). How is this choice that many kids make, as part of the process of growing up, even more difficult for LGBTQ kids?

8. Have you ever read a book before that was explicitly about the lives of gay young-adult characters? How do you think the "coming of age" process for LGBTQ kids is similar to, and different from, the choices and challenges of heterosexual kids?

FUN ACTIVITY

Traditionally, a silhouette is the outline of a person, in profile, filled in with black and placed on a white background. The technique was made famous by Étienne de Silhouette. Before photography was invented, it was a less expensive alternative to commissioning an artist to sketch or paint a portrait.

You can make your own silhouette art of people, birds, animals, or any objects you like! Tape a white piece of paper to the wall, seat your subject in front of it in profile, and shine a light to cast a shadow onto the paper. Another person uses a pencil to trace the profile, and then it can be cut out and mounted on black paper. Likewise, for a more authentic look, use black paper on the wall and a white crayon for tracing. Then mount on white paper. You do not need to have expert artistic skills to make a beautiful silhouette.

In the book *Silhouette of a Sparrow*, each chapter begins with a different bird silhouette, possibly as a metaphor to represent the characters in the book. As a mother-daughter book club you can make silhouettes of each other, or of any objects that are meaningful to you. How do you feel while making the silhouettes? Is it calming? Are you able to "look for the borders between things and trace those dividing lines"? When you are finished, can you set them all out and identify which one belongs to whom, and what makes them different?

Reflection from Charlotte

My mom has sometimes described me as a "late bloomer" in terms of my interest in and experience with romantic relationships. Other people who have known me throughout my life probably would too. Personally, I agree and I think the term fits, but at the same time, I find it troubling. "Late" how, and according to whom or what? Being "late" means you are not on time, not in step with everyone else, and are therefore not acting according to the schedule you're supposed to follow.

(cont'd on the next page)

This schedule is not so much biologically predetermined as it is socially constructed. Unless kids are completely blind to the media around them as well as their social environment, they get the message at a young age that they *will* be dating and exploring sexuality during the early teen years. I didn't do any of this until I got to college. I didn't follow the schedule.

It took me a relatively long time—the duration of both middle school and high school—to figure out my sexual orientation, and even longer before I wanted to explore it with another person. It was not until I met my girlfriend in college that I felt ready to "bloom" because for me, truly getting to know each other over time, trusting each other, and being in love needed to come first. I think that "early blooming" can hurt girls of all sexual orientations because their emotional development, self-knowledge, and ability to make safe judgments are often not yet on par with their physical development. For girls who turn out to be gay, bisexual, or transgender, the pressure from popular culture as well as their own peers to engage in sexual activity is arguably even more harmful than it is for their heterosexual friends because these girls often need time to reflect and "come out" to themselves before getting involved with other people.

My orientation does not define who I am any more than a straight woman's orientation defines who she is. It is simply one aspect of my identity. Because of this, I appreciate books that present LGBTQ characters as whole people whose sexuality is not the main focus of the book, and I think this is the most meaningful kind of representation of LGBTQ people in literature because it normalizes them in a society that has long stigmatized them. This kind of representation also shows all people—male or female, heterosexual or not—that plunging prematurely into relationships before they figure out who they are is problematic. I, along with the other girls in our book club, had the luxury of enjoying our childhoods and not growing up too fast, and I want that for today's girls too.

RECOMMENDED BOOKS

TITLE	AUTHOR	AGE RANGE	MOVIE ADAPTATION?
Alanna: The First Adventure	Tamora Pierce	9+	
Am I Blue?: Coming Out from the Silence	Marion Dane Bauer, editor	13+	
Dairy Queen	Catherine Gilbert Murdock	12+	
Happy Families	Tanita S. Davis	13+	
Hard Love	Ellen Wittlinger	13+	
My Mixed-Up Berry Blue Summer	Jennifer Gennari	10+	
My Most Excellent Year: A Novel of Love, Mary Poppins, and Fenway Park	Steve Kluger	12+	
Parrotfish	Ellen Wittlinger	13+	
Silhouette of a Sparrow	Molly Beth Griffin	12+	
The Story of Ferdinand	Munro Leaf	all ages	Yes

RECOMMENDED MOVIES

TITLE	MPAA RATING
Harriet the Spy	PG
Pippi Longstocking (1950, 1988)	G
The Hours	PG-13
Tomboy	NR
Chely Wright: Wish Me Away	NR

RECOMMENDED MEDIA

Use an Internet search engine to locate these videos on YouTube, Vimeo, or other video hosting sites.

"It Gets Better" Project

"Zach Wahls Speaks About Family"

"Ellen Degeneres Stands in Her Truth"

"Portia De Rossi on Coming Out"

"High School Senior Comes Out in Assembly"

"My Tide Detergent TV Commercial"

"Gender Roles in the Media"

"J. Crew's Gender Bending Kids Advertisement"

"Fifty Shades of Gay" TED Talk

"Androgynous Model Walks Runway As Man and Woman"

10

Girls are Leaders!

LAYING THE FOUNDATION FOR
FUTURE ADULT FEMALE LEADERSHIP,
ONE GIRL AT A TIME

"One day I would have all the books in the world, shelves and shelves of them. I would live my life in a tower of books. I would read all day long and eat peaches. And if any young knights in armor dared to come calling on their white chargers and plead with me to let down my hair, I would pelt them with peach pits until they went home."
—from The Evolution of Calpurnia Tate
by Jacqueline Kelly

Key Takeaways

- The world needs more female leaders, but leadership has long been reserved for boys and men.

- Although our society in many ways discourages female leadership, there are nonetheless various avenues girls can take to pursue it.

>■ Mothers have great influence over how girls view their potential, their opportunities, and their abilities. Moms can emphasize, demonstrate, support, and reward girl power!

When I was in my early thirties, I went through a rough patch with my health and was feeling particularly low on inspiration. A friend of mine came to visit me in the hospital after I'd had surgery, and she brought me a copy of what is now my favorite autobiography, *The Road from Coorain* by Jill Ker Conway. It is the story of a young girl who grew up lonely and isolated on a huge ranch in the Australian outback, helping her family tend sheep and mend fences in a dangerous and unforgiving terrain. After the accidental death of her father, her mother moved the family to Sydney, where Conway could finally receive a formal education. She overcame many gender-related obstacles and eventually made her way to America where, in 1975, she became the first female president of Smith College, an all-women's institution that, like almost all US colleges, had historically been led by men.

Reading about Conway's achievements helped me regain my physical and emotional strength, and still tickles my brain today, because it was back in that hospital that I first realized that our culture of pervasive male leadership creates a mind-set by which there is nothing odd about a man running a women's college, yet the reverse seems unimaginable. *That* truth, in a country that is 51 percent female, is not only invisible to most people, but is applicable to every single elite sphere of leadership from Wall Street to Hollywood to Congress.

Here's what *is* unusual—that those boardrooms and film sets and political chambers are *not* at least half female. Anywhere that power rests that is overwhelmingly male-dominated should look very, very odd to everyone. Women are not a minority. Like heterosexuals and Christians in this country, women are a statistical majority, but they do not have the same power that those other groups wield.

When Women Lead, the World Gets Better

For hundreds of years in the United States, people have looked to an extraordinarily narrow pool of candidates to fill our leadership positions. From community agencies to private sector corporations to state and federal government, our chosen and elected leaders have primarily been males. White males. The talents of women (as well as people of color and other marginalized groups) have been off limits for consideration until relatively recently in our history. And although significant improvements for women have started to take root in our society, as a gender we are far from equally represented by our government, in corporate boardrooms, and among other key entities that together determine the nature of the playing field we all strive on. Forget representation—we do not even receive equal pay for equal work! The field is not level, and it is still true that women reside further down the incline than men, with an uphill climb that weeds many of us out before we can reach South Base Camp, where the men with their Sherpas and yaks are already acclimatized.

This gender gap should not be only a women's issue. When women lead alongside men, everyone benefits. In politics, female leaders tend to bring a sharper focus to international peace efforts, create more transparency and accountability in government, and lend greater compassion for struggling groups in our society, among many other known positive attributes brought to the table especially (but not exclusively) by women. Of course, they also shine a brighter light on issues of greater importance to women specifically, such as equal pay for equal work, reproductive rights, and protection from violence.

I submit that many if not most of the challenges facing girls and women that are discussed in this book—plus many of those that aren't—would cease to exist if 50 percent of all power rested in female hands. It is sad but true that a substantial number of male power brokers are not keen to either share their power or use it to improve or secure the rights of women. Unless and until women attain their fair share of power and leadership, their fates will continue to be determined primarily by men. This is not to demonize men, but just to say that it is human nature for any group in power to struggle to hold onto it for itself. Many of the current challenges facing girls and women today can be understood more deeply in that context.

If you have ever worked on a team that was heavily or exclusively comprised of a single gender, you have possibly experienced what I have in my last two school administrative jobs. Teams that do not have enough diversity of voices within them are at risk of going down the wrong path, together, smoothly. The presence of divergent opinions forces a team to closely examine facts and opinions and options for action in a way that sometimes does not happen if group members are too similar. My last school had an entirely female administrative team, and my school before that had an almost entirely male administrative team. I struggled a lot more on the mostly male team, but the experience gave me the insight to recognize that the comfort of being on an all-female team was also something to be concerned about. Ideally—in schools and other workplaces of little or great significance to our population on the whole—teams of mixed gender (and race, sexual orientation, socioeconomic level, and other human characteristics) are most effective in the long term, even when, in the moment, it may not feel that way!

When we aspire to see more women in leadership positions, we must obviously figure out how to make that happen. It must start in childhood. Waiting until women are adults to steer them toward political office and other positions of power is too late.

How can we encourage girls to imagine themselves as leaders when they grow up? It is important to first understand and examine some of the factors that are holding girls back, and then to brainstorm how these obstacles can be overcome. So let's do it, with the guidance of Lyn Mikel Brown, professor of education at Colby College, founder of Hardy Girls Healthy Women, and cofounder of SPARK Movement. She is a guru in the world of girl empowerment and female activism!

My interview with Brown was beyond inspiring. We first discussed the most common reasons girls give for shying away from leadership. Although factors such as girls worrying they won't be liked, or their lack of exposure to adult female role models for leadership are at play, Brown emphasizes that what is really missing are the support and structures necessary for girls to *practice* leadership from a young age. If girls are given opportunities for leadership through activism, this is a great way for them to exercise those critical "muscles" and build the actual skills they will need throughout their lives.

"If girls can work together to identify something in their lives that really matters to them, and then go deep with it, they will learn how to build coalitions and think creatively about solutions," Brown explains. "We tend to plug girls into preestablished leadership or civic-engagement programs, often modeled after what works for males, and then wonder why they don't 'lean in.' If we give girls the opportunity to work together as allies to identify a problem—say, gender safety, sexualization, or any other problem they observe in their daily lives—and challenge them to develop creative solutions together, they will begin to imagine new possibilities, figure out who to go to and where to turn for help, and anticipate how their actions might result in social change. They need to experience building something from the ground up to gain confidence and a sense of personal efficacy so key to leadership."

I asked Brown how mothers might provide these opportunities for their daughters, and she explained that her organization, Hardy Girls Healthy Women, is a great place to start. Its elementary school program (Stronger Together) and middle school program (From Adversaries to Allies: A Curriculum for Change) are designed to support Girls' Coalition Groups. Outlines for both programs are available online to help girls identify and talk about topics that need to be addressed, develop critical-thinking skills, and then move girls "from conversation and critique to social action." Any parent can help establish and mentor a girls' coalition group in his or her own community. Brown recommends inviting a diverse group of girls, not only to extend opportunities for activism to less privileged kids, but because coalition building is about working across differences and learning from one another.

Drawing upon her extensive expertise in training girls for leadership, Brown pulls no punches when she explains, "Girls really need to understand cultural capitalism, existing power structures, and how to step up and make a difference in the world." This is how a communal "village" works. Moms can make a huge difference! Youth activism can be an extraordinary opportunity to practice leadership, and it is a gateway to future adult leadership for women. Our world needs more engaged girls, who grow up with meaningful goals, to step into leadership roles alongside boys and men.

RECOMMENDED BOOK

My Life with the Chimpanzees by Jane Goodall (age 8+)

Ever since she was a young girl, Jane Goodall dreamed of becoming a scientist and working with animals. Her children's autobiography, *My Life with the Chimpanzees,* describes not only her contributions to the field of primatology, but the personal and family sacrifices she made along the road to becoming a leader at a time and in a place where women were still expected to conform to traditional gender roles. Her stories of life among the chimpanzees of Tanzania through several generations of chimp families are as funny and engaging as her life story is inspirational.

Goodall's autobiography is about adventure and discovery and bravery. It directly encourages young people to recognize the importance of their human friends and relatives, and mirrors these relationships in the world of primates. She stresses the need for humans to coexist with nature—as a part of nature, rather than as superior beings in nature who use it to suit their needs. As a woman leader, Jane Goodall is imperfect, as are all humans. Her choices were her own, and make for meaningful conversation between mothers and daughters. This book is very fun to read, and yet it quietly stimulates reflection from readers about what it means to be human and the imperative to remain emotionally in touch with our own humanity. Our children are our future, and our future will require more adults who have the compassion, ambition, and leadership qualities exemplified by Jane Goodall.

DISCUSSION QUESTIONS

1. What were the factors that led to Jane Goodall becoming a leader in her field of research?

2. Goodall had to balance her work with her family life. In what ways do you feel she succeeded? Are there ways in which you think she failed?

3. What sacrifices did she have to make? Are those same sacrifices commonly discussed with regard to men, or just for women?

4. What did Goodall learn about chimpanzees that made them seem almost human?

5. What is the "alpha position" in a group of chimps? Do humans have alpha positions? Are there alpha positions among your friends at school?

6. What does Goodall learn about individuality among chimps? Did it surprise you?

7. In the book, Goodall writes a special message to her child readers: "The most important thing I can say to you—yes, you who are now reading

this—is that you, as an individual, have a role to play and can make a difference. You get to choose: do you want to use your life to try to make the world a better place for humans and animals and the environment? Or not?" How does this make you feel? Why do you think Goodall delivers this message so strongly?

8. Goodall also writes, "Young people, when informed and empowered, when they realize that what they do truly makes a difference, can indeed change the world. They are changing it already." How do you think children are changing the world? How should they? Do you believe children have this much power?

FUN ACTIVITY

Visit this page on Jane Goodall's website, called "Jane's Reasons for Hope": www.janegoodall.org/janes-reasons-hope.

Goodall writes, "It is easy to be overwhelmed by feelings of hopelessness as we look around the world. We are losing species at a terrible rate, the balance of nature is disturbed, and we are destroying our beautiful planet. We have fear about water supplies, where future energy will come from—and most recently the developed world has been mired in an economic crisis. But in spite of all this I do have hope. And my hope is based on four factors."

Read about Goodall's four factors. Do you agree with her? Do you ever feel hopeless about the planet? Does thinking about Jane's reasons for hope help you feel more optimistic?

Goodall further writes, "I meet many young people with shining eyes who want to tell Dr. Jane what they've been doing, how they are making a difference in their communities. Whether it's something simple like recycling or collecting trash; something that requires a lot of effort, like restoring a wetland or a prairie; or whether it's raising money for the local dog shelter, they are a continual source of inspiration. My greatest reason for hope is the spirit and determination of young people, once they know what the problems are and have the tools to take action."

How could *you* be a part of Jane Goodall's vision for children making the world a better place? How could you become a leader in your community, on a large or a small scale?

Why Does It Seem That Many Young Women Don't Want to Lead? For Those Who Do, What Structural Impediments Are Getting in Their Way?

These are difficult questions. H. L. Mencken is notably quoted as saying, "For every complex problem there is an answer that is clear, simple, and wrong." Our foremothers fought hard for us to gain the same opportunities as men. Even though this goal has not yet been reached, much progress has been made. And yet, despite the changes in laws and policies that have allowed women to ascend to more leadership positions, a lot of young women turn away from opportunities that were not available to their mothers and grandmothers. The pink-collar job market (made up of jobs traditionally held by women, such as teachers or nurses) has not changed a lot, and the vast majority of our rainmakers are intractably still male.

I believe we have not successfully addressed how to create a culture that is accepting of female leadership rather than undermining of it, a culture in which more girls will *want* to lead and will be able to see all of the positives rather than the exaggerated negatives that the media loves to give oxygen. As long as girls feel that to be a leader they have to be perfect, that they must "have it all," they will shy away from trying. Boys and men do not fall victim to this paradigm. In fact, they often succeed despite all manner of imperfections and microfailures that girls are less likely to overcome with the same resilience.

What are some of the pressures unique to girls and women? Well, for one thing, whether they are fourteen or forty, females feel that they must perform their duties extremely well *while maintaining thin bodies, beautiful hair and makeup, up-to-date and fashionable clothing, and magnetic sexual attractiveness.* That makes several full-time jobs!

June Cohen, executive producer of TED Media, plays an extremely active role in cultivating female leadership at TED, and has many thoughts on why women tend be more reticent to step forward than men. I interviewed her about the various challenges of recruiting more women to speak at TED conferences, which, especially for the smaller, regional conferences, can at first glance seem like a man's world. Cohen explained that her initial assumption was that men running the local TEDx conferences tended to recruit people most like them—mostly other white, middle-aged men—to be speakers. But she found out that there are other, equally salient factors.

"Women tend to prioritize differently than men and to value different things. If I invite an amazing female expert to a speak at a TED conference, she is more likely than a man to decline for reasons related to family, team responsibilities at the office, home/work balance, and because she does not feel ready in that she does not want to take the risk until she is more confident in her expertise. While men are more comfortable putting themselves out there and more interested in that opportunity as a personal achievement, women are more likely to decline invitations, and slightly more likely to cancel if they have accepted. I feel like half my job is smoking out women!" Cohen quips. "Women lean towards perfectionism. They also know that they are far more likely than their male peers to be attacked in the media and online when they speak publicly and appear on the Internet. They even worry about scrutiny of their physical appearance, having seen that happen to other women, and will sometimes shy away for that reason also.

"On my local news stations, the women are expected to wear tight dresses and be younger. If not—if they're putting on a little weight or getting a little older—they're out, to be replaced by a younger woman. Yet the guys are older, and many times overweight. How many times are women expected to be mere eye candy in these fluffy 'news' programs? And how many times are women attacked for their physical appearance rather than what they say, as compared to the men? And I don't even want to get into game shows, where there isn't a one I know of that's hosted by a woman."

I joke with them, 'You're letting down the sisterhood!' and then I offer wardrobe tips. Seriously. I know they are anxious about it, so I offer to talk it through."

We discussed the ways in which women can become more confident about presenting themselves as experts, and Cohen pointed out the need for women to believe that it is not inconsistent to be powerful *and* feminine, despite societal messages that may suggest otherwise. "A woman does not have to decide between those things," explains Cohen. "She can be *both*. And, the best leaders—male or female—exhibit characteristics of the expected leadership styles of both men and women. The best teams are diverse—made up of many types of voices. Teams function optimally when they include some members who are individually very direct and decisive, and others who are more reflective and collaborative; members who are competitive, and those who are more nurturing. Men and women can embody any combination of these qualities, and women need to give themselves permission to lead in their own way—not to lead like a man. The earlier in their careers they learn this and practice it, the sooner they will feel ready to go on stage—literally and figuratively—and the less they will worry about the scrutiny they receive as powerful women."

For women, there is also the expectation that the job of wife and mother will not "suffer." When it comes to careers, boys and men only have one expectation put on them by society: to succeed. When was the last time you heard a reporter ask a male political candidate how he plans to juggle his job and family? When was the last time you heard a TV news anchor critique a male politician's haircut or choice of clothing or facial wrinkles? It happens to female politicians *constantly*, but most of us are desensitized to this sexist double standard. Female politicians and other leaders are *often* (often, often, often!) reduced to how they look and also made to feel as if they are hurting their families when they pursue substantive careers outside of the home.

No wonder young women doubt themselves and their ability to be leaders! They also hear and read gendered messages like the following:

- Men are not attracted to powerful women.

- Women in powerful roles often must forgo having children to be successful.

- It is impossible to be both powerful and feminine.

- Being a successful woman "in a man's world" involves dealing with sexism and the good-ol'-boys' club on a daily basis, which is exhausting.

- To be successful leaders, women have to "be like men."

- Women are often not supported by other women, and even get undermined or attacked by other women, when they try to lead.

- For women, it's hard to be both successful and liked.

- Both men and women seem to prefer male leaders, be they bosses or politicians.

- Both men and women perceive men to be better "natural leaders." They vote and promote and behave accordingly.

Sheryl Sandberg, Facebook COO and author of the book *Lean In: Women, Work, and the Will to Lead*, was once talking about female leadership when she brought up the ubiquitous T-shirts for boys emblazoned with the words SMART LIKE DADDY while the girls' version reads PRETTY LIKE MOMMY. Sandberg said, "I would love to say that was 1951, but it was last year. As a woman becomes more successful, she is less liked, and as a man becomes more successful, he is more liked, and that starts with those T-shirts."

Women are not raised to feel entitled to leadership the way men are. They are taught they must work very hard for it, that it is not "natural" for their gender, and that it will be very difficult to attain. They see the culture around them that holds women up as objects to be looked at, and as accessories to the lives of men. It is in the pages of magazines, on the silver screen, in song lyrics, and right there on the stages of political debates. I recently saw the video of a debate for a local election in neighboring New Hampshire—I forget which one, and did not know the candidates—but the women were asked whether they had read *Fifty Shades of Grey*. As Charlotte says, "Epic fail!" I read an interview in which Hillary Clinton was asked which clothing designers she prefers. Yes, *really*. And at the 2013 CPAC conference, a member of the audience shouted out that Hillary Clinton needed a facelift. (Insert expletive of your choice *here*.) What kind of message does this send to aspiring female leaders?

> "My daughters, my students (I'm a literacy specialist at an elementary school), and I have been especially inspired by Sonia Sotomayor lately. She was on Sesame Street twice and we have been obsessed ever since. Frida Kahlo is also a favorite role model. We have the children's book about her written by Jonah Winter."

We must redefine female leadership. It will be hard work. It must begin with the children. Let's look more closely at the world of our children, of girls in particular, and see what messages they are getting about leadership from the youngest ages. How can we use books and movies with strong female protagonists to spark conversations about the importance of female leadership, and help them recognize what female leadership in its many forms actually looks like?

RECOMMENDED BOOK

The Evolution of Calpurnia Tate by Jacqueline Kelly (age 10+)

In the scorching summer of 1899, in a small Texas town outside of Austin, eleven-year-old Calpurnia Tate is growing up in a well-to-do family as the only daughter sandwiched between three older brothers and three younger ones. The times are changing fast—the town's first telephone line is on its way, and the first automobile makes its debut at the county fair. As the Tate family rings in the new century, Calpurnia wrestles with what it means to be a girl, and how to reconcile her mother's aspirations for her to be a housewife with her own aspirations to be a scientist. Her close relationship with her grandfather is central to the book.

Set against a backdrop of Charles Darwin's *Origin of Species,* the story focuses on Calpurnia's "evolution" into a budding young naturalist who resents the gendered demands placed upon her to sew and cook and prepare for a domestic life she considers boring and monotonous compared to the excitement of studying nature and biology.

At the end of the book, Calpurnia and her grandfather discover a new species of plant, which is received with much fanfare at the Smithsonian Institution, the National Geographic Society, and, to a lesser degree, within the Tate family. Calpurnia's role model, Granddaddy, is her only hope for an ally when she asserts her desire to take a different path in life than other girls. His careful and loving mentorship of his only granddaughter is one of the most beautiful and inspiring parts of story, and it can't help but make you think about how many girls could benefit from this kind of relationship in today's world.

Calpurnia has to create her own path to leadership, much like how she bushwhacks her own paths in pursuit of plant and animal observations to record in her special notebook. Her fierce intelligence, tireless curiosity, and steady ambition allow her to stand out, even among a family of boys, as someone who knows who she is and who is determined to become a leader in a time and place where girls are actively discouraged from pursuing careers and are pressed into traditional roles by their parents. Calpurnia is determined to outsmart them all, and she does!

DISCUSSION QUESTIONS

1. What do you think of the title of this book? Why did the author choose it?

2. Throughout the story, there is tension between what Calpurnia wants for herself and what her mother wants for her. What does she want for herself? What does her mother want for her?

3. At the beginning of the book, Granddaddy says, "It's amazing what you can see when you just sit quietly and look." Do you think that children are taught this today? What did Calpurnia get out of practicing this kind of patience, observation, and reflection?

4. When Calpurnia is being prepared for her piano recital, she says, "Then they slathered me with Peabody's Finest Hair Food, Guaranteed to Produce Lustrous Locks, and set me out in the sun to bake for yet another hour with this revolting sulfur grease on my head. *This*, I thought, *this is what ladies go through?*" What is she upset about? What other examples can you find in the book of Calpurnia's view of gender expectations for females?

5. What factors do you think laid the groundwork for Calpurnia to demonstrate leadership?

6. How did you feel when Mrs. Tate says to Mr. Tate, "Your father feeds her a steady diet of Dickens and Darwin. Access to too many books like those can build disaffection in one's life. Especially a young life. Especially a young girl's life." What do you think she means by this comment? How would you feel if you overheard your parents talking this way about you?

7. After overhearing her parents' conversation, Calpurnia thinks to herself, *I had never classified myself with other girls. I was not of their species; I was different.* What is Calpurnia expressing, and why does she use this language?

8. What do coyotes symbolize to Calpurnia? Why does she feel like a coyote? Why does she also feel like a firefly?

9. Toward the end of the book, Granddaddy lists for Calpurnia many famous female scientists, whom she had never heard of in school. How was this a tipping point in the book? In what other ways did her relationship with her grandfather help her envision creating her own path in life?

10. As a girl, do you believe that all paths are open to you? If so, why? If not, why not?

FUN ACTIVITY

Put away your iPads and smartphones, grab your notebooks and some pencils and a magnifying glass or butterfly net, and get outside onto the lawn, into the woods, or anywhere a slice of nature can be found. Look around for any living creature or interesting plant specimen. Quietly observe it for a while, then sketch it in your notebook, write a description, and chart your location as best you can. Don't talk about anything but what you're doing. Don't even listen to music on your iPod. Be *in* this experience!

Once everyone has had a chance to do this, gather as a club and share your notebooks and discuss your experiences. How did it feel to be immersed in nature emotionally and intellectually? How do you think Calpurnia felt escaping piano lessons and embroidery to explore her grandfather's world?

The Smurfette Principle and the Bechdel Test: Analyzing the Media's Role in Transmitting Regressive Ideas to Girls

The average child today consumes more than seven hours of media per day—more than ten if you include multitasking. (That's a figure reported by the Kaiser Family Foundation resulting from its comprehensive, widely circulated study published as *Generation M2: Media in the Lives of 8- to 18-Year-Olds*). We've examined the messages girls get about the importance of their physical appearance and how they should perform femininity. But what explicit and implicit messages do girls get from media about the importance of women in society, including female leadership? By closely considering what is on offer to children on television, in the movie theaters, in online videos, and via other mediums, we can begin this conversation. Using a couple of specialized lenses, the Smurfette Principle and the Bechdel Test, we can actually describe and measure what media is feeding our girls.

Remember *The Smurfs*? You know, those funny blue creatures that began as a comic strip and morphed over many years into action figures, books, movies, a TV series, DVDs, music CDs, video games, theme parks, and even *Smurfs on Ice*? Full disclosure: I've always hated them and could not understand their wild popularity.

A number of years ago I discovered that the Smurfs had yielded an extremely valuable media-literacy tool called the Smurfette Principle. Remember Smurfette, the lone female character among the seventy-five-plus characters created over the many years during which the Smurfs were popular? Read that again. You read it correctly. *The lone female character.* There was the Smurf who was Brainy, the one who was Grouchy, the one who was a Doctor, the one who was an Architect, the one who was . . . *female.* Yep, the unique characteristic that Smurfette added to the menagerie was her gender. Thus, the Smurfette Principle came to refer to any instance of a cast of characters (human or animated) in a book, movie, or television show that was skewed heavily male, or in fact included literally only one token female (usually stereotyped and in the role of sidekick/ little sister/love interest or any other version of an ornament beside the male characters and their adventures).

When I first learned that there was a name for this phenomenon, I fell down the rabbit hole of childhood memories searching for instances of the Smurfette Principle that I had not noticed as a child. It was a long daydream. Kanga in *Winnie-the-Pooh* came to mind first. Wow, in all of the Hundred Acre Wood, the only female to be found was the doting, docile mother of Roo! Then there was *Sesame Street* and *The Muppet Show*. Let's see . . . there was the highly glamorous Miss Piggy and . . . hmmm. I thought about my beloved Saturday morning cartoons: Bugs Bunny, Daffy Duck, the Road

Runner, Yosemite Sam. I ended up with almost one hundred male characters on a list, plus Olive Oyl, Jessica Rabbit, Minnie Mouse, Natasha Fatale, and a few other stereotypical female characters. (Yes, I spent a lot of time obsessing about and writing that list.) Then I moved on to cereal box characters. Whoops, same problem there! I started Googling current popular kid movies. That felt like getting punched in the eyeballs and the soul at the same time.

Finally I started thinking back on Charlotte's childhood. Of course, many of the same characters in books, television, and movies I'd loved as a child were still around. I looked at what was different. Although PBS seemed to have a few shows that defied the Smurfette Principle, most shows demonstrated it, especially on the Disney Channel, Nickelodeon, and the Cartoon Network. Charlotte watched little TV, but had beloved videos back in the days of VCRs, and an all-time favorite video series was *The Land Before Time*, about a bunch of animated dinosaurs and their prehistoric adventures. It features Cera (the triceratops) and Ducky (the duckbill)—*two* girl dinosaurs!—and then there are lots of other dinosaur characters that left me wondering if the real reason the dinosaurs died out was because all of the species of dinosaurs suddenly starting having only male babies, and eventually there were no females left to reproduce.

I could go on, but I'll stop here. You will undoubtedly think of many more of your own examples. So what effect does the Smurfette Principle have on girls, who grow up as 51 percent of the population but see their gender appear in media in token numbers? For starters, they learn they don't matter very much. (And boys learn that too.) Clearly, we need more female leaders, so more female leadership can be represented in our culture, so we will have more female leadership! Mother-daughter book clubs are where the seeds of female leadership can be sown.

The Smurfette Principle is relevant to children's books as well as movies—and it is why I started our mother-daughter book club in 2000. I just had to *do something*! Sure, there are current and older television shows, books, and movies we could all name that feature girls as protagonists and/or include multiple female characters. Some are great, while others perpetuate stereotypes and do more harm than good. But these are all *greatly* outnumbered by those that demonstrate the Smurfette Principle, and girls and women have never experienced anything else throughout history. It's the same dynamic for adult women who bankroll Hollywood by purchasing well over 50 percent of the movie tickets sold in this country, yet see themselves onscreen in small numbers, usually under age forty, and often sexualized. That brings us to the Bechdel Test!

Here is a great YouTube video that explains the origin and function of the Bechdel Test (www.youtube.com/watch?v=bLF6sAAMb4s), a way of assessing the presence and relevance of female characters in movies, which can be summarized very simply by posing three questions:

- Does the movie have two or more women, with names?
- Do they talk to each other?
- Do they talk to each other about something other than a man?

Seriously, this changed my life. I find myself assessing every single movie I see now in terms of whether it passes the Bechdel Test. I think we'd all agree the bar is pretty low. If for ten seconds, two named female characters talk to each other about makeup, the movie passes, even if for the other two and a half hours, you see nothing but men onscreen. Start thinking about your favorite movies. Maybe get a glass of wine first.

I recently saw the fantastic Academy Award-nominated movie *Lincoln* in the theater, and found myself in anguish on the car ride home, asking my husband if he could remember whether Mary Todd Lincoln ever talked to either of the other two women who had extremely minor roles in the film. Then I started making excuses for the film—because I loved it so much— saying that it was *historical*, and that during the Civil War, of course all of the soldiers were male, and all of the politicians were male, and gosh, the Lincolns only had sons, not daughters, and so, and so . . . it could not be *expected* to pass the Bechdel Test! How badly I wanted to give Hollywood a pass. The reality is, it could have passed if Steven Spielberg had wanted it to. (I bet Spielberg does not care about the Bechdel Test. Perhaps he has never heard of it.) And why should he or any other male directors, writers, producers, or other powerbrokers in Tinseltown if women continue flocking to movies about men? Which they will. It just makes me sad.

Now think about our daughters. We want them to be *empowered*. We want them to be *strong*. We want them to be *leaders*. But what do they see? When they are young they see Disney princess movies that, with a few exceptions, show them the opposite of female leadership. They see movies depicting boys' and men's stories as the norm, and girls' and women's stories labeled as "chick flicks." They see most roles go to males, as well as speaking parts, lines, and plots, just to name a few of the injustices. They see girls and women sidelined.

Girls hardly ever see women over fifty in movies, even though this is currently the largest segment of society. If they do see older women onscreen, the actresses have often had plastic surgery to still get the roles. (That's an interesting message.) They see teenage girls presented as sex objects and peripheral characters to the stories being told about boys. Ditto on television; ditto in books. They rarely see girls and women playing roles involving leadership. The popular screenwriter, producer, and director Joss Whedon, known for creating courageous and substantive female characters including Buffy the Vampire Slayer, was once asked in an interview, "Why do you write strong female characters?" Whedon answered, "Because you're still asking me that question."

Despite the positive changes for women in our society (e.g., women being breadwinners in almost half of all households, women outnumbering men in college admission and in earning advanced degrees), films and television programs do not reflect these achievements and realities. Instead, they persist in presenting very archaic, regressive, and stereotyped views of the role of women that for some reason still sell. There is a saying, "You can't be what you can't see," (Marie Wilson, founding president of the White House Project). Depictions of girls and women in film have not evolved with the times. Anyone alive today has *never* experienced gender balance in movies, on television, or in books. The extreme imbalance seems normal; in fact, it is not even noticed most of the time. How do you solve a problem if you can't see it?

A lot of parents think that pop culture doesn't matter because, if they are being good role models who expose their daughters to a variety of healthy imagery and activities, none of the media's messages can harm them. (Check out the "Third Person Effect" on Wikipedia.) This notion is wonderfully idealistic, but the reality is that, with the exception of children who are raised in remote geographies or communities without media, our girls do absorb media messages. The older they get, the less time they spend supervised by parents, the more they spend out in the larger world with peers and technology, and the less influence parents have—even the best ones. So how do you hold on to your daughters? Hold on too tight, and they slip from your grasp. You have to build a strong foundation of trust with them that allows room for increasing amounts of media consumption, *while also* teaching them to be critical consumers of media. This will help them make good choices in their teen years and beyond. That is why teaching media literacy is so important, and a crucial skill to foster from an early age.

Accepting that all of our girls (no exceptions!) are negatively affected by media, to at least some degree, is crucial. It paves the way for us to talk seriously about what we can do as moms to counter these very disempowering messages, and raise girls to believe they can be leaders. The "village" of your club is where girls can try on leadership surrounded by nothing but support!

RECOMMENDED MOVIE

Whale Rider **(PG-13, but considered suitable by "mom reviewers" for much younger girls. I think this should have been PG, and feel it is fine for ages 8+)**

This is one of my all-time favorite kids' movies. It is a beautiful adaptation of the book of the same name by Witi Ihimaera, which I also recommend highly. Ihimaera wrote the book in just three weeks after he took his daughters to several action movies and they asked him repeatedly why the heroes were always boys, and why girls were always helpless. Ihimaera decided to write this book for his daughters to show that girls can be heroes, too.

Whale Rider takes place in a small village, Whangara (the actual hometown of Ihimaera), on the coast of New Zealand. The town is inhabited by people of Maori descent who believe that in every generation, one male heir to the chief is born who will eventually inherit the position to lead them. The people have lived in the same place for more than one thousand years and trace their ancestry back to a single man, Paikea, who, legend has it, escaped death when his canoe capsized by riding on the back of a whale all the way in to shore. The first-born boys of chiefs are considered to be the direct descendants of this ancestor. Even in the modern day, this mythology is alive in the people.

Enter eleven-year-old Pai, the twin sister of the boy who, had he not died at birth along with the twins' mother, would have been that chosen male heir. Pai is given up by her grief-stricken father (who abdicates becoming the next chief) to be raised by her grandparents. She believes her grandfather, the current chief, should recognize her as the rightful heir in the patriarchal tribe, even though she is female. Koro, the grandfather, repeatedly rebuffs his granddaughter, who is determined to win over both her rights to succession and Koro's love and respect. Only Nanny Flowers, Pai's grandmother, understands Pai's true destiny and drive to become a leader in a male-dominated community, and supports her efforts to train for it alongside the boys of her village. Koro's inability to recover from the loss of both his son and his grandson as future chiefs, as well as his entrenched prejudice toward females, blinds him to what only the viewer can see: Pai's natural leadership abilities and her special gift for communicating with whales. To say more would require a spoiler alert!

This movie gives me goose bumps every time I watch it. It is stunningly beautiful, ethereal, and mysterious. You'll be captivated, and your daughter will see an extremely special story about a young girl who never gives up on her dream to become a leader.

DISCUSSION QUESTIONS

1. In *Whale Rider*, the grandfather, Koro, comes from a long line of first-born sons, and tries to stay true to the teachings of his ancestors. However, in some ways he is a throwback to an earlier era. In what ways did you notice this?

Prompts

- What is the town like? Is it the same as one thousand years ago or is it different today? How?

- How are the old traditions viewed by Pai's father, Porourangi? How is Porourangi viewed by his father, Koro?

- What are the boys like who Koro tries to train?

2. What causes Koro's blindness to Pai's talents?

Prompts

- Do you think Koro is stubborn? Do you think he is prideful? How has he become so hardened?

- How much effect do culture and tradition have on a person's beliefs and attitudes? Is it different for older people than younger people?

- What role do you think grief plays in Koro's behavior?

- Do you feel Koro respects girls and women? Why or why not?

- Do you feel Koro loves Pai?

3. Name some examples of times when Pai is willing to go along with a system where girls are considered less important than boys. What are some examples of times when she tries to prove that girls are equal to boys?

4. Why does Pai support her grandfather even though he keeps hurting her?

Prompts

- What has her grandmother Nanny Flowers taught her?

- What lessons has Pai learned from her time with her father?

- How does Pai continue trying to win her grandfather over?

5. What are some examples of Pai's leadership abilities coming through?

6. What about this movie did you find uplifting? What did you find painful? What did you think about the ending?

7. Is leadership easy or hard for you? Talk about some times you have had to prove your abilities to someone who did not believe you had them.

8. What types of leadership (besides riding whales and becoming a chief) do you aspire to?

FUN ACTIVITY

Interview an older woman in your family or community about the cultural or religious traditions of her family and the role of women within those traditions. Find out how she navigated any obstacles to leadership when she was growing up, or as an adult, and how she did or didn't over-come them. Then share your interview experiences with the members of your book club and see if they have anything in common!

Raising Girls to Be Self-Confident and to Be Leaders: What Can Moms Do?

You can start a mother-daughter book club—and I hope by now you've decided to! As a group of moms and daughters, you can have discussions that may sometimes be more powerful than one-on-one conversations. Here are some ways a mother-daughter book club can be fertile ground for growing female leaders.

- Help girls learn to identify with female heroes and leaders through literature and film. Celebrate their accomplishments within your club! There are lots of great recommendations at the end of this chapter, and even if you can't get to them all as a club, moms and daughters can pick and choose from these examples of female leadership (or search for their own).

- Use the Smurfette Principle and the Bechdel Test when consider-ing books and movies for your daughters. To the greatest extent possible, I did this when compiling the recommendations!

- Try to focus the girls on assessing other girls and women in the club (and elsewhere) on the strength of their character, intel-lect, and other positive attributes rather than on their looks. When girls are together in groups, you are more likely to hear things like "Yeah, she's a good athlete, but she's kind of fat, isn't she?"

- Remind girls that they are equal to boys. Let them hear this from all of the moms, together, perhaps with personal anec-dotes. This sounds clichéd and oversimplified, but it needs to be explicitly pointed out to girls that gender differences are hyped up and exaggerated by media, our sports culture, in schools, and often by religion. Obviously, this is not to say that girls should quit sports or school or religion, but that they should understand that *they* get to determine their role in their future marriage (or lack thereof), family, career, and life, regardless of the stereotyping messages they may get from society.

- Choose field trips and other activities—such as those suggested in this book, and others you think of yourselves—to *show* girls the many accomplishments of women.

- As moms, talk about what you have each experienced in your own lives pertaining to leadership. Discuss with the girls your goals, hardships, failures, and successes as you pursued positions of leadership as children and later, as adults.

- Ask the girls to dream, and dream big. Talk as a group about what each of you aspires to, famous or familiar women you view as role models, and how you can support each other's goals. Revisit this often, especially as girls approach middle school, a time when some girls tend to abandon their prior ambitions and begin talking about wanting to be a celebrity or model when they grow up.

- Work on leadership skills within the club. Give girls ample opportunities to lead discussions, suggest books and movies, run activities, and more. Your club will be a safe and nurturing place for girls, even more reserved ones, to practice asserting themselves, supporting others while they do the same, and to learn to deal with setbacks.

- Deal swiftly and directly with any incidents of bullying between the girls. Use the conflict as a teachable moment. Don't scold, stay positive, and model leadership as mothers.

- If the opportunity arises, mentor another mother-daughter book club once you've got your sea legs with your own. Girl power!

You can also support your daughter at home in these ways:

- Encourage her to take healthy risks—physically, emotionally, academically, and in other ways.

- Encourage her to consider leadership opportunities available through school, sports, or any other extracurricular activities, and support any steps she takes in that direction, no matter how small.

- Teach her to express and be comfortable with emotions often reserved for boys, such as anger.

- Help her pursue her passions and develop at least one deep interest or talent about which she can feel good.

- Let her experience small failures, and resist the temptation to rush in to solve them for her.

- Encourage female camaraderie and teamwork, and verbalize why collaboration is so important for girls and women.

- As much as possible, let her choices and her body be her own— let her choose her clothes, her haircuts, and her activities (within reasonable limits, of course). Send her the message that she has a voice in who she is, what she does, and how she expresses herself.

- Find ways to connect your daughter with other girls who will inspire her, provide mutual support, and be her peers in girl activism. (See next two bullet points for ideas.)

- Consider signing her up for Girl Scouts if she's amenable. Did you know that a majority of women in Congress were once Girl Scouts, and many attribute some of their leadership skills to what they learned in scouting?

- Consider reading about or joining girl-empowering groups such as Girls on the Run, Hardy Girls Healthy Women, Powered By Girl, Girls Leadership Institute, or SPARK Summit. (There are even more recommendations at the end of the book.)

These suggestions are just for starters. There are plenty of other books and online resources presented at the end of this book to help you further explore ways of encouraging your daughter to develop her leadership skills.

I long for the day when girls will look in the mirror and see their potential to be leaders and change agents in society rather than simply seeing the physical features they wish they could improve. More girls must grow up believing that they can and should strive to change the way the deck is stacked, and be able to imagine themselves in positions of leadership at

"My first leadership position was as patrol leader in Girl Scouts. Girl Scouts actually is a great place for a girl to learn leadership. Their current national focus is leadership (and encouraging girls to enjoy science, technology, engineering, and math). I loved Scouts."

school, on the sports field, and in the future. But first they need to be able to see themselves as they really are, not as media, pop culture, and the beauty industry define them. If I did not believe moms could have a positive impact on their daughters' self-confidence, I would not be as excited as I am every day in my work, because I *know* we can make a difference if we try!

Reflection from Charlotte

Since I'm fairly introverted, I've never felt suited to traditional leadership roles that involve a lot of action and communication with large groups of people, but in middle school I discovered my own way to be a leader. In seventh grade, I arranged an interview with the editor of my local newspaper to apply for the position of student columnist. The former columnist who'd been writing for the paper in the past few years had just left for college. The editor loved my writing portfolio and thought I would do a good job, so I got the assignment. I was excited for the opportunity to take on that role.

It was a big commitment to write a one-thousand-word newspaper column every month, but I loved that job and I kept it from seventh grade until I graduated high school. With this unique venue for self-expression through writing, and the freedom to write on nearly any topic I desired, I had the ability to draw public attention to issues that I thought were

(cont'd on the next page)

important. Some of the subjects I covered included the conflict between hate speech and the First Amendment, Western society's pressure on women to remain youthful and attractive instead of aging naturally and gracefully, and the experience of children in violent areas of the Middle East during the Iraq and Afghanistan wars. Sometimes I interviewed people who I felt had important stories to tell, such as a teacher at my mom's school who was a Vietnam veteran, as well as my aunt, who emigrated to the United States from Vietnam with her family during the war.

When I entered high school, my position as a columnist became even more important to me after I tried to get involved in other student clubs and organizations on campus. The literary magazine and the student newspaper functioned more like popularity contests than open forums for creative expression and public discourse, and were not conducive to the type of leadership I wanted to continue to practice. I also involved myself in a couple of social-activism groups, but I found myself more content to work as I was needed rather than to assume the role of directing others and organizing large projects. I realized at this point that I did best as a leader on my own, using writing to encourage my readers to think about and engage in various issues—sometimes troubling ones—of the world we live in.

Contributing to this book itself is a manifestation of my leadership style, as I see it. I don't believe that I, or any other girls, necessarily need to be very outspoken, well-known, or visibly active in order to contribute meaningfully to society and work toward the changes that are important to us. Each girl has her own way of making a difference by expressing herself and her own interests, talents, and hobbies. That is what's important, because if each girl can use her voice on behalf of the causes she believes in, in the way that best works for her and plays to her strengths, then she has the ability to be an inspiring leader.

RECOMMENDED BOOKS

TITLE	AUTHOR	AGE RANGE	MOVIE ADAPTATION?
Counting on Grace	Elizabeth Winthrop	10+	
Divergent	Veronica Roth	12+	
Fly Girl	Sherri L. Smith	12+	
My Life with the Chimpanzees	Jane Goodall	8+	Yes
Rachel Carson: A Twentieth-Century Life	Ellen Levine	13+	
The Evolution of Calpurnia Tate	Jacqueline Kelly	10+	
The Lions of Little Rock	Kristin Levine	11+	
The Road from Coorain	Jill Ker Conway	13+	Yes
Toliver's Secret	Esther Wood Brady	8+	
Where the Ground Meets the Sky	Jacqueline Davies	10+	

RECOMMENDED MOVIES

TITLE	MPAA RATING
Akeelah and the Bee	PG
Gorillas in the Mist	PG-13
Miss Representation	NR
Temple Grandin (miniseries)	PG
Whale Rider	PG-13

RECOMMENDED MEDIA

Use an Internet search engine to locate these videos on YouTube, Vimeo, or other video hosting sites.

Rachel Simmons's TED Talk about Girls' Leadership

"Cause and Effect: How the Media You Consume Can Change Your Life"

"Colin Stokes: The Hidden Meanings in Kids' Movies" (TED Talk)

Jennifer Siebel Newsom's TED Talk on *Miss Representation*

"'I will be a hummingbird'—Wangari Maathai"

"Adora Svitak: What Adults Can Learn from Kids" (TED Talk)

"See Jane" Video from the Geena Davis Institute on Gender in Media

"Sesame Street: Sonia Sotomayor and Abby—Career"

"Megan Kamerick: Women Should Represent Women in Media" (TED Talk)

"Sheryl Sandberg: Why We Have Too Few Women Leaders" (TED Talk)

11

The Welfare of Girls and Women Around the World and Why That Matters to All of Us

"I've always been the breadwinner and men don't like that. They turn on you. They bite the hand that feeds them."
—from The Breadwinner *by Deborah Ellis*

Key Takeaways

- The challenges faced by girls and women in developed and developing countries differ in many ways, but overlap in others.

- It can be difficult for mothers to decide how much to share with daughters about the struggles of girls and women in other countries, especially when it comes to violence.

- Both one-on-one with their daughters, and within mother-daughter book clubs, moms can raise girls who are informed, empathetic, and engaged in the struggles most women and girls face for human rights and dignity. Understanding is one of the greatest gifts a mother can give her daughter.

In August 2012, President Obama issued an executive order aimed at preventing global violence against women and girls. He explained that the issue of violence against women is not only about the human rights of affected women, but also about economic stability, public health, and national security everywhere. As secretary of state, Hillary Clinton helped spearhead Obama's executive order. Several months later, when she stepped down from her post, she gave an extraordinary speech, capping off years of dedicated work on behalf of women and girls. Speaking about the marginalization of females, she stated, "Just ask young Malala [Yousafzai] from Pakistan. Ask the women of northern Mali who live in fear and can no longer go to school. Ask the women of the Eastern Congo who endure rape as a weapon of war. And that is the final lever that I want to highlight briefly. Because the jury is in, the evidence is absolutely indisputable: If women and girls everywhere were treated as equal to men in rights, dignity, and opportunity, we would see political and economic progress everywhere. So this is not only a moral issue, which, of course, it is. It is an economic issue and a security issue, and it is the unfinished business of the twenty-first century. It therefore must be central to US foreign policy."

It is too easy to compartmentalize the problems of girls and women in developing countries, to see them as different than our own, and to shield our daughters from them because we don't want them to know of such suffering. It is also too easy to say that here in the United States, women and girls are "equal enough," and to look at women's greater oppression in other countries as proof that we Americans have nothing to complain about. The fact of the matter is, we live in a global society. Our lives and fates are intertwined. As Caribbean American writer and civil rights activist Audre Lorde said, "I am not free while any woman is unfree, even when her shackles are very different from my own."

> "I have two sons. No daughters but many nieces. From the time my sons were young, I asked them to treat girls like they would want their cousins treated. To always keep in their minds what was best for the girl they were with. There is still so much work to do in this country, and around the world."

Education: The Key to Better Lives for Girls and Women

Malala Yousafzai, the fourteen-year-old Pakistani schoolgirl who was shot in the head and seriously injured by members of the Taliban for insisting on going to school and advocating for girls' education, has become an international symbol and spokesperson for gender equality in education. In 2013, she was nominated for a Nobel Peace Prize, and it is a shame she did not win because I cannot imagine anyone more deserving than this brave young teen. In many countries around the world, girls are not allowed to reach the same levels of education as boys; in some places, they are not allowed to attend school at all or even learn to read.

According to the World Bank, "Educating girls yields a higher rate of return than any other investment in the developing world." It is the opinion of many human rights activists that educational opportunity must be the number-one goal for improving the lives of girls and women—and men and boys—around the world. With female education comes:

- later marriages
- fewer children
- healthier mothers and children
- less poverty
- greater safety from abuse
- reduced infant and maternal mortality rates
- greater opportunities for these girls and the next generation, their children
- greater respect for women

The problem is that in many countries with highly patriarchal social systems, girls and women are deliberately denied the education many girls in America take for granted. They are either not allowed to leave the house at all, or are pressured to drop out of school at a young age. Some of the many obstacles girls like Malala face include:

- sexual abuse perpetrated against them in school buildings or on the way to or from school

- threats and acts of brutality against the parents of those girls allowed to go to school

- early pregnancies

- sexist curricula that reinforce traditional gender roles, and the resulting impoverishment of female economic and social opportunity

- the lower status of educated girls compared to educated boys

- curricula designed for girls that prohibit the study of many of the subjects available to boys

- taboos and superstitions about menstruation that result in many girls remaining at home when they reach puberty

- lack of safe, accessible, and hygienic ways for girls to deal with their periods while at school

- expulsion of girls who have been raped, who are viewed as having shamed their schools as well as their communities

I spoke with Pam Allyn, founder of LitWorld, a global nonprofit organization that works with teachers, parents, community members, and children to support the development of literacy as a human right. Allyn created LitWorld after going to Kenya to do teacher training and noticing the absence of girls in sub-Saharan high schools. She decided that the illiteracy rate of girls in the developing world was a grave injustice, and that a grassroots effort was needed to cut through the political red tape and get inside communities to bring programming, funding, and other resources directly to the people who could most effectively partner with LitWorld to allow more children, especially girls, access to education so they could learn to read.

LitWorld is now on the ground in countries throughout Africa, as well as in Haiti, the Philippines, Peru, Kosovo, and elsewhere. Work is also done domestically, in America's poorest communities. Although there is a more pressing need to address the educational inequalities of girls around the world, boys in need are also served. Allyn explains, "It's hard not to focus most of our energy on girls, because they are struggling so much relative to boys in the developing world, but we try to help all children. We also know that for there to be improvements to the lives of girls and women, boys and men must be educated."

I asked Allyn to talk about some of the obstacles she has observed in her travels that uniquely affect girls' ability to receive an education and become literate. She mentioned many of the issues I have already listed above, plus others that are extremely poignant. "One of the first things you notice in working with these girls is how little they value themselves and how low their perception is of themselves as learners," Allyn notes. "In the poor areas of America where we work, and in other developed countries, the issue we often see is girls buying the message that their looks are the most important thing about them. In poorer countries, the issues are obviously different. It is hard for girls to stand up for themselves within their families and communities and to push back against the cultural norms that they should assume the same responsibilities their mothers and grandmothers did (that kept them out of school). It is very hard to convince the families of girls to forego the labor girls could provide on a daily basis to help the family and instead commit to educating them for an economic payoff many years down the road. The family truly needs their labor within the system that has always existed for females."

Allyn continues, "Also, the expectation that they will have babies, and have them young and often, prevails. How do you break that cycle when the pregnancies are often the result of rape, and when sexual violence is generational and accepted? This is the great untold story—the systemization of misogyny and violence toward girls and women that keeps them 'in their place' within their families and communities. We encounter a few such stories in the media, but most are never spoken about because they are so common and expected."

It is hard for girls in developed countries, who anticipate and expect educational opportunities equal to boys, to imagine what life would be like for them if they couldn't read, perform basic arithmetic, or have any knowledge of history, science, and other subjects. I remember that Charlotte's favorite game to play by herself in her room when she was only three or four years old was "school." She would arrange all of her stuffed animals to be the pupils, and would teach them lessons by writing with a dry erase marker on a whiteboard on an easel. These lessons could go on for hours. How many of our daughters played or still play this way? It brings such great joy to them.

Helping our daughters understand that education is both a right and a privilege, and one denied to millions of girls around the world simply because they are female, is important. Girls are viewed as either unworthy

"Being literate empowers people, especially now with the Internet and eBooks available through cell phones. Having girls and women able to access this wealth of information must be incredibly destabilizing for cultures built around their subjugation. But it will happen. Girls will learn to read. I'd love to be alive a hundred years from now, and see the social changes this will drive."

of education, or must fulfill the roles assigned to them by sacrificing education.

The degree to which the broad array of global problems for girls and women should be discussed within your book club depends on daughters' ages and maturity, and is up to the discretion of each mother. I do believe that an inalienable right to education, however, is a concept every girl can understand. The desire for *all* girls to receive educations, no matter where they live, is a powerful and unifying concept. If all girls really could receive an education, it would change the world.

As Ghanian scholar Dr. James Emmanuel Kwegyir-Aggrey said, "If you educate a man, you educate an individual. But if you educate a woman, you educate a nation."

RECOMMENDED BOOK

The Breadwinner by Deborah Ellis (age 10+)

For her research, author Deborah Ellis, a psychologist by profession, spent several months talking to girls and women in Afghan refugee camps in Pakistan and Russia, and used these interviews as the basis for her description of daily life in Afghanistan. *The Breadwinner* is based on true stories that came from these interviews. This book was a labor of love for Ellis. She donates all proceeds she receives from book royalties to Women for Women in Afghanistan, and the money goes toward girls' education in the refugee camps. Talk about walking the walk!

The Breadwinner is the first book in a trilogy. Eleven-year-old Parvana, like other girls and women in Kabul, is not allowed to go to school, go shopping, or even play outside since the Taliban has taken control of Afghanistan. She spends most of her time indoors, stuck in her family's one-room home. When Taliban militants take her father away, Parvana must cut off her hair and pose as a boy in order to economically support her family.

Like many girls and women oppressed by the Taliban's regime, Parvana actually comes from an educated family. The changes instituted under Sharia law dismantle the rights and quality of life women and girls had experienced before the Taliban gained control. Although now dressing in a chador (veil), Parvana's feelings about the repressive Muslim regime she now struggles against are always clear. This is must-read literature for American girls who have grown up with the Afghan War in the news and are curious about the lives of the people there, especially the plight of females.

DISCUSSION QUESTIONS

1. At first, Parvana is happy that she doesn't have to go to school, but Nooria is upset about it. What does Nooria understand that Parvana does not?

2. Parvana's family has to be careful about trusting people. Why? Is it the same way or different in the United States?

3. Why must Parvana become the breadwinner of the family?

4. Under Taliban rule, what freedoms are lost by Parvana and her family? What would you do if you lost those same freedoms?

5. Parvana's mother and sister have not been outside in more than a year, and this is typical of cultures in which men tightly control women's lives. How would you feel, emotionally and physically, if you were rarely allowed to go outdoors? How would you feel if you saw that your father and brothers *could* go out, and had a lot more freedom than you because of their gender?

6. What choices do Parvana and Shauzia have to make to earn money? Would you have done the same if in their circumstances?

7. Shauzia decides to leave Afghanistan in search of a better life. How does this affect her family? What would you choose to do?

8. An old man who helps Parvana plant flowers says, "They may look scraggly and dying now . . . but the roots are good. When the time is right these roots will support plants that are healthy and strong." What do you think this means?

9. This book takes place before the United States went to war in Afghanistan. Mothers: give your daughters more context by sharing your observations of the war and its effect on the people of Afghanistan. With the pending (at the time of this writing) withdrawal of troops from the region, what do you think will happen to girls and women?

10. What did you learn from this book that you did not know before? How can what we learn about the lives of females in other countries change our own lives? How can we help the world become a more fair and equal place?

FUN ACTIVITY

In the book *The Breadwinner*, Parvana's mother and Mrs. Weera publish an underground magazine. They want to educate people in other countries about the difficulties of living under Taliban rule. Now that you have read the book and understand more about life in Afghanistan, pretend that you are a contributor to this secret magazine. Write a short article that you would like people around the world to read. Combine everyone's entries to make your own underground newspaper!

"It's a Girl": The Three Deadliest Words in the World

The first time I heard the words of the above heading, in relation to the movie *It's a Girl*, I got chills. The documentary explores the social, political, religious, economic, and legal reasons that some two hundred million girls are "missing" in the world today, either selectively aborted (by those who can afford it) or killed, abandoned, or neglected to the point of death (by those who are poor). Clearly, in some parts of the world, the violence directed toward females begins at—or before—birth. In some places, baby girls are born unwanted, born in shame, born into lives that will be characterized by oppression, abuse, and hatred simply because they are female.

As cruel as this is, I see particular cruelty in the irony that women are the chief perpetrators of female infanticide. They have no good choices. They often must decide between killing their girl children and saving themselves. The birth of daughters can result in beatings, rapes, and even murders for mothers who have failed to produce male heirs. Some fathers—not understanding or not caring about the fact that it is *their sperm* that determines the gender of offspring, not a mother's egg—are willing to kill their wives in the hope of remarrying someone else who will produce infant sons. Because some countries now have significantly fewer females than males, this contributes to other problems, such as sex trafficking, mail-order brides, and gang rape.

Why are females—who give *all* human beings life—viewed in some places as so worthless, as such bad luck, as so deserving of abuse and death? The reasons are complicated and differ somewhat by country and culture, but some of them include the following:

- Females, because they have been born into patriarchal societies in which they may not work, own property, or inherit wealth, are always seen as a financial burden.

- Females, because they may only marry and leave home if parents supply a dowry (even in places where dowries have been legally abolished but still culturally thrive), are viewed from birth as money losers for their families.

- China, specifically, has a birth control policy of one child per family. Since males are valued above females, many parents take drastic measures to ensure their one child is a boy.

- In patriarchal societies, male children confer status, while females confer the opposite.

All of this becomes even more unbearable in light of statistics from a report published by the United Nations Development Programme (UNDP) in July 2011. The report reveals that women perform 66 percent of the world's work, produce 50 percent of the food, but earn only 10 percent of the income and own only 1 percent of the property.

For those activists working to create the *enormous* cultural shift needed to combat this complex problem, the solution requires many efforts, including the reduction of poverty, laws against selective abortion and female infanticide that are actually *enforced*, a campaign to change anti-female social and religious attitudes that have been around for thousands of years, and education of girls and women, so that they will learn their rights and fight for the rights of their daughters. Change will not come quickly, and will be hard won to the degree that it is won at all.

It is hard for American girls to imagine many of the challenges facing girls in developing countries. I spoke with Regina Yau, founder of the Pixel Project, a California nonprofit that works globally to end gender-based violence. The Pixel Project is a "first step" organization—geared toward getting people who are new to the cause to start taking action to help end violence against women and girls. I asked Yau, who is ethnically Chinese but was born and raised in Malaysia and is currently based in the capital city Kuala Lumpur, to talk about the preference for sons in China and other parts of Asia and the Middle East. I asked her to help me think of a way for moms in Western countries to explain to their daughters how the lives of girls halfway around the world differ so greatly from their own.

"First of all, because there is a preference for sons in many Asian countries, boys grow up in parallel to girls, but with significantly more opportunities and freedoms, and significantly fewer rules and punishments than their sisters and other girls. That causes them to grow up feeling entitled, which often translates later in life to the entitlement to control and abuse women and girls. Boys grow up seeing that dynamic between their parents, within their families, and in their larger communities, and they naturally perpetuate it," Yau explains.

"Also, laws in many of these countries give men tremendous power and leverage in the lives of females . . . if girls are even allowed to be born and to survive their childhoods. In many parts of Asia and the Middle East, fathers still get to decide if a daughter goes to school or not, when and whom she marries, even whether she can leave the house. The entire life experience of many girls in the world hinges on the goodwill of their fathers and other men in their communities. Men decide everything. They are the default. Mothers in conservative families have very little authority in the raising of children, and they end up contributing to patriarchal systems because they know nothing different and are brought up to be duty-bound to tradition."

Yau feels that a good way for mothers to explain this to daughters is to ask them a series of questions, such as:

- "Imagine how you would feel if, from birth, your parents always put your brother first, simply because he was a boy, and regardless of who you both were as individuals. How would it feel if you worked very hard and were well-behaved, but your brother was always misbehaving, yet he was still always favored?"

- "Imagine how you would feel growing up and knowing that your brother would be allowed to make his own decisions, but you would have them all made for you by men. What would you do in that situation?"

- "Imagine how Malala Yousafzai would have felt if her father had not been supportive of her becoming an educated girl in Pakistan. How different would her life be?"

- And finally, the very provocative, "Imagine you are a baby girl in the tummy of your mother, somehow able to hear conversations outside the womb, and you hear your parents talking about whether you should be allowed to be born since you are a girl, or whether you should be killed when you are born . . . simply because you are not a boy. How do you think girls in other countries feel knowing their lives have such little value?"

Yau believes that the education of children (both girls and boys) in countries like the United States must begin early if they are to grow up with empathy for the plight of females around the world. By asking girls simple questions like the ones above, parents can help kids put themselves into the shoes of oppressed girls and women in different cultures, and instill in them both an appreciation for what they have and the desire to fight for social justice elsewhere.

What about here in the United States? Gender bias against the birth of girls could not possibly exist, could it? Apparently it does, but to a much smaller degree than in some so-called third-world countries, and without the violence directed at babies who enter the world without a Y chromosome. A recent Gallup poll asked both men and women whether, if they could only have one child, they would prefer a girl or boy. The women surveyed stated no measurable preference, but the men had a strong preference for a boy. This data has remained unchanged for more than seventy years.

In "first-world" countries like the United States, an argument could be made that girls are of great value based upon their current achievement in school. They are excelling more than ever, going to college in higher numbers than boys, and obtaining more of the advanced degrees. This is new. The future of our economy will surely involve the participation of a record number of women. Indeed, in the book *Half the Sky: Turning Oppression into Opportunity for Women Worldwide* by Nicholas Kristof and his wife, Sheryl WuDunn, WuDunn writes, "An important future indicator for a developing economy is its treatment of women." Any country that gives girls equal rights to boys and educates them will have double the talent pool of countries that don't. She considers girl power to be "the best way to fight poverty and extremism."

RECOMMENDED BOOK

Tua and the Elephant by R. P. Harris (age 8+)

I was drawn to this tale of a ten-year-old girl rescuing an abused elephant in Thailand in part because I love elephants, and in part because I once saved one myself. I didn't do it by slipping its chain like Tua does; I did it by writing a letter. Tua was far braver!

This is a delightful story about courage and friendship and empathy set amidst the sights, sounds, and tastes of Thailand. There's a fair amount of new vocabulary in this book, but it is not heavy-handed. Tua's quest for a sister takes her to the city marketplace and results in her sudden acquisition of Pohn-Pohn, an elephant she sees being mistreated by two villainous "mahouts" (men who train and ride elephants). Tua and her fugitive elephant must make their way to the safe haven of an elephant refuge before they are caught by Pohn-Pohn's evil captors. Along the way, many kind people help Tua and Pohn-Pohn. The usual hilarious hijinks occur, making this a fun and light story despite the seriousness of issues including animal abuse, the plight of the Asian elephant, and the many very real problems facing the girls and women of Thailand.

This is an easy introduction to Thai culture for young readers. The protagonist, Tua, is the kind of girl the members of a mother-daughter book club can look up to and admire.

DISCUSSION QUESTIONS

1. Tua, which means "peanut" in the Thai language, received her name because of her physical size. Does her name fit her personality?

2. When Tua rescues Pohn-Pohn, she is doing what she knows is right—even though at the time she has no idea what to do with the elephant she has just rescued! Can you think of a time you followed your heart and did the right thing?

3. What qualities make Tua a strong character and a leader?

4. Throughout the book, Tua receives assistance from many people—friends, relatives, and total strangers. She—and her new companion—are clearly beloved in her community. Do you think Tua could have gotten Pohn-Pohn away from the horrible mahouts and to safety in the elephant refuge without help? Or do you think her courage trumped everything else?

5. One person does not help Tua: her own mother. Why not?

6. Have you ever gone out on a limb to help an abused, ill, or abandoned animal? Would you?

7. When Tua says, "One simply can't toss a blanket over an elephant and call it a job well done," what does this tell you about her?

8. Moms: This book touches on a few social problems in Thailand, such as children living in extreme poverty and mothers begging with infants, but due to the reading level of the book and the age of the children reading it, the author does not go more deeply into issues that could be upsetting to young children. Thailand is a beautiful but struggling country with many environmental and political problems, not to mention a huge amount of child prostitution and sex trafficking. To the

degree you are comfortable, discuss some of these issues in your club meeting. Why is it important to *both* read uplifting and cheerful books like *Tua and the Elephant,* and to talk realistically about the unique challenges facing girls and women in many developing countries like Thailand?

FUN ACTIVITY

The book mentions some Thai cuisine. Thai food may be unfamiliar to some readers of this book, but it's delicious! Most children who enjoy Chinese or Indian food will enjoy Thai food too, especially the noodle and rice dishes. Cook a Thai meal or some Thai snacks to accompany the discussion of this book and set the mood. Or, if it works for your club, go out to a Thai restaurant and be adventurous eaters in honor of Tua, an adventurous girl!

Understanding Violence Toward Women and Girls Around the World, and Making Individual Decisions About How Much to Share with Daughters

I remember the very first, rather generic conversation I had with Charlotte when she was in elementary school about how her life compared with the lives of other children on this planet. I drew a triangle for her and said, "The tippy-top point is where the richest and most fortunate people in the world are. There are a few of them. At the bottom of the pyramid is where the poorest people who struggle the most are, and there are a lot of them. Where do you think you are?" She pointed to the middle of the triangle. Gah!

Part of me was surprised and part of me wasn't. After all, in her immediate world of her town, neighborhood, and school, she was in the middle socioeconomically. I learned something that day. I had not thought much about it before that impromptu drawing lesson, but I thought about it a lot afterward. I realized I wanted to raise a child who understood very clearly how fortunate she was and who did not take her advantages for granted. More important, I wanted her to feel that the rental fee for her place at the top of the global wealth pyramid was some sort of activism, philanthropy, or simple exercising of informed citizenship.

After that day, I came to the conclusion that it was important for me to begin teaching Charlotte about current events, history, politics, and what was going on sociologically and culturally around the world. I did not want her to grow up like so many kids I saw—bubble-wrapped and self-absorbed. Let's be honest—that's how it is by and large for many American children from reasonably well-to-do homes.

Sometimes other mothers thought that I shared too much too soon with Charlotte. I sometimes let her watch the news along with me, explaining things to her (and, sure, occasionally changing the channel when the material was truly not age appropriate). I talked to her a lot about what was going on in the world, even when it was ugly. Lots of times there were wonderful things to talk about: female presidents getting elected in other countries, cool scientific discoveries, civil rights victories in other places. Lots of times there were very difficult things to talk about, but we talked. I tried to do it carefully, age-appropriately, and while reassuring her that she was safe and loved. But I did not shelter her from everything. And I did not listen to friends who thought telling her "scary" things was tantamount to child abuse. I think she is not only a better informed and more compassionate human being today, but also more resilient for it.

Charlotte's father and I had the advantage when raising Charlotte of never being scooped by the Internet. This is a new dynamic that bears *much* consideration. In all of my years working with kids in schools, I can tell you this: they almost always know more, about all kinds of things, than their parents think they do. Kids are reading online and hearing from friends about many of the issues parents might want to shelter them from altogether. Worse, they often misunderstand complex issues they read about, or get misinformation from friends. The decision about how much to share, and when, must necessarily take into account the risk that if we as parents do not get out ahead of certain pieces of information, our girls will still encounter them—and without us there to help them process that information.

> "I try to ask open-ended, exploring questions to see what she knows and what she doesn't and then I proceed forward from that point. I think getting out ahead of it is key, though difficult to do."

All of that said, my decision was mine, as all moms must make these individual decisions for themselves and their daughters. We all have different perspectives on how much "news" to share with children, and mutual respect is important, especially within a mother-daughter book club, where there can be great intimacy but not always precisely shared personal values and parenting styles.

I leave it to individual mothers to decide how deeply to delve into human rights abuses directed at girls and women around the world and how much to share with daughters as they grow. The recommended books, movies, and media offer plenty of side doors to open dialogue with daughters on many different topics, so moms can pick and choose. Although it may sound paradoxical, by showing girls what less fortunate girls in other countries face as obstacles to living safe, free, and happy lives, we ultimately lift our girls up because we give them good reasons to *use* the opportunities they have been given. In the best of circumstances, we are growing tomorrow's leaders and role models, and the world's girls and women need lots more of those!

RECOMMENDED MOVIE

Rabbit-Proof Fence (PG)

Set in 1930s western Australia, *Rabbit-Proof Fence* is the story of three "half-caste" Aboriginal girls—sisters Molly and Daisy, and their cousin Gracie—who are stolen from their mother and grandmother and relocated fifteen hundred miles away to a reeducation camp for children of mixed race. The idea—and indeed, government policy—was that these children needed to "have the black bred out of them" for their own good. They would be trained to enter a life of indentured servitude to wealthy white families, and then, once in that world, if they were ever to marry and have children, they would most likely do so with white people, so that successive generations would progressively become whiter.

Based on a true story, the girls escape and walk for nine weeks without food and through harsh desert terrain along a rabbit-proof fence to find their way back to their mother and grandmother. The fence, thousands of miles long, was constructed at the turn of the century in an effort to keep rabbits and other agricultural pests in the eastern part of the country from crossing over into the western pastures and destroying them. The girls were able to use it as a landmark while making their way home. Alternately finding strangers who would feed and shelter them, and others who wanted to turn them in, the girls made their courageous journey while outsmarting a full-blooded Aborigine tracker who was a traitor to his own people. This story reminded me a lot of movies I've seen about the capture and reeducation of Native American children here in the United States in the 1800s.

Be sure to pay special attention to the last few minutes of the movie, when the real-life Molly and Daisy, now old women, are shown. This movie is riveting. It has been a long time since I've seen a movie starring girls who are so completely unadorned, and whose bravery shines so brightly against such a stark setting. This movie is about the triumph of the human spirit, and even more so, of the feminine spirit.

DISCUSSION QUESTIONS

1. How does the mother react when she sees white policemen? Why does she shout in her own language, "Hide the children"?

2. When the children are captured, how do the mother and grandmother react? How is this like or unlike your own culture?

   Prompts

   ▰ Who can they turn to for support?

   ▰ How do they express their grief?

   ▰ Why does the grandmother hit herself in the head with a rock?

3. How does the reeducation camp attempt to "civilize" and "Christianize" the children? Why are they told, "We don't speak that jabber here"?

4. Despite what happens to Olive, why does Molly decide to make a break for it?

5. Do you think that children have rights? What rights do they have? How have Molly, Gracie, and Daisy's rights been taken? What does "the stolen generations" mean?

Prompts

> Think about physical needs, emotional needs, and identity.

6. How do the girls demonstrate courage? Cleverness? Strength?

7. What do you think about the title of the movie? What do you think the fence symbolizes?

8. How did you feel at the very end of the movie, when you found out it was based on a true story and discovered what later happened to Molly, Gracie, and Daisy?

9. What would you have done in Molly's place? What characteristics of Molly do you think you might have within yourself?

FUN ACTIVITY

Get a large paper map of your country, determine the scale, and draw a line on it that represents a walk of fifteen hundred miles, radiating outward from your hometown. Talk about what it would be like to walk that far, how long it might take, what you would do for food and shelter, and how it would feel to be doing it alone at fourteen years of age and while responsible for two younger girls. Did you think this was realistic while watching the movie? Were you surprised to find out it was a true story? How would you summon the courage to go on a long journey like Molly's?

Sisterhood and Solidarity: Why It Matters

Whether thinking about gender bias in America or halfway around the world, the fundamental issue is the same: the entrenched belief that females have less value than males. The differences in degree and consequence are also extremely important to bear in mind, and for our daughters to understand. While a bias against girls is rather pervasive throughout the world, daughters in most developed countries have tremendous assets—from free public education, to nutrition and medical care, to greater physical safety and dignity—that girls their own age in many parts of the world can only dream about.

In our relationships with our daughters, both personally and as a book club village, we must help them oppose gender bias, but we must also help them appreciate all the ways in which they are incredibly fortunate. In addition to the above, our girls will grow up to be women who are allowed to pursue higher education, work, start businesses, own property, manage and inherit money, decide if/when/whom they will marry, plan their families (although this is currently threatened in some states), vote (although this is now being obstructed in some states), and in so many ways determine their own destinies. When such freedoms are denied to millions of girls and women in other parts of the world, we have an obligation to open this window for our daughters, and to teach them that when, for example, they invest their energy in their appearance instead of their education, they are disrespecting an opportunity that other girls like Malala Yousafzai are willing to die for.

When I was a child, I had no idea that so many girls were not allowed to go to school. I had no idea how much higher the illiteracy rate was for girls than for boys in the world. I hope this will improve significantly during my lifetime, and next generations will be instrumental in getting us there. We must all be the change we want to see in the world.

Reflection from Charlotte

Beginning when I was really young, my mom always made sure that I was aware of the world outside this country. She talked with me about human rights issues in other countries as well as in America, and let me watch the news with her each night, explaining anything I didn't understand. There were some things she didn't discuss with me until I was older, like rape, but I understood concepts including racism and sexism earlier than many of my peers. As I got older, I became aware that such attitudes were also often the cause of violence and oppression throughout the world. My mom always struck a good balance

(cont'd on the next page)

between assuring me that I was reasonably safe from such things, and stressing the importance of empathy and activism on behalf of people who are struggling, as well as why their lives and problems matter, regardless of what part of the world they're in.

Some parents avoid discussing difficult or upsetting subjects like the suffering of other people with their children because they don't want them to be afraid. I never found myself worried that the things I learned about would happen to me, though. I think that if parents develop open and trusting communication with their kids and make it known that they will always support and do their best to protect them, children can transcend any fear they may have of the realities of the world and instead gradually come to understand and empathize with problems affecting other people. If parents want to make a difference in the world, one of the things they can easily do is to raise children who also want to make a difference.

We all need to challenge the idea of American exceptionalism, and it begins with teaching kids to look outside our own borders for other perspectives and solutions, and to incorporate a global lens when looking at ways of improving our own society. The Internet makes it easier for everyone to be a citizen of the world, but parents need to foster this attitude in their kids first. Mother-daughter book clubs can have this broader mission, and the books and movies chosen could help girls think more globally. My mom and I both wish we'd done more of this in our book club, and it is my hope that the mother-daughter book clubs of the future will delve even more deeply into world issues, especially those affecting females. If I ever have a daughter of my own someday, we'll have our own club, and that's exactly what we'll do!

RECOMMENDED BOOKS

TITLE	AUTHOR	AGE RANGE	MOVIE ADAPTATION?
An Ocean Apart, A World Away	Lensey Namioka	12+	
The Breadwinner	Deborah Ellis	10+	
Esperanza Rising	Pam Muñoz Ryan	11+	
The Firefly Letters: A Suffragette's Journey to Cuba	Margarita Engle	11+	
Inside Out and Back Again	Thanhha Lai	11+	
No Laughter Here	Rita Williams-Garcia	10+	
Seven Daughters and Seven Sons	Barbara Cohen & Bahija Lovejoy	12+	
Shabanu: Daughter of the Wind	Suzanne Fisher Staples	12+	
Shadow Spinner	Susan Fletcher	10+	
Tua and the Elephant	R. P. Harris	8+	

RECOMMENDED MOVIES

TITLE	MPAA RATING
Life, Above All	PG-13
Mulan	G
PBS's Wide Angle "Time for School" episodes	NR
Rabbit-Proof Fence	PG
Wadjda	PG

RECOMMENDED MEDIA

Use an Internet search engine to locate these videos on YouTube, Vimeo, or other video hosting sites.

"Taking Root: The Vision of Wangari Maathai"

"Interview with Author/Activist Somaly Mam"

"Kakenya Ntaiya: A Girl Who Demanded School" (TED Talk)

"2011 YPO Global Leadership Summit: Rose Mapendo"

"Shabana Basij-Rasikh: Dare to Educate Afghan Girls" (TED Talk)

"Leymah Gbowee: Unlock the Intelligence, Passion, Greatness of Girls" (TED Talk)

"Sheryl WuDunn: Our Century's Greatest Injustice" (TED Talk)

"Hawa Abdi and Deqo Mohamed: Mother and Daughter Doctor-Heroes" (TED Talk)

"Sunitha Krishnan: The Fight Against Sex Slavery" (TED Talk)

"Elders Speak: A New Dawn for Women in Kenya"

Conclusion

||||||||||||||||||||||||||||||||||||||||||||||||||||||||||||||||||||||||||||||||||||||||||||||||

While writing this book, I managed a Facebook page about mother-daughter book clubs. One day I received this comment. I can't think of a better way to end this book:

> *"I'm from Madison, Wisconsin. I don't have children but I joined this page because I was in a mother-daughter book club from age nine to eighteen. I'm twenty-three now and still close with many of the girls in our group. As the daughters got older and busier we read less but still gathered every month to just hang out or to watch a film. It has empowered me to say my opinions out loud to a room full of people, to be a good and loyal friend, to trust my mom and to find female role models, to be silly, and of course—it had me reading all the time! I just graduated from UW-Madison in December. I studied gender and women's studies and now that I think about it, the book club was my first GWS classroom. I think it's one of the best things my mom has ever done for me. Great job, moms!"* —Lydia

The mother-daughter book club that so deeply changed my life and Charlotte's ended years ago, but only in a certain way. It lives on in our hearts, and now in the pages of this book. It lives on in other mothers and daughters. Together, from one generation to the next, we can change the world—one girl at a time, one book at a time, one voice at a time. Welcome to the village! May it be everything for you that it has been for us, and more.

Resources

||||||||||||||||||||||||||||||||||||||||||||||||||||||||||||||||||||||||||||||||||||||||||||||||||||||

Books

Let's Hear It for the Girls: 375 Great Books for Readers 2–14 by Erica Bauermeister

Raising Girls: Helping Your Daughter to Grow Up Wise, Warm and Strong by Steve Biddulph

Where Has My Little Girl Gone? by Tanith Carey

Once Upon a Heroine: 450 Books for Girls to Love by Allison Cooper-Mullin and Jennifer Marmaduke Coye

100 Books for Girls to Grow On by Shireen Dodson

The Mother-Daughter Book Club: How Ten Busy Mothers and Daughters Came Together to Talk, Laugh, and Learn Through Their Love of Reading by Shireen Dodson

The Lolita Effect: The Media Sexualization of Young Girls and What We Can Do About It by M. Gigi Durham

Pink Brain, Blue Brain: How Small Differences Grow Into Troublesome Gaps— And What We Can Do About It by Lise Eliot

Strong, Smart and Bold: Empowering Girls for Life by Carla Fine

Delusions of Gender: How Our Minds, Society, and Neurosexism Create Difference by Cordelia Fine

Bullied: What Every Parent, Teacher, and Kid Needs to Know About Ending the Cycle of Fear by Carrie Goldman

How to Say It® to Girls: Communicating with Your Growing Daughter by Nancy Gruver

Growing Up with Girl Power: Girlhood on Screen and in Everyday Life by Rebecca Hains

The Mother-Daughter Project: How Mothers and Daughters Can Band Together, Beat the Odds, and Thrive Through Adolescence by SuEllen Hamkins and Renée Schultz

Princess Recovery: A How-to Guide to Raising Strong, Empowered Girls Who Can Create Their Own Happily Ever Afters by Jennifer Hartstein

Book by Book: The Complete Guide to Creating Mother-Daughter Book Clubs by Cindy Hudson

Just Between Us: A No-Stress, No-Rules Journal for Girls and Their Moms by Meredith and Sofie Jacobs

The Gender Trap: Parents and the Pitfalls of Raising Boys and Girls by Emily Kane

Deadly Persuasion: Why Women and Girls Must Fight the Addictive Power of Advertising by Jean Kilbourne

Half the Sky: Turning Oppression into Opportunity for Women Worldwide by Nicholas Kristof and Sheryl WuDunn

Packaging Girlhood: Rescuing Our Daughters from Marketers' Schemes by Sharon Lamb and Lyn Mikel Brown

So Sexy So Soon: The New Sexualized Childhood and What Parents Can Do to Protect Their Kids by Diane Levin and Jean Kilbourne

The Case For Make Believe: Saving Play in a Commercialized World by Susan Linn

Consuming Kids: Protecting Our Children from the Onslaught of Marketing & Advertising by Susan Linn

Great Books for Girls: More Than 600 Books to Inspire Today's Girls and Tomorrow's Women by Kathleen Odean

Cinderella Ate My Daughter: Dispatches from the Front Lines of the New Girlie-Girl Culture by Peggy Orenstein

Pink and Blue: Telling the Boys from the Girls in America by Jo B. Paoletti

Reviving Ophelia: Saving the Selves of Adolescent Girls by Mary Pipher and Ruth Ross

Born to Buy: The Commercialized Child and the New Consumer Culture by Juliet Schor

Good Girls Don't Get Fat: How Weight Obsession Is Messing Up Our Girls and How We Can Help Them Thrive Despite It by Robyn Silverman

Odd Girl Out: The Hidden Culture of Aggression in Girls by Rachel Simmons

The Curse of the Good Girl: Raising Authentic Girls with Courage and Confidence by Rachel Simmons

Off the Beaten Page: The Best Trips for Lit Lovers, Book Clubs, and Girls on Getaways by Terri Peterson Smith

Redefining Girly: How Parents Can Fight the Stereotyping and Sexualizing of Girlhood, from Birth to Tween by Melissa Atkins Wardy

The Body Image Survival Guide for Parents: Helping Toddlers, Tweens, and Teens Thrive by Marci Warhaft-Nadler

Queen Bees and Wannabees: Helping Your Daughter Survive Cliques, Gossip, Boyfriends, and the New Realities of Girl World by Rosalind Wiseman

Websites

Adios Barbie: www.adiosbarbie.com

Amy Poehler's Smart Girls: http://amysmartgirls.com/

Beauty Redefined: www.beautyredefined.net

Brave Girls Alliance: www.bravegirlswant.com

Campaign for a Commercial-Free Childhood: http://commercialfree childhood.org

Center on Media and Child Health: www.cmch.tv

Common Sense Media: www.commonsensemedia.org

Day of the Girl: http://dayofthegirl.org

Dr. Jennifer Shewmaker's Operation Transformation: http://jennifer shewmaker.com/operation-transformation

Dr. Robyn Silverman: www.drrobynsilverman.com

Fearlessly Girl: www.fearlesslygirl.com

Geena Davis Institute on Gender in Media: www.seejane.org

Girls for a Change: www.girlsforachange.org

Girls Leadership Institute: www.girlsleadershipinstitute.org

Girls on the Run: www.girlsontherun.org

Girls, Inc.: www.girlsinc.org

Go! Go! Sports Girls: www.gogosportsgirls.com

Hardy Girls, Healthy Women: www.hghw.org

Her Next Chapter: www.motherdaughterbookclubs.com

In This Together Media: www.inthistogethermedia.com

Miss Representation: www.missrepresentation.org

Mother Daughter Book Club: http://motherdaughterbookclub.com

The Mother-Daughter Project: www.themother-daughterproject.com
National Coalition of Girls' Schools: www.ncgs.org
New Moon Girls: www.newmoon.com
Peggy Orenstein: http://peggyorenstein.com
Pigtail Pals & Ballcap Buddies: http://pigtailpals.com
Pink Stinks: www.pinkstinks.co.uk
Powered by Girl: http://poweredbygirl.org
Princess Free Zone: http://princessfreezone.com
Project Girl: www.projectgirl.org
Rachel Simmons: www.rachelsimmons.com
Rebecca Hains: www.rebeccahains.com
Reel Girl: http://reelgirl.com
Rookie Magazine: http://rookiemag.com
Scarleteen: www.scarleteen.com
Shaping Youth: www.shapingyouth.org
SheHeroes: www.sheheroes.org
SPARK Summit: www.sparksummit.com
Strong Women, Strong Girls: http://swsg.org
Toward the Stars: www.towardthestars.com

Index